Learning and the
E-Generation

Learning and the E-Generation

Jean D. M. Underwood
Division of Psychology
School of Social Sciences
Nottingham Trent University, UK

&

Lee Farrington-Flint
Centre for Research in Education & Educational Technology
Faculty of Education & Language Studies
The Open University, UK

WILEY Blackwell

This edition first published 2015
© 2015 Jean D. M. Underwood and Lee Farrington-Flint

Registered Office
John Wiley & Sons, Ltd, The Atrium, Southern Gate, Chichester, West Sussex, PO19 8SQ, UK

Editorial Offices
350 Main Street, Malden, MA 02148-5020, USA
9600 Garsington Road, Oxford, OX4 2DQ, UK
The Atrium, Southern Gate, Chichester, West Sussex, PO19 8SQ, UK

For details of our global editorial offices, for customer services, and for information about how
to apply for permission to reuse the copyright material in this book please see our website at
www.wiley.com/wiley-blackwell.

The right of Jean D. M. Underwood and Lee Farrington-Flint to be identified as the authors of this work
has been asserted in accordance with the UK Copyright, Designs and Patents Act 1988.

Library of Congress Cataloging-in-Publication Data

Underwood, Jean D. M.
Learning and the e-generation / Jean D. M. Underwood & Lee Farrington-Flint.
    pages   cm
    Includes bibliographical references and index.
    ISBN 978-1-118-89759-1 (cloth) – ISBN 978-0-631-20860-0 (pbk.)   1. Education–Great Britain–Data
processing.   2. Educational technology–Great Britain.   3. Computer-assisted instruction–Great Britain.
4. Generation Y–Great Britain.   I. Farrington-Flint, Lee.   II. Title.
    LB1028.43.U53 2015
    371.33′4–dc23
                                                    2014017306

A catalogue record for this book is available from the British Library.

Cover image: Little nerd with music player. Photo © deucee_ /iStockphoto

Set in 10/13pt Sabon by SPi Publisher Services, Pondicherry, India
Printed and bound in Malaysia by Vivar Printing Sdn Bhd

1   2015

Contents

Foreword

We envisaged this sequel to *Computers and learning: Helping children acquire thinking skills* (Underwood & Underwood, 1990) would appear as a belated millennium offering but work pressures and the rapidity of change in this field caused us first to delay and then to rethink roles. Those pressures led to Geoff Underwood stepping aside while a new co-author joined me in completing the text. I would like to thank Geoff for his generosity and Lee for his hard work in producing this text for Wiley.

We would like to thank the many Blackwell's production staff associated with this project for their tireless support and patience. At times they must have despaired of ever seeing a completed manuscript.

Much of our own work reported here emanates from a very fruitful and long-standing association with BECTA and there are many of the staff of that now lost champion of digital learning we could and should thank. Please forgive us if we name just three: Peter Avis, Di Levine and Vanessa Pittard have always acted more as partners than sponsors of our research.

Several teams of researchers contributed to studies reported in this text. Central to those teams have been: Alison Ault, Thom Baguley, Phil Banyard, Sue Cavendish, Emily Coyne, Gayle Dillon, Mary Hayes, Tony Lawson, Ian Selwood, Bridget Somekh, James Stiller and Peter Twining. Firstly Sue, then Gayle and Phil, have been rocks on which much of this work has been built.

Finally, thank you to the many children, teachers and schools that allowed us access and gave their time to help identify how and why technology can contribute to effective teaching and learning.

Chapter One
Learning in a Digital World

Starting Points

It is two decades since *Computers and learning: Helping children acquire thinking skills* was published (Underwood & Underwood, 1990). This sequel text is entitled *Learning and the e-generation* as a recognition that the digital contexts in which individuals now learn has irrevocably changed. The new generation of students, for whom digital technologies are the norm, has grown up during the rise of the World Wide Web and uses technology at home and in school for learning and entertainment. Their use of digital media is expanding and their culture will have a major impact on the rest of society. They now use online resources as a preferred option and as a consequence headlines such as 'Libraries dump 2m volumes' (Atwood, 2007, p. 1) mark the move from paper to digital technology storage and the demand from students for more space for virtual-learning study areas. It is not that the students have abandoned libraries; they are simply reshaping their use. Video game playing, for example, has taught them to place less reliance on manuals or experts. Students use Google rather than use the library's web pages: they are used to figuring things out for themselves and their reliance on the expert, in this case the librarian, is diminishing (Lippincott, 2005). Outside the classroom, everyday events such as paying the London congestion charge or finding the time of the next bus are facilitated by a savvy use of technology.

In 1990 we noted that classroom computers were now commonplace and we asked the question would any good come of it? We were cautiously confident of the value of educational computers. Has that state of restrained

Learning and the E-Generation, First Edition. Jean D. M. Underwood and Lee Farrington-Flint.
© 2015 Jean D. M. Underwood and Lee Farrington-Flint. Published 2015 by John Wiley & Sons, Ltd.

optimism changed and, 20 years on, is there reliable evidence of the impact of computer use on the cognitive, and indeed social and emotional development of the learner? There is compelling evidence that technology is changing the lives of many children and young adults in ways that we had not originally anticipated. With the rise in Web 2.0 technologies and new social media, learners have greater access to a range of digital tools for collaborating, communicating and exchanging ideas. Learners can share common interests, photos, music and videos and maintain active social relationships with friends, acquaintances and even strangers through a range of online communication tools. Facebook along with other social networking tools such as YouTube (video sharing), Flickr (photo sharing) and Blogger (interactive online diary) are incredibly popular among many learners and this popularity reflects a shift towards acquiring a range of new digital literacy skills beyond those of simply using a traditional computer. Technology is also being used in quite creative and innovative ways, invading every aspect of our lives, as Palmer acknowledges below:

> It is only in the last couple of decades that electronic speed has overtaken real time, as technology has invaded every aspect of our life and work. PCs, the Internet, the web and mobile phones mean that the (Marshal McLuhan's) electronic (global) village is around us 24/7, whether we like it or not.
>
> (Palmer, 2006, p. 253)

It seems that we are now part of this extensive, global electronic village that shapes every aspect of our social lives. However, the rise in Web 2.0 technologies and the affordances of digital tools now challenges the relevance of our initial question. The digital world is here to stay and even if we decide not to fund resources into schools, as some are arguing should be the policy, the net generation will use the technology from home, in the streets and in every other aspect of the lives. The current generation of students is able to work with technologies in ways not thought of by even their elder siblings. The Test Bed project has shown children as young as 5 years of age happily working with digital cameras and editing photos to produce their own web pages, while in the secondary sector students are producing home movies and composing and recording music (Underwood, Dillon & Twining, 2007). Furthermore, communication has been transformed through the Internet. It is estimated that there are in excess of 27.2 million weblogs and the blogosphere continues to double about every 5.5 months. There are about 75,000 new weblogs created every day and 1.2 million posts per day on average (Sifry, 2006). These creative activities are not just for home or school consumption, the audience is now worldwide using YouTube or GoogleVideo for videos or Myspace, Facebook or Bebo to link to friends. As Green and Hannon (2007) point out these students are connecting, exchanging and creating in new ways, which appear quite unfamiliar to many parents and teachers (Banyard, Underwood, & Twiner, 2006).

So the question now is how do we make the best use of these digital technologies? There are many who would argue that the functions offered by Web 2.0 technologies have the potential to offer increased learning opportunities for students and young adults (see, for example, Bennett, Bishop, Dalgano, Waycott, & Kennedy, 2012; Contarello & Sarrica, 2007). Can we identify the 'what' and the 'how' of the impact that the major advances in and increased accesses to digital technologies are having on the development of the net generation? A second equally important question is can we identify and support those who have not yet joined the net generation? Throughout our own research (Underwood, Baguley, et al., 2007, 2009) there has been a persistent minority of some 10 per cent of students who have minimal access to computers and the Internet outside school, a finding confirmed by Madell and Muncer's (2004) survey of 1,340 11-to-16 year olds in the north of England, which showed a large proportion of students simply did not have access to new digital technologies. These findings highlight the equity issues associated with the use of digital technologies for learning. Although cheap technologies such as the Raspberry Pi[1] and the £30 UbiSlate 7Ci tablet[2], which have recently entered the educational marketplace, is suspected to go some way to alleviating the issue of access, there are still a minority of individuals for whom this technology is unavailable.

There is little doubt that the prolific rise in our access to digital technologies is having a marked effect on how we learn and think. Johnson (2005) asserts that popular culture, to a large extent stimulated by rapid developments in digital technologies, has presented us with an increasingly complex, problem-orientated and intellectually challenging world. This is the antithesis of the 'couch-potato' perspective of the impact on the cultures evoked by digital technologies. Johnson's book, *Everything bad is good for you*, has reinvigorated and redirected the debate on the impact of technology in a way reminiscent of Papert's (1980) *Mindstorms: Children, computers and powerful ideas*. However, surprisingly three decades after the first computers were introduced into mainstream classrooms, the educational use of digital technologies still remains controversial. As with the introduction of earlier technologies, the spread of digital technologies, especially the Internet, arouses passionate debate about the consequences ensuing from

[1] http://www.bbc.co.uk/news/technology-24426414
[2] http://www.bbc.co.uk/news/technology-25402621

technological change and innovation (Marvin, 1988; Southwell & Doyle, 2004). As Underwood (2006) points out the digital world is now an everyday reality but does this new reality bring benefits or costs to education? Is this too simplistic a dichotomy and, as Southwell and Doyle have argued, can both divergent positions be simultaneously correct? Here we investigate the challenge of digital technologies on learner behaviours across both formal and informal settings.

Hopes, Dreams and Nightmares

There are many who question the importance of digital technologies for education (see Selwyn, 2006; Underwood & Dillon, 2004, for a fuller debate) and vociferous arguments have been put forward to support the conclusion that, far from enhancing education, ICT is a drain on our educational system (see Cuban, 2001; Cuban, Kirkpatrick, & Peck, 2001; Oppenheimer, 2003). This perception clearly articulated in the title of Oppenheimer's text, *The flickering mind: The false promise of technology in the classroom and how learning can be saved.* Notwithstanding this doom-laden title, Oppenheimer acknowledges, 'Computers can, in select cases, be wonderfully useful to school' (p. 411). For instance, the effectiveness of technology in supporting students with special educational needs is accepted by most. This is exemplified by work such as that of Standen and Brown (2005), which has shown the benefits of virtual reality as a tool to practise skills needed to function in society. These vulnerable students manipulated a virtual world safely, without being exposed to potentially humiliating or dangerous consequences, thus allowing them to develop skills such as grocery shopping, preparing food, orientation, road safety and manufacturing skills before facing a bewildering, and for some threatening, real world. The aim of this learning experience was to facilitate independence by transferring skills acquired virtually to the real world. Parsons and Mitchell (2002) have similar positive findings from virtual reality training of social skills with adults on the autism spectrum. The use of technology also allows those with special educational needs to demonstrate competencies thought to be beyond them. For example, young children on the autistic spectrum can match those skills of their typically developing peers on imaginative storytelling under the right circumstances and situations (Dillon & Underwood, 2012).

While recognizing the benefits of such experiences for special groups Oppenheimer nevertheless adds the caveat that 'high technology is steering youngsters away from the messy fundamental challenges of the real world … toward the hurried buzz and neat convenience of an unreal virtual world' (2003, p. 411). It is Oppenheimer's reasonableness that makes him such a powerful critic of the value of technology as a learning tool. His scepticism raised three key questions:

1. Can digital technologies enhance the cognitive, social and emotional development of the learner?
2. Which learners benefit and under what circumstances do they benefit?
3. Are there losers: students for whom technology is at best an irrelevance but possibly a hindrance to their development?

For many working in the field there is a growing acceptance that, as Southwell and Doyle (2004) have argued, the answer cannot be a simple yes or no. Debates concerning the educational value of technology rage on. On the one hand Johnson (2005) asserts that popular culture alludes to the issue that new digital technologies are mind enhancing, that is technology makes smart kids; while Hancox (2005) warns that the rising number of 'couch potatoes', a consequence of the popularity of entertainment technologies, is fuelling the obesity epidemic in the Western world. Central to this debate is the argument that digital technologies are actually damaging and eroding young people's social lives (Palmer, 2006). For example, in the affective domain, there is a growing body of research evidencing the deleterious effects of video game playing on the socio-emotional development of adolescents. There are also genuine concerns of some parties that computer games are even dangerous and damaging to young people's intellectual and social capabilities (Guan & Subrahmanyam, 2009).

Why Is the Supportive Evidence so Hard to Find?

So with the potential for new digital technologies to revolutionize both learning and education, why is the evidence so hard to find? In our review of the research on Integrated Learning Systems (ILSs) in UK schools a decade ago, we made the following argument:

> we need, but do not currently possess, a well-founded 'language' which we can use to classify, relate and communicate about the different kinds of tasks we use to assess learning, so that we can refine our claims about the impact of teaching and learning outcomes and our assessment of what a learning gain means.
>
> (Wood, Underwood, & Avis, 1999, p. 99)

Although many teachers and students in the UK ILS evaluation, as well as other similar international studies, recorded strong positive attitudinal and motivational changes to learning (Hativa, 1989) and a strong belief that learning gains were substantial (Barrett & Underwood, 1997), there was no evidence of ILSs conferring benefits on the standard indices of school and student achievement such as SATs or GCSE scores. This clear discrepancy between hard outcome measures and the experiences of teachers and students led us to re-evaluate both the questions we were asking and the methods by which we were seeking to capture educational experiences (Underwood & Dillon, 2004). A partial explanation for the discrepancies exemplified by the ILS evaluation is that we were measuring the wrong thing.

A brief aside, as we finalize this manuscript the headline news is that the government is looking once again to computers to teach children. Under the disparaging headline '4 reasons to be happy about the end of teaching', Harriet Green (2013)[3] reports that the Minister for Skills and Enterprise, Matthew Hancock, has plans to use computers and personalized online tuition to impart knowledge. Green posits four reasons why the technology will deliver, of which the need to help teachers combat large class sizes seems the most important. Interestingly she reports that the Minister feels this approach will free teachers' time in the classroom to focus more on mentoring, coaching and improving the motivation of learners. When ILSs were first mooted in the 1980s they were seen as a cost-efficient way to reduce teaching staff and, if Hancock is true to his word, the current government's view is that personalized systems will reduce the workload of teachers allowing them to function in more meaningful ways. Of course, the counter argument is simply to employ a higher proportion of teachers although this seems an unlikely route for any government to take in the near future. What we do know, however, is that headlines such 'League Tables 2013: Hundreds of schools below new targets'[4] put a very real pressure on both the government and the educational professionals to up their game and deliver.

While the usefulness of digital technologies in education is an open debate, few would challenge the major impact of digital technologies on our everyday lives. The iSociety's report on the impact of increasing bandwidth into the home, schools and the workplace exemplifies this impact (Crabtree & Roberts, 2003). Their report identifies the ways in which people use technology to extend and enhance their everyday lives, arguing that this information is 'the basis for any sensible understanding of technological change' (Crabtree & Roberts, p. 3). They too say that positive impacts of technology in the world outside the classroom are elusive but point to

[3] http://www.cityam.com/blog/1387211628/4-reasons-be-happy-about-end-teaching
[4] http://www.bbc.co.uk/news/education-25332808

proof by existence as one way forward. They point out that it is difficult to capture the economic gains using standard metrics of digital technologies on say a small business such as a local painter, yet every painter and plumber is now an active user of the mobile phone. There is the existence proof of the importance of technology, which Crabtree and Roberts argue is a valid affirmation of the effectiveness of the technology.

Children's interactions with digital texts in out-of-school settings have revealed the playfulness, agency and creativity with which the children engage with the technology (Burnett, 2010). For example, Marsh's (2004) study of the literacy practices of pre-school children in the home found that engagement with television, computer games and mobile phones provided the children with pleasure and self-expression.

> Literacy as skills development was embedded within children's techno-literacy practices, whether that related to learning grapheme/phoneme relationships from watching television or reading texts on the screens of computer games. In short, children's home literacy events within this study could be mapped on to existing literature in the field, differing only in the extent to which techno-literacy practices were involved.
>
> (Marsh, 2004, p. 63)

There is also a growing recognition that technology can shift the goals of education. One example would be how the use of calculators has shifted the focus of mathematics towards estimation and the meaning of operations and away from the mechanics of the arithmetic operations themselves. Or a more current change in the way texting on mobile phones is allowing new forms of written communication to evolve among our digital natives (Baron, 2010). Where generations of well-meaning spelling reform have failed to introduce simplified spellings, mobile phone texts have succeeded admirably.

It remains clear that merely adding digital technology into the classroom is unlikely to produce any notable improvements in either the quality of teaching or the outcome of students' learning. We are also aware that for some teachers there is a lack of necessary knowledge or experience to successfully incorporate such new technologies into their own teaching practices (Underwood, Baguley, et al., 2010). The association between affordances of the technologies and learner-engagement is key to understanding what works, what does not and why. Furthermore, within education there is a need to go beyond simply understanding technological change, important though this is, to understanding the impact of such change on the actual processes of learning. It is also important to recognize that much learning takes place outside formal settings. One of the very real impacts of digital technologies is that much of the learning process may be taken out of the formal arena and into less formal contexts, although the extent to which this may become the norm is not part of the discussion here. However, by identifying the active use of digital technologies in both formal and informal learning environments, as Crabtree and Roberts (2003) suggest, represents only the first stage in realizing the true potential of digital technology for educational learning.

The impact of digital technologies on the process and products of education have proved difficult to assess for a number of reasons but, as Eisenhart (2005) asserts, the search for causation is a fixation as we seek to establish the events and processes that will promote an effective educational system. In brief, education is a complex system of interrelationships of checks and balances and we neglect this inherent complexity at our peril for such neglect will not facilitate an in-depth understanding of this reality.

Contextual factors do not provide a neutral backcloth on which the teaching and learning are played out. These factors may in turn hinder or help the task of embedding any innovation into the educational environment. These influencing factors include learner variables such prior knowledge but also investment in learning (Underwood, Baguley, et al., 2007) and organizational structures put in place by the school. Some are directly influential at the learner level, and these include elements of the home and community environments. While factors such as national and local policies do have a secondary impact and often influence the behaviour of teachers and the policies of schools, they often fail to impact the individual learner directly.

In addition, it is clear that technological innovations are rarely a direct cause of change but rather act to facilitate existing educational practices. It is clear such evidence is beginning to emerge especially within the findings of Impact studies that have been carried out within the United Kingdom (Underwood, Ault, et al., 2006; Underwood, Baguley, et al., 2007, 2010). While much thoughtful and illuminating research has been conducted into the impact of ICT on education, the story so far is confused and confusing. To capture a greater proportion of this complexity, a necessary prerequisite for the development of predictive dynamic models of the impact of ICT on the educational process, we first need to develop analytical tools, which allow the synthesis of multiple-sourced data. Knowing how these factors interact with one another is important and worthy of our research endeavours.

Evidence of effectiveness in the ordinary classroom is what has been questioned. While a body of anecdotal evidence or existence proof ('I've seen it with my own eyes') has been available for some time, what one might term hard evidence has been patchy at best. However, evidence of effect is beginning to emerge, for example, from the large-scale four-year Test Bed project, which was an investigation of how the sustained and embedded use of ICT in learning spaces can improve learner outcomes, classroom practice and institutional development (Underwood, Dillon, & Twining, 2007). Schools within this project were provided with funds to upgrade their technical resources and to train staff in the use of those resources. One of the key findings from the final phase of this project was the confirmation of the existence of, and recovery from, the previously reported technology dip (Underwood & Dillon, 2011). The research has also shown that the post-dip recovery can be swift and strong as staff ICT competence and confidence rose in the year after the technology was introduced. This in turn was followed by an expansion of staff pedagogic skills in year three, finally leading to verifiable gains in core national test scores in year four of the project (Underwood & Dillon, 2004). This successful incorporation of technology was achieved over a four-year period and through the development of the staff and student skills base, which in turn was stimulated by good school leadership. The findings from this innovative project showed that technology alone is not that effective but effective use of technology does reap dividends. Therefore, while recognizing the importance of changing educational structures, it is vital to recognize that the interaction of teachers and learners with technology remains pivotal and it is here that psychology has important contributions to make to the debate about effective learning.

As Green and Hannon suggest, the fact that our current generation of students are able to work with technologies in ways unthought of by adults, is indicative that they are on the other side of a digital divide:

> The current generations of decision-makers – from politicians to teachers – see the world from a very different perspective to the generation of young people who do not remember life without the instant answers of the Internet or the immediate communication of mobile phones.
>
> (Green & Hannon, 2007, p. 15)

The term 'digital divide' became part of the lingua franca in the 1990s but the early economic definition of that time is now seen as simplistic and has given way to a rich and complex concept of interacting physical, digital, human and social resources (for a description of the ontogeny of this concept, see Underwood, 2007). One aspect of that definition, and the focus here, is the digital divide between teachers and their students. Prensky (2001) argues that the implications of this discontinuity are profoundly important. He argues that the emersion in digital worlds means that the current cohort of students, and those that will follow them, think and process information in fundamentally different ways from those that have gone before, and this includes their teachers. These students termed as digital natives who are born immersed within a technologically rich digital environment, use technology in qualitatively different ways to other 'digital immigrants'. Prensky (2001) makes quite a coherent argument regarding the problems of education:

> single biggest problem facing education today is that out digital immigrant instructors, who speak an out-dated language (indicative of the pre-digital age), are struggling to teach a population that speaks an entirely new language.
>
> (Prensky, 2001, p. 2)

The concept of the digital native is at least partly grounded in the belief that students are effective managers of their own digital world, based on the premise that students are information savvy and able to effectively multitask with various technologies. There are a number of strong voices questioning the importance of being a digital native. Kirschner and van Merriënboer (2013) dismiss the concept of digital natives as an 'urban myth'. They argue that, for example, Veen and Vrakking's (2006) characterization of the net generation is not tenable. This generation sees learning as playing, is endowed with the skills to construct learning from the flow of digital data and so relegates school to the place for meeting and socializing rather than learning. Others have also questioned the concept of the distinct net generation. For example, Margaryan, Littlejohn, and Vojt (2011) found that current university students use only a limited range of technologies for learning and socialization. When used for learning, technology was largely restricted to the passive consumption of information. If more advanced technology use was required, as in say a problem-solving scenario, then direct training was required if any effective learning was to take place.

A significant finding from much of the research in this area is the lack of homogeneity of the net generation. Jones, Ramanau, et al.'s (2010) survey of first-year undergraduates studying a range of pure and applied subjects found a complex picture that they describe as a *collection of minorities*. There was a small group of non-technology users. The largest group of users showed a reliance on simply downloading or uploading materials to the Internet; while most active users of more advanced functionalities were confined to a small minority of students. These results are not confined to the net generation. Underwood and Stiller's (2013) descriptions of technology use by teachers in technology-friendly schools found four distinct groups of teachers based on levels of technology awareness but when actual use was taken into consideration, there was clear division between a small group of teachers resistant to technology at all costs and three groups which, while having different perceptions of the technology, essentially used the same functions due to institutional constraints such as access time, timetables and workloads. To conclude that any one cohort is a homogeneous group as far as its response to technology is concerned is too simplistic.

Selwyn (2006) has queried whether these concerns as exemplified by, but not limited to, Prensky are really so important. His interviews with 84 UK secondary school students revealed students' frustration at not being able to use technology, particularly the Internet, because of resource levels and risk-aversive measures taken by their schools (see Underwood, Ault, et al., 2005). However, most students understood and accepted the problems faced by their schools although a minority did display frustration and disenchantment. This is a worrying minority trend because such students are likely to be demotivated and possibly disruptive if such feelings persist. However, Prensky (2001, 2006) and Green and Hannon (2007) are concerned with a digital divide that is perhaps more profound than simply feelings of frustration and demotivation. From their own research these authors argue that teachers (and very often parents) do think and operate in remarkably different ways to the younger generation who have been immersed within this technologically-rich digital environment from birth. It could be argued that while teachers remain serial thinkers from the book-age, students' parallel process and multitask. Students are more graphical while teachers are still focused on the written word, the former producing multimodal presentations rather than an essay to express their thoughts and arguments.

There is then a growing realization that, as in the old world of books where poor readers abound, the current generation may be digital natives but some have only a basic level of digital literacy. Education, as ever, has a pivotal role in ensuring that all young people attain the necessary competencies, in particular because those who seem most likely to be left behind are already socio-economically marginalized (Facer, Furling, et al., 2003; Selwyn 2009a).

How does Psychological Theory Illuminate the Educational Debate?

In the past two decades of the twentieth century within the United Kingdom it has been government-led policy to focus on classroom pragmatics resulting in an undervaluing of theory. Thus, educational practice was cut off from its feeder roots within psychology, sociology and other key disciplines. There is now a greater willingness to accept that psychological theory might have a place in supporting and developing pedagogic practice and the promotion of effective learning, due in part to the excitement aroused by recent developments in the areas of cognition, education and neuroscience. However, translating learning theories into practice is not always easy, not least because there are seemingly competing theories, which represent learning as response strengthening, information processing or knowledge construction (see Lajoie & Derry, 2013, for a fuller debate). But psychological theories and models have a great deal to offer the debate around learning through digital technologies.

Psychological models focus not simply on the affordances of the technology but how the learner's cognitive, behavioural and affective characteristics can be improved or sustained through their own engagement with the use of these technologies. The shift from 'content' to the 'process' of learning, which du Boulay (2000) records, has been accompanied by the shift in the recognition of the importance of the affective dimension of learning, which emphasizes that students' motivation is pivotal. The concept of Self-Regulated Learning (SRL) has emerged from the more extensive literature on Self-Regulated Behaviour (SRB). Vancouver (2000) defines self-regulation as the *processes involved in attaining and maintaining (i.e., keeping current) goals, where goals are internally represented desired states (i.e. within the self)*: a mechanism for maintaining and restoring wellbeing and avoiding negative status in all aspects of life and SRL is a subset of that more general concept (see Banyard, Underwood, et al., 2006). Self-regulated learners draw on their knowledge and beliefs to devise an interpretation of a given academic task. These learners will set goals and think about the skills and strategies for achieving their goals. They monitor their progress by judging their success against their goals (Zimmerman, 1989) and they recognize deviations from their expected rate of progress. Of course self-regulation is not always the most strategic or effective approach to achieving academic success. Deci and Ryan (2000), for instance, make a clear distinction between autonomous and controlled behaviour regulation. In the former, goals emanate from the individual and are set as a result of personal importance. In the latter, controlled regulation occurs when the individual feels coerced or pressurized into achieving a goal set by external but also internal forces. This may lead to less effective or less sustained learning in the long run.

Larson (2000) approaches the issue of 'what' and 'how' we learn from the perspective of positive youth development and places particular emphasis on how we motivate individuals and develop their capacity for initiative. He argues that the capacity for initiative is an essential twenty-first century skill that is restricted among our younger generation, who have few opportunities to learn given the closed experiences provided within the school environment coupled with unstructured leisure time. He has established that organized activities, such as participating in sporting teams or

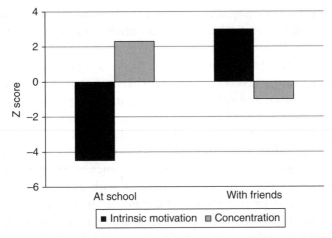

Figure 1.1. Mean rating of intrinsic motivation and levels of concentration from Larson (2000)

clubs, are effective ways of developing this capacity for initiative. These activities are productive because they engender intrinsic motivation, concentration and cognitive effort. They also require cumulative effort over time to achieve a goal. Figure 1.1, taken from Larson's data, demonstrates a crossover effect between levels of intrinsic motivation and concentration, when adolescents are in school or with friends. The adolescents in his study often reported feeling bored and unmotivated in school but had relatively high concentration levels. However, motivation rose when socializing with friends although concentration levels slipped.

In a further study the impact of structured activities such as team sports was investigated (Larson, Hansen, & Moneta, 2006). For such activities the motivation stayed high, as it was when socializing with friends; however, there was no dip in concentration. Concentration remained at a level consistent with school activities. Furthermore, organized activities, such as football, often involve sustained effort over time in order to meet goals. The team sports investigated here captured the positives of school and out of-school activities without the downsides of loss of motivation or concentration. Larson concludes that developmental benefits come from activities that, while of interest to the learner, are also organized and require sustained effort over time in order to meet desired goals.

The advantages of learning with new technologies, particularly those supported through the Internet, include the flexibility of 'anytime and anywhere' learning (Brandon & Hollingshead, 1999). New technologies can accommodate different learning styles, increase motivation and have the potential for widening access beyond the constraints of the traditional classroom context (see, for example, Cavendish, Underwood, et al., 1997). Pintrich (1999, 2000) outlines three general types of motivational beliefs: self-efficacy beliefs (that is, judgements of one's capabilities to complete the academic task); task value beliefs (that is, beliefs about the importance of, interest in, and value of the task); and goal orientations (that is, whether the focus is on mastery and learning of the task, grades or extrinsic reasons for doing the task, or relative ability in relation to social comparisons with other students). They have shown that self-efficacy is positively related to self-regulatory strategies such as planning and monitoring: strategies that are often associated with academic success. We should also remember that the use of technology itself is considered more exciting to the digital generation of students, with numerous papers documenting the motivating effects of different technologies (Passey, Rogers, et al., 2003).

Personality factors impact on self-regulatory behaviour but they also impact on the propensity for risk-taking. While risk can be evaluated cognitively, it also evokes an emotional reaction. However, cognitive evaluations of risk are sensitive to variables such as assessment of probability of success or failure, while in contrast emotional reactions are sensitive to the vividness of associated imagery, and proximity in time (Loewenstein, Weber, et al., 2001). How individuals perceive risks of various kinds is an important influence on the choices that they make. The role of potentially damaging risky or illicit behaviour such as school truancy, drug abuse and criminal activity are challenging areas for society in general, and education in particular. In this monograph risky behaviour is explored through analysis of the use of the Internet by learners of all ages.

Another area in which psychological research illuminates the educational debate is in its recognition for, and understanding of, enhanced social interactions. Social grounding, the mechanism by which an individual seeks to maintain a mutual understanding with a co-worker, requires that the speaker monitors the listener's understanding and, in case of misunderstanding, attempts to repair the communication. There is an element of sustaining effective lines of communication through monitoring and comprehending spoken and written forms. Whether learners use mobile phones, instant messaging or Skype, there is a strong emphasis on effective communication. In such situations verbal and non-verbal cues are important to detect misunderstanding and disambiguate dialogues. Clark and Brennan (1991) have shown that the communication medium impacts the ability to maintain such grounding. While in face-to-face exchanges, conversational turn-taking is achieved easily, for conversations in cyberspace, where there are delays between the emission and the reception of a message, turn-taking becomes difficult because of the loss of facial cues. This is most evident in the use of social networking, like Facebook and Twitter. As we shall illustrate in subsequent chapters, the changing nature of these social interactions is having a profound impact on these types of online communications and on how learners engage with traditional notions within conventional written language (Underwood & Okubayashi, 2011).

How Can We Bridge the Home School Digital Divide?

The issue of home and school use of ICT is an important one that has been increasingly mentioned in the literature and deserves more attention. Several major reports conclude the huge impact that home use of computers has on school children, often suspecting that it is greater than the impact of school use. One report that investigated ICT use at home is ImpaCT2, a strand of which looked at students' attitudes, conceptions and experiences of ICT use. It was found, among other factors, that for most students the time spent on ICT at home greatly exceeded the time spent on ICT at school (Somekh, Lewin, & Mavers, 2002). There is an association between students' awareness of computers in today's world and the level of access to home computers. Although students spent more time on their home computers playing games, it was found that sometimes students use home computers for learning, although they may not recognize it (Lewin, Mavers & Somekh, 2003; Somekh, Lewin, & Mavers, 2002). Additionally, students who have access to home computers also use ICT more at school. Such links are important and through ICT use at home students can extend their learning beyond the school day. Although there are several benefits to using ICT at home it should not lead to turning a blind eye to the potential divide between students with different levels of access and opportunities (Hayward, Alty, et al., 2003). Other studies have also referred to possible benefits of the high level of use of home computers, such as students at the Millennium Primary School using home computers for schoolwork (Priest, Coe, et al., 2004).

However, it is not simply computers that are helping to break through this home–school divide. Digital technologies include an expanding variety of technologies available both inside and outside educational settings, particularly in the area of small mobile digital technologies such as mobile phones and MP3 players as well as social networking tools such as Facebook, Twitter and Bebo. The importance of these technological developments lies not in the number of digital technology devices currently available but in their up-take by the young and in the convergence of functionality of the technologies. This functional convergence means that modern desktop and laptop computers now incorporate the functionality of a communication device and communication devices such as mobile phones are taking on the functionality of a computer (Yoffie, 1997). These functionalities are readily accepted and exploited by the young (Underwood, 2006, 2007) and are having profound effects on their patterns of behaviour, including their responses to formal education. However, teachers and parents often see these technologies as tools for enhancing social forms of communication rather than having any educational relevance to learning, an issue to which we return in later chapters.

Risks, Skills and Opportunities

The educational potential of digital technologies is evident and offers a range of possibilities to transform education and learning. However, with the increase of new technologies come a number of risks that need to be recognized, many of which we have alluded to in the current chapter. Many schools and educational institutions often implement new technology in the classroom context without thinking through the pedagogy behind such use and this could be detrimental to the learner. Moreover, many teachers hold negative perceptions about using social collaboration tools, like social networking and online gaming, as a potential resource for learning. While new technologies can promote effective learning through collaboration and engagement, as the IMPACT and Test Bed projects confirm, this is unlikely to occur without effective implementation by schools, teachers and of course the individual learners themselves (Underwood, Baguley, et al., 2007, 2008, 2010; Somekh & Underwood, 2007). There is a need to move beyond studying technological change and to acknowledge how the implementation of new technologies can influence the learner. There is also a need to bridge the home–school divide otherwise effective teaching methods can be displaced by a lack of engagement with technology within the home (Fuchs & Woessmann, 2005). To take full advantage of the opportunities available, a culture change is necessary if digital technologies are to be a vehicle for bringing about improvements in learning.

Conclusions

The prolific rise in new digital technologies can, even at first glance, appear to offer at least some educational promise. This introductory chapter has outlined some of the key themes and debates arising from the range and variety of digital technologies within society in general and within education specifically. The paradox is that many aspects of these ubiquitous technologies have not provided strong evidence of impact, either in the world beyond the classroom or indeed within the constraints of the classroom environment. There is little doubt that digital technologies can support, and are supporting, a range of teaching and learning styles. The functionalities of digital technology are readily accepted and exploited by the young as they often embrace many of these features as possible tools for collaboration, communication and learning (Underwood, 2007; Underwood, Baguley et al., 2008, 2009). The focus on the role of social interaction has led to an increasing interest in collaborative and co-operative learning and new technologies can be a key to such social interaction. However, while technology has the potential to shift the goals of learning and to make the learning process more authentic and engaging, this can only occur if the technology is focussed on enhancing the learning process itself, a recurring theme that is addressed in the following chapters.

Chapter Two
How do People Learn?

Introduction

One of the most divisive issues within education concerns the role of digital technologies in supporting the teaching and learning. There is no doubt that online technologies have unique properties that have the potential to support learning (see Garrison & Anderson, 2003). It could be argued that the greatest affordance of the web, for example, is that it has created a myriad of ways to communicate and interact with others, including family, friends and peers. Anderson (2004) suggests that these interactions are formed through a range of online tools including wikis, blogs, social networking sites, podcasts, and syndicated content.

There is some support showing that digital technologies may have a sustained effect on promoting an individual's cognitive understanding, through enhancing their thinking, learning and problem-solving skills. However, despite quite compelling evidence of strong positive attitudinal and motivational changes to learning (Hativa, 1989; Underwood & Dillon, 2011) many studies have failed to show any benefits of using these digital technologies. This lack of supporting evidence of the effectiveness of these costly tools can be taken at face value but many would argue that it is the nature of the questions that researchers are asking that has resulted in these disappointing data (Underwood & Dillon, 2004; Jenkinson, 2009). There is a need to move beyond measuring the mechanistic or procedural aspects of how these technologies are used to facilitate learning so that we can comprehend how such technologies are affecting the cognitive, behavioural and effectual aspects of the learning process. Our focus on the technology alone

Learning and the E-Generation, First Edition. Jean D. M. Underwood and Lee Farrington-Flint.
© 2015 Jean D. M. Underwood and Lee Farrington-Flint. Published 2015 by John Wiley & Sons, Ltd.

has often neglected the role of the learner. As Jonassen, Howland, et al. (2003) assert, technology should be seen as a vehicle to learn rather than simply a vehicle to teach and therefore a greater awareness of the learning process is required before we may see any notable changes in the use of technology for educational gains.

So how can technology provide educational benefits for the learning process? To address this question, it is necessary to refer to psychological theory around learning and instruction. Such approaches offer a rather valuable insight into addressing some of the key issues highlighted in the previous chapter given that they have a specific central focus on understanding the learner and their learning process. The current chapter focuses neither on the affordances of the technology nor on the procedural aspects of implementing technology into the curriculum, but on the individual learning process and the skills and requisites for educational gains. It is only when we consider these psychological approaches, and the importance of the biological, cognitive and social dimensions of learning that the benefits of technology for students' learning can be recognized.

What is Learning?

One of the very real difficulties in establishing the what, the when and the how of learning is that there are so many, often competing, theories each with an entrenched group of supporters who reject other views of learning. As we pointed out in Chapter 1 translating learning theories into educational practice is not always easy. This is made even more difficult by the plethora of competing psychological theories, emphasizing either the biological, cognitive, behavioural or affective dimensions of learning.

Traditionally there has been a keen focus on the importance of the application of behaviourist theory to education and learning, which reinforces traditional drill-and-practice models of learning, particularly to help encourage the learning of key facts. The use of reward charts to celebrate or reinforce positive behaviour is an example of the application of behaviourist theory found in many mainstream classrooms. However, despite evidence of their success, there is widespread agreement that such an approach fails to embed creativity and deep-level engagement with the learning process itself. There is now an increased focus on recognizing the importance of learner's active construction of knowledge through their engagement with their own learning process. Although, as an aside, we should not reject the accumulation of factual information as it often provides the building blocks for creative thought.

The current dominant theoretical position within education marries constructivism with situated action, and emanates from Gestalt psychology. It states that learning is an active and collaborative process whereby students engage in solving authentic real-world tasks (Bransford, Brown, & Cocking, 2000; Merrill, 1992). The constructivist metaphor focuses on the learners' active participation involving their actions and thoughts within a particular context when solving any given problem. Current views of cognition have started to explore 'the relationships between the person and the environment, and the conditions under which they can exert reciprocal influence' (Bransford, et al., 2006, p. 28). The concept of 'context', 'environment' or 'activity' is divergently expressed within constructivist perspectives and this view of learning has usurped the 'cognitivists', and even the 'behaviourists' before them, to focus specifically on the role of authenticity and of active learning within educational contexts (Greeno, 1998).

However, these are not competing theories rather they represent an evolution from simply learning by association and extrinsic rewards to the more active construction of knowledge within the learning process (Mayer, 1983). It has a number of pedagogic implications, the most significant being the shift of focus from teaching per se to creating a meaningful learner-centred learning environment. At its most extreme, constructivists argue for minimal guidance allowing learners to discover or construct essential information for themselves and technology provides a fruitful tool to allow this active exploration to occur. However, there is evidence that some level of guidance or direction is required by most learners and scaffolding this exploration is important especially within the context of formal learning (see Kirschner, Sweller, & Clark, 2006).

It could be argued that focussing solely on the cognitive solutions provides only a partial answer to our understanding of the learning process and the biological and social dimensions to the construction of knowledge cannot be ignored or simply overlooked. For example, although Caine and Caine (1990) argue that all learning is physiological, they recognize the affective aspects of learning. Learners need to be engaged with the learning process to recognize the potential gains that can be provided. They assert that meaning, and hence learning, occur through patterning and that emotions are critical to that patterning. The importance of practice also has biological roots as those neurons that repeatedly fire allow for the strengthening of neural connections (Zull, 2002). In his own work, Zull makes a compelling argument in support of the role of biology and emotion within the learning process. Chemicals, including adrenaline, serotonin and dopamine, which are often released during the act of learning, lead to changes in the neural networks. Neuroscience, then, confirms that practice is central to successful

Table 2.1. Basic brain functions and Zull's (2002) four pillars of learning

Basic brain functions	Brain sites	Pillars of learning
1. Getting information	Sensory cortex	Gathering
2. Making meaning of information	Back integrative cortex	Analysing
3. Creating new ideas from these meanings	Front integrative cortex	Creating
4. Acting on those ideas	Motor cortex	Acting

learning especially when that practise occurs in a meaningful way and when the learner is engaged with the task in hand. According to Zull the art of teaching is to find ways that allow learning to become intrinsically rewarding as exhibited in his model of the four pillars of learning, each of which promotes brain activity and so collectively exercises the whole brain as individuals gather, analyse, create and act on new sources of information (Table 2.1).

The perception of learning as a brain exercise rather than as pure knowledge acquisition is gaining currency outside education, not least because there is a need to maintain the mental wellbeing of an ageing population (Doige, 2007). Brain training is seen as one way to slow down and even reduce the inevitable decline in cognitive functions of the 'silver' generation and results from the recognition that the brain is not immutable and that environmental influences are capable of altering or rewiring the neural connections within brain structures. This has led both researchers and educators to question the capacity of the brain to respond to enrichment for learners of all ages. Some of the most vivid accounts of the susceptibility of the brain to training, that is its plasticity, occur in Doige's descriptions of individuals with brain damage. These individuals, who have lost functionality in, for example, perception or motor control, have been shown to recover a certain level of functionality as activity is routed through non-standard, rather than the damaged standard, pathways in the neural network. Diamond (2001) points out that ascertaining the nature of what constitutes 'enrichment' for humans is often quite a difficult and complex task given the importance of individual biological and environmental differences. However, what evidence there is confirms the basic finding that dendritic growth in response to environmental stimulation correlates with learning, suggesting that newness and challenge are as important for the development of the human cortex. As Diamond notes, enrichment effects on the brain have consequences for behaviour, and she argues that parents, educators and policymakers can all benefit from such knowledge.

There is also growing evidence for the role of neuroscience in education, particularly in regard to promoting brain activity as a learning process that emphasizes the biological foundations of learning (Small & Vorgan, 2009). There is a large body of scientific research, for instance, documenting the effectiveness of neuro-feedback for ADHD and many areas of psychological or neuro-developmental difficulty (Knox & Anderson-Inman, 2001). In partnership with NASA, 'SmartBrain Technologies' has created a number of interactive games, including a non-violent driving game that improves visual tracking skills, hand-eye coordination, planning, concentration, memory and patience. Orlandi and Greco (2004) tested the impact of playing this driving game on boys aged 9–11 years who had a primary diagnosis of ADHD. The results showed that the non-game playing group experienced a 47 per cent study dropout rate from clinical support. However, the experimental group had only 6 per cent study dropout rate and showed a number of positive behaviour changes. Such studies add further credibility to the argument that changing brain structures can have a profound and pervasive impact on learning both within and outside formal educational settings.

Beyond General Theories of Learning

Psychological theories of learning have therefore focused on emphasizing, to various degrees, the biological, cognitive and affective dimensions of the learning process. Alongside general theories of learning there are also a number of theories closely associated with the engagement with technology. Mayer and Moreno (1998, 2002) for instance have applied the Dual Coding Theory from cognitive psychology (Paivio, 1986) to multimodal learning in digital environments. The basic premise of the Dual Coding Theory is that cognition involves two subsystems: a verbal subsystem to process language and a non-verbal imagery subsystem to process non-linguistic information. The theory assumes that visual and auditory information is processed via different verbal and visual systems that can be activated independently but are also connected, thus allowing dual pathways: this permits more efficient coding of information but is limited by the capacity of each pathway. The view that there is limited capacity overlaps with Sweller's (1988) Cognitive Load Theory, which states that a learner's attention and working memory is limited. According to this cognitive load theory, if the amount of new information is too great and places additional constraints on working memory, then learning is likely to be impeded. Coupled to this model of processing, Mayer (2005) argues uncontroversially that learning is an active process, which supports both the cognitivist and constructivist descriptions of learning.

Cognitive load theory has been used to explain the superiority of collaborative learning compared to individuals acting alone when working on highly complex but not low-complex tasks (Kirschner, Paas, & Kirschner, 2009). The authors argue that collaboration circumvents the individual's working memory limitations by creating an expanded cognitive capacity and by distributing the cognitive load among group members. Although there is an increased work associated with the necessary organization of the group and the recombining of individual disparate pieces of information, the costs are minimal compared to the gain achieved by this division of labour if the task is complex. For low-complexity tasks, however, an individual can adequately carry out the required processing activities, but the costs of recombination and coordination are relatively more substantial.

The third theory finding currency in the online learning community is Flow Theory (Csikszentmihalyi & Csikszentmihalyi, 1975). Flow is described as a mental state that occurs when an individual is fully immersed in an activity. Flow experiences are intrinsically rewarding as they require intense involvement, focused attention, clarity of goals that lead to a lack of self-consciousness, and a feeling of full control over the activity. Athletes often describe this state of consciousness as 'being in the zone'. A state where self and task merge results in the individual being intrinsically motivated to repeat the activity that is now deemed to be worth doing for its own sake. Flow Theory has also been widely used to explain the feeling of telepresence in the virtual environments, that is, the state of consciousness that gives the impression of being physically present in a mediated world. This theory has been extensively used to explain the nature of online social interactions and the lure of video games (Kiili, 2007; Weibel, Wissmath, et al., 2008).

What About the Quality of Learning?

The preparation of young people for life, leisure and work in a rapidly changing world is a concern for parents, educational practitioners and, of course, young people themselves. The view that the learner is an active participant rather than a receptacle for knowledge is coupled with the concept of deep learning. Entwistle (2000) defined a deep learner as one who is able to:

- relate new knowledge to previous knowledge
- use theoretical ideas in everyday experience
- distinguish evidence and argument

- organize and structure content into a coherent whole
- relate knowledge from different sources
- is self-motivated.

According to Entwistle, these are attributes that are highly desirable as they describe the flexible and independent learner who will succeed in a changing society. By contrast, surface learning tends to be superficial and the learners themselves tend not to grasp the point of the learning as an act within itself. It is all about passing the test. However, we should be wary of classifying any student as a 'deep' or 'surface' learner as one person may use both approaches at different times depending on the context of their learning. For example, disciplines with high content knowledge such as history lend themselves to surface learning, while mathematics requires deep learning; although to advance as an historian, deep learning is also essential. There are also cultural differences in the value placed on these two types of learning with Chinese students' associating memorization with understanding and academic performance. Deep learning has been shown to correlate with intrinsic motivation, and surface learning with extrinsic motivation. Once again we should be wary of thinking the terms are interchangeable as any person can adopt either approach at any time. It is important to consider how these individual characteristics influence the process of learning and how technology can engage and promote an authentic form of active, deep learning.

Active Versus Passive Learning

A key focus in the literature concerns the distinction between active and passive learning and has strong foundations within cognitive psychology. The active-learning hypothesis predicts that learning from interactive systems increases learning by engaging individuals more closely with the material. On the other hand, the passive-learning hypothesis predicts that learning from interactive systems has no special effect on learning since the information content is no different from that contained in a non-interactive system. The active-learning hypothesis derives from constructivist models of learning (Jonassen, 1992; Mayer, 2005). Under the constructivist model, the learning process involves learners constructing their own individual knowledge of a subject on the basis of their prior knowledge and new information that they receive. When they learn, students play an active role in receiving and processing information. When required to interact with a learning system, learners have to make decisions about when to receive information (e.g., by button-clicking), and what information they receive (e.g., by selecting from a number of options). They have an active relationship with the material. As a consequence the active-learning hypothesis predicts that learning should increase when learners use interactive as opposed to non-interactive multimedia systems. While for Drave (2000) the quality of interactivity is more important than content for the success of learning Sim, (1997) believes that the level of interactivity plays a crucial role in knowledge acquisition and the development and refinement of cognitive skills.

A number of principles have already been formulated for the design of multimedia learning systems to promote interactivity, which often consist of a combination of words and images (Mayer, 2005). These include the *multimedia principle* (using both words and pictures), the *coherence principle* (avoiding extraneous media), the *modality principle* (using narration rather than text), the *spatial contiguity principle* (placing words and pictures close together) and the *temporal contiguity principle* (presenting words and pictures at the same time). The empirical evidence for these principles is strong. The systems developed to establish these principles were generally non-interactive, that is, they required no input from the learner in the form of mouse-clicking or key-pressing in order to finish a lesson. Commonly the lessons consisted of uninterrupted narrated animations such as Mayer and Anderson's (1991) 30-second narrated computer-based pump lesson and Mayer and Moreno's (1998) continuous 140-second narrated computer-based lightning lesson.

From a cognitive perspective, the utility of incorporating interactivity in computer-based systems is that it allows the learner to influence the flow of information in terms of timing or content. For example, button-clicking can be used to allow the learner to indicate when they want the next portion of text to be displayed; and interactive multiple-choice questions can be used to provide meaningful feedback for self-assessment. Supporters of the constructivist model usually contrast it with the information or knowledge transfer model of learning (e.g., Mayer, 2005). The passive-learning hypothesis has its origins in this model. Under the information-transfer model, the learning process involves the transfer of information from subject experts (e.g., through lectures or textbooks) to learners. The role of the learner in this process is primarily as a passive recipient of knowledge, whose task is simply to store information to memory. What matters is the quality of the content to which they are exposed. As a consequence, the passive-learning hypothesis predicts that for two systems with the same multimedia material, the level of learning should be the same regardless of whether the systems are interactive or non-interactive. However, is not simply the level of interaction and the distinction between passive and active learning that remains crucial to the learning process. A further aspect is tailoring the educational experience to meet the individual learning styles of the student.

Preferred Learning Styles

The central principle of learning styles is that children learn in different ways. Enthusiasts of learning styles claim that everyone has a preferred style and it is possible to test children to determine their preferences and the success they have in storing, processing and retrieving information as part of this learning process.

Gardner's (1993) influential theory of multiple intelligences takes a holistic and general approach to identifying the cognitive building blocks and views intelligence as an ability. This principle can be extended to recognize individual differences in student's approaches to learning. Although logical and linguistic forms of intelligence are perhaps the most valued ways of thinking within education, these represent just two of the eight intelligences outlined in Gardner's original theory. However, if we translate these intelligences into different modes of learning (or preferred learning styles) this offers a real potential to personalize the learning experience for all students and to tailor the teaching and learning activities to meet the preferred styles of individuals. While many educators would see the perceived benefits in such a personalized approach, in reality this is often difficult to implement given time constraints. This raises additional questions about the feasibility of such attempts and whether the pedagogy of teaching and learning should actually be closely aligned to the individual, and often preferred, style of the learner, especially given that individual learners' rarely know how best to learn. It could be argued that a preferred style of learning may not be the most effective way of learning new information.

Within the literature, there is a clear suggestion that educators can not only identify individual learning styles but can also deliver pedagogy that tailors to these particular modes of learning (Pashler, McDaniel, et al., 2008). Perhaps one of the most influential and widely recognized approach is Kolb's classification of learning styles, which focuses on experiential learning and identifies four distinct styles: diverging, assimilating, converging and accommodating. Each of these four styles places a slightly different emphasis on the actions and perceptions required for learning (Kolb & Kolb, 2012). According to Kolb's theory, the impetus for the development of new concepts is provided by new experiences and each learning style represents a focus on concrete experience and abstract conceptualization. *Diverging* emphasizes an innovative and imaginative approach and requires observation rather than acting. *Assimilating* emphasizes the ability to reason inductively and draws on different observations to influence thinking. Both of these approaches focus on the reflective nature of learning. In contrast, there are more active approaches to learning. For example, *converging* emphasizes the practical application of ideas and problem-solving while *accommodating* emphasizes problem-solving through trial-and-error rather than reflection. This has led to a number of measurement instruments, both questionnaires and inventories that help teachers identify individual student's preferred learning styles. For instance, Honey and Mumford (2000) developed a learning questionnaire that remains one of the most popular learning styles resources, identifying four discrete categories of learner: activists, reflectors, theorists and pragmatists. Activists learn best when confronted with new ideas; reflectors prefer to observe others and listen to several viewpoints; theorists learn by drawing on their existing knowledge to analyse complex situations; and pragmatists make progress by making clear links between work in the classroom and life outside it.

Perhaps a more widely recognized approach is the VAK theory (visual, auditory or kinaesthetic learners) often seen as an extension from neuro-linguistic programming models and offering a more simplistic differentiation between learning styles. There has been a profound lack of understanding especially in the use of VAK styles within the school context (Sharp, Bowker, & Byrne, 2008). Many school activities are not purely visual, auditory or kinaesthetic, but a mixture of all three. A learner may be reading a book (visual) while listening to instructions (auditory) and actively making written notes (kinaesthetic). However, there is a real emphasis on promoting teaching and instruction that targets all pupils with all styles of learning and part of this remains reliant on delivery rather than content.

Does meeting the preferred learning styles of students actually enhance their learning outcomes? The evidence is mixed at best although there is some partial recognition that new technologies can help to support personalized learning in some way. New technology affords both teachers and learners the opportunities to embrace new ways of working, particularly using a broad spectrum of applications such as: social networking sites (SNSs), e-communities, collaborative authoring, and information sharing to create material using a range of social networking tools such as YouTube (video sharing), Flickr (photo sharing) and Blogger (interactive online diary). It is perhaps easy to see how multimodality is addressed. Our own work, among others, illustrates the pedagogic potential of allowing greater flexibility and choice of medium from which learners can select, editing and producing material for classroom activities and assessment to offer greater opportunities for visual or kinaesthetic learning styles rather than a reliance on the purely written form (Fisher & Baird, 2005; Underwood, Baguley, et al., 2007, 2008).

However caution is needed. As Hargreaves and colleagues (2005) suggest, the evidence in support of promoting preferred learning styles for effective learning is, at best, highly variable and lacks scientific validity. Similarly, Kirschner and van Merriënboer (2013) talk about the myths or 'urban legends' around learning styles arguing that the effects of tailoring teaching methods to accommodate preferred learning styles lacks any rigorous scientific evidence. Identifying individual student learning styles is problematic in itself, and accommodating these preferred styles in teaching may not, in fact, lead to positive measurable outcomes. As they also acknowledge: a *learning style that might be desirable in one situation might be undesirable in another situation due to the multifaceted nature of complex skills* (Kirschner & van Merriënboer, 2013, p. 175). We need to be wary, especially given the lack of robust evidence to show that matching the instructional style to individual learning style improves learning outcomes.

What About the Learner?

While good pedagogic design and new tools for delivery, specifically through the means of technology, can provide a potentially effective learning environment, our own work (Underwood and Banyard, 2008) and that of Entwistle (2000) reminds us that learners have to take up those affordances. The use of interactive multimedia systems and digital technologies may, for example, appear engaging and appealing, especially among enthusiasts. The technology must also promote learning in some meaningful way for the individual. Entwistle describes three main approaches to learning each of which involves an intention and a process. These different approaches generally lead to a qualitatively different outcome. Students may adopt:

- A deep approach to learning, that is, work to *understand the information for oneself (linked to intrinsic motivation)*. This brings into play the integration of ideas and uses evidence and logic in reaching conclusions.
- A surface approach where the learner's aim is *pass without too much effort* or thinking. This may result in inappropriate attempts to rote learn or to follow procedures blindly.
- A strategic approach where the intention to *do well and/or achieve personal goals* depends on organizing studying, effort, concentration and monitoring studying.

While we might describe the deep approach as the gold standard of learning (the type of learning that produces an Einstein), a strategic approach can also be very effective – we might call it the silver-gilt medal perhaps? However, it is the case that we all despise surface learning or so we argue. In his essay on deep and surface learning Entwistle emphasizes the power of deep learning, a learning that can be encouraged through the use of technology; but, as the quote below shows, deep learning does not always deliver rewards.

> A deep strategic approach to studying is generally related to high levels of academic achievement, but only where the assessment procedures emphasise and reward personal understanding. Otherwise, surface strategic approaches may well prove more adaptive.
>
> (Entwistle, 2000, p. 4)

Indeed Entwistle (2000) found that although Chinese students are more prone to the use of rote memorization and are more passive and less interactive than most students, they achieve well academically. A small fly in the ointment, is that these so-called rote learners also have higher deep and strategic scores than their Western counterparts (Biggs & Watkins, 2001). Those who reject content for process should remember that we need material to process and that is the content. The deep learning comes from making new connections between old content, but connections are not possible in a knowledge vacuum. Entwistle is arguing that if we assess facts then a learning strategy that emphasizes deeper understanding may not provide higher grades. If, as many educators have argued, technology is best used as a support of deep learning, then surface-level assessments are unlikely to be able to tap into the growing skills and knowledge of the tech-savvy student.

What has been called the Chinese paradox is understandable from Ericsson's theory of expertise (Ericsson & Smith, 1991). Ericsson downplays innate capacities and focuses on hard work and practice when discussing the acquisition expert performance. He argues that specific training and practice provide the opportunity for all individuals, regardless of perceived talent, to have the potential to achieve expert performance if they are sufficiently motivated to endure a significant amount of time engaged in intense deliberate practice. Ethnic Chinese, wherever they reside, show that motivation is crucial to success and as a consequence they consistently appear at the top of the academic performance league tables. But what of rote factual learning you cry! The more facts you have at your fingertips the more likely you are to be able to see new patterns in data, thus enabling the capacity to indulge in creative thought. The current political debate in the United Kingdom around the value of a more content-rich factual curriculum and the assertion that such a curriculum is detrimental to children's development misses the point. Learners need both facts and problem–solving abilities; the former providing the building blocks on which the thinking tools operate.

Risks, Skills and Opportunities

Tailoring teaching and learning activities to meet the needs of individual students and focusing on the learning process (rather than the technology itself) can provide real opportunities for improving the overall educational learning experience. Technology may assist in supporting, developing and refining the learning process but only when digital resources are incorporated into the curriculum in an authentic and meaningful way. Technology can be valuable in applying those psychological theories of learning into educational contexts. For example, the promotion of cognitive strategies that facilitate student learning can be achieved with the effective use of multimedia instruction (Smith & Woody, 2000). Individuals can effectively control their own rate and style of learning when using multimedia and other digitally pervasive online learning environments. Moreover, the development of video games as educational tools can support learning styles in quite innovative ways. These are often based on a range of instructional designs focusing on the principles of cognitive psychology and exemplify how best to manage cognitive load and the flow of information for learners (see Kester, Kirschner, & van Merriënboer, 2005). Nonetheless, such opportunities are not without their risks and attempting to create a new curriculum that caters for all individuals and their various approaches to learning may be an unrealistic and rather complicated process.

Conclusions

In our quest to improve teaching and learning practices, we are often susceptible to the 'Silver Bullet Syndrome' believing that new technological advances will be an easy-fix for all individuals (Watson, 2012). However, despite strong attitudinal and motivational improvements in learning through the implementation of digital technology, it has been argued that focusing solely on the mechanistic aspects of the technology will provide an incomplete picture at best. As we have discussed there is a need to look at the processes involved in learning and to allow some discussion concerning the relative stability versus variability in student learning and its implications for instruction. When we consider the relative impact of cognitive neuroscience on our understanding of styles and abilities, we are fully able to explore what a deep approach to learning involves and how to ascertain a student-centred approach to teaching and learning. However, focusing on the individual and their own learning process is far from easy and raises a number of equally challenging issues (Goswami, 2006). Perhaps one of the greatest challenges facing education is how we engage individuals with the learning process and design and tailor instructional methods to sustain positive changes that are feasible, accessible and realistic.

Chapter Three
Social Interactions and Written Communication

Introduction

Language plays a crucial role in our social communications and how we form meaningful interactions with others. While the current evidence suggests the possession of language remains a defining characteristic of what it is to be human. In some cultures the status of being a person is not attributed until language is acquired. Such is its importance, for example, in some African groups that a newborn child is termed a 'kintu' or 'thing' only becoming a 'muntu' or 'person' once some semblance of language has been acquired and developed (Fromkin, Rodman, & Hyams, 2013). However, it is not simply culture that shifts the goal posts as to the nature of language. Language has always been shaped by technology – the printing press is a case in point (Blake, 1969; Crystal, 2012). There is also a feeling that new digital technologies have accelerated that change, particularly with the rise in online communication tools and the sheer popularity of social networking sites, such as Facebook. Undoubtedly, technology has had a profound impact not only on how we communicate but how we engage with new orthographic features of written text, particularly when communicating through social networking sites, instant messaging (IM) and text messaging. Many children enter school with an unprecedented amount of technological experience and skills that many parents lack, especially in the form of online communication and social networking skills (Revelle, Reardon, et al., 2007). As their engagement with new technology increases so does their range of styles of online communication. For example, teenagers spend considerable time sending text messages, 'tweeting'

Learning and the E-Generation, First Edition. Jean D. M. Underwood and Lee Farrington-Flint.
© 2015 Jean D. M. Underwood and Lee Farrington-Flint. Published 2015 by John Wiley & Sons, Ltd.

friends, or communicating through IM and are continually in touch with a phenomenon that is currently unknown to older generations. The Ofcom (2010) UK-wide survey shows that typically 16–24 year olds declared greater time spent on their mobile phones and the social networking sites than time spent watching television. Over a quarter of adults (27%) and almost half of teenagers (47%) now own a smartphone and the frequency of sending text messages is highest among smartphone users; 79 per cent of smartphone owners claim to make and receive SMS texts on their mobile every day, compared to 50 per cent of standard phone users.

This chapter considers how learners' engagement with online social interaction and communication has had a prolific effect on their use of language practices. According to Prensky (2001), the rapid dissemination of digital technologies has seen a rise in the number of 'digital natives', that is individuals who are native speakers in the digital language of computers, video games and the Internet. With this increase towards using new digital forms of communication, and a reliance on mobile technologies, there is a notable change in the orthographic and phonological features found within written language, one that has given rise to new forms of abbreviations to facilitate effective communication. The evolution of new forms of written features of language illustrates the effect of being part of a digital revolution. Given that we are facing a digital revolution then perhaps teachers and other educators need to rethink the traditional conventions of spoken and written language.

Communicating Online

The very nature of our social interactions is changing through the introduction of new communication tools: is this a good thing? Social presence is often thought to be crucial to learning, and social exchanges and interactions can help guide thinking and reasoning on a number of levels. As Vygotsky (1978) suggests, language and learning are primarily a human activity occurring within a highly valued social context and higher cognitive processes such as thinking, problem-solving and reasoning can arise from such intimate social interactions. The use of online communication may, therefore, prove to play a critical role in developing our communication styles and our ability to engage with others in order to promote those higher-order cognitive skills most often associated with learning.

Despite initial concerns that technology would reduce human interaction and impoverish the language this has not proven to be the case. Analyses of electronic discourse show that conversational language rules are still adhered to (Crystal, 2006; Greenfield & Subrahmanyam, 2003). Indeed, the evidence to date suggests users appear to be aware that they need provide contextual information resulting in a honing of the individual's pragmatic language skills. A study by Greenfield and Subrahmanyam that investigated adolescent interactions in chat rooms showed that the participants were developing new communication strategies and creating a new communicative register.[1] Crystal (2006) argues that there is evidence that chat groups and online forums are developing dialects. Users appear to be very aware of social context (Mesch, 2009) and adapt their relational tone, personal language, sentence complexity and message composition time depending on their target recipient (Walther, 2007). All of which suggests a high level of cognitive awareness in terms of pragmatic skills.

In line with Vygotsky's assumptions about the role of language within social interactions, we can see how learners' engagement with digital communication tools, such as Twitter and Facebook, may be influencing their understanding of written language. One notable change is the shift from private to public forms of online communication. Traditionally, with the use of the telephone or handwritten letter, this involved a one-to-one form of personal communication among friends, families or close acquaintances. Essentially you knew whom you were conversing with. However, given the rise in internet chat rooms and social networking sites like Facebook, Bebo and Myspace, which thrive on the one-to-many forms of conversations, those interactions are frequently published online for anyone to see within more open and unrestricted arenas. The shift towards sharing ideas, thoughts and personal opinions is becoming increasingly more apparent online and our interactions are observable by others (Lankshear & Knobel, 2003, 2006).

A related point concerns the level of ownership and the extent to which our communications can be restricted or unrestricted. As learners begin to engage more with public forms of communication it brings with it greater opportunities for engagement with unrestricted levels of communication. An example of how technology is supporting this change is through unrestricted student blogging and online discussion boards, both of which are becoming more popular within educational environments. Blogs have become a very popular way of producing digital text and illustrate learners' tendency to blend the personal with the public (Davies & Merchant, 2009; Lankshear & Knobel, 2006). This move towards unrestricted forms of communication is often considered to be beneficial given that it allows greater freedom of expression, opportunities for collaboration, discussion and reflection: all indicative of higher levels of cognitive processing (Deed & Edwards, 2011).

---

[1] Register: in linguistics, a variety of language used for a particular purpose or in a particular social setting.

So rather than the solitary activity of sending a letter or making a telephone call, each of which are likely to be directed towards one specific individual, learners are using a range of new communication tools to interact with a range of individuals at any specific time: one-to-one, one-to-many, and many-to-many. One-to-one types of social interactions can be most commonly found in the use of email, text messaging and IM. Often the content of these communications are aimed at one particular individual, and provide a direct, immediate point of contact (Schiano, Chen, et al., 2002). If we take IM as an example here, it seems to be the only form of one-to-one synchronous online activity that is currently available. It is designed for one-to-one dialogue that allows real-time, spontaneous discussions with friends, family or acquaintances allowing for an almost immediate response (Paolillo, 1999). Through a series of studies, Valkenberg and Peter (2009) have consistently found positive associations between IM and the quality of adolescents' existing friendship networks online, often indicative of their willingness to disclose intimate information or reduce social anxiety that can often be found in more face-to-face forms of communication (Pierce, 2009). However, like many of these new forms of technology, they are primarily developed to encourage adolescents to communicate with existing friends rather than encourage interactions with complete strangers online. The use of one-to-one forms of online communication is therefore allowing greater control over the types of networks established and strengthens existing friendship groups.

However, one-to-many forms of online interactions are increasingly popular, and can be seen in the sheer rise in student's engagement with Internet chat rooms and social networking sites (such as Facebook and Myspace). Within these social networks, individuals create a public or semi-public profile, with connections made with close friends, relatives and even partial strangers. We are relying less on one-to-one interactions and focus on sharing ideas with a larger group of individuals online. Facebook remains an interesting case because although profiles are open to many, and often seen to be a one-to-many form of interaction, not all individuals behave in the same way. Underwood, Kerlin, and Farrington-Flint (2011) in their exploration of undergraduate students' interactions with the increasingly popular social-networking site Facebook, identified two distinct groups: broadcasters (one-to-many communication) and communicators (one-to-one or one-to-few) and these groups varied in how they chose to communicate with others. The communicators had smaller social-knit groups, had regular high-quality interactions and often sent messages to one person or a small group. Broadcasters, by contrast were found to have less quality interactions and engaged in self-promotion online, often engaging in one-to-many forms of communications. What the research does show is how we communicate on Facebook and with whom we choose to communicate with may be very similar to everyday face-to-face communications practice (Ellison, Steinfield, & Lampe, 2007).

Another example of one-to-many forms of interaction is through the use of Twitter, a micro-blogging tool, which offers free-flowing just-in-time social connections and interactions. Given that it happens in real time, the exchange of information is immediate and allows individuals to respond almost immediately to tweets and feeds. Twitter can be seen as unidirectional – used for the sharing of resources and following individuals online, namely celebrities. However, more recently there has been a shift towards using tweets to engage in direct conversations with other people, often by using the @ symbol to send messages directly to others. Tweeting, seen as a new form of literacy experience, can lead to improving distributed cognition through the sharing, collaborating and brainstorming that can be seen in many one-to-many forms of interactions and illustrate how individuals construct meaning through their sustained communications (Dunlap & Lowenthal, 2009). However, an important question remains with regard to how these forms of online communication are changing the nature of our writing and the orthographic representations of written language.

Changes in Written Language

There is no doubt that changes have occurred in our access to textual resources, and this engagement with new technologies, and the availability of digitized materials, questions the very relevance of what we mean by reading and literacy, something which Healy (2000) clearly acknowledges.

> Terms such as 'screening' and 'visual acuity' are accepted as aspects of reading the media and texts on digital screen. Text now refers to multiple forms of communication including information on a digital screen, video, film and other media, oral speech, television, and works of art as well as print materials. Electronic texts in particular have become part of children's everyday lives to the extent that before they commence school, a growing number of children have more experience with electronic texts than they do with books. It is important to recognise that print is now only one of several media which transmit messages in our culture.
>
> (Healy, 2000, p. 156)

So if, as Healy suggests, if electronic texts and written communication are clearly changing in response to cultural expectations, how are these texts affecting our written communication? Given the ubiquitous nature of mobile phones, and one-to-many forms of online communication, it is hardly surprising that the conventions around written language are changing within our current generation of learners. Certainly earlier chapters have alluded to the notion of a digital divide occurring between children and adults and current data around social networking and mobile phone uptake certainly supports that assertion. For example, the UK-wide data from Ofcom (2010) suggests that a new digital divide is emerging, with 16–24 year olds almost ten times more likely to go online via their mobile phone to access social networking sites than older adults. This is also true with regard to the frequency of text messaging behaviours. The Ofcom data also shows how 8 to 11 year olds send an average of 27 texts per week with 12 to 15 year olds sending on average 113 messages per week. Text sending was much less frequent in adults. This resulted in the emergence of terms, such as 'Net Generation' (Rosen, 2007) and 'Generation txt' (Thurlow, 2003) that are often seen within the popular media.

This sheer increase in text messaging is also having a profound effect on learner's written language skills. As it is now widely recognized, text messaging has evolved as a new language, often seen as a hybrid between traditional forms of written and spoken English because of its representation of features often found in spoken language. This new form of abbreviated messaging is commonly referred to by many as text speak or textisms (Wood, Kemp, & Plester, 2013). Changes to the structure of written language come out of necessity as a result of the limitations imposed by the technology itself. For example, with Twitter, a 140-character limit is imposed for any individual tweet while for text messages these were originally constrained to 160 characters per text. This meant that individuals needed to find a more efficient and cost-effective way of communicating as much information as possible within the shortest space available.

Showing some similarities to speech, text abbreviations are spontaneous, loosely structured and focus on the invention of new spelling–sound patterns. Many of these abbreviations, despite deviating from the grammatical structure found within traditional written forms of English, do share many similar features with the phonological aspects of speech. For example, common abbreviations can include letter/number homophones (gr8 for *great* or 2day for *today*), phonological contractions (txt for *text*), non-conventional spellings (foned, nite for *phoned* and *night*), shortenings (Uni, poss), *G clippings* (goin, borin), other clippings (hav, wher), acronyms (BBC), initialisms (lol), symbols (@, :-)), and accent stylizations (wanna, wivout) (see, Wood, et al., 2013). So while the phonological aspects of our language are preserved, the orthographic written features are constantly changing with this exposure to new forms of online communication.

However, there are some arguments that the use of text message abbreviations serves to threaten more traditional forms of literacy leading to a generation of 'linguistic ruin' (Cingel & Sundar, 2012; Crystal, 2008; Thurlow, 2006). There are similar arguments to the use of messages on Twitter, suggesting that abbreviations found in tweets are often shorthand, which reflects nothing more than examples of poor grammar (Grosseck & Holotescu, 2008). For many people, both educators and researchers alike, the use of abbreviations has been seen as having a detrimental effect on traditional aspects of the English language. The social popular media has regularly expressed ongoing concerns about how the use of text message abbreviations may serve to threaten more conventional standards of literacy, particularly in relation to reading and writing. In his review of media headlines from 2001–2005, Thurlow found that many national and international media sources represented this new communicative discourse in a relatively pessimistic light, citing specifically the pervasive nature of the discourse and the potential degeneration of some of the traditional aspects of the English language.

Many educators fear that the use of alternative language forms, such as phonological contractions or non-conventional spellings, is filtering inappropriately into students' academic work and serves to threaten the very premise of academic literacy. The study by Cingel and Sundar (2012) reports that the culture of text messaging raises concern among parents and teachers that 'textual adaptations' are altering their child's sense of written grammar. Furthermore, their own study shows broad support for a general negative relationship between the use of text speak in text messages and scores on a grammar assessment. However, this study has been roundly criticized by Mark Liberman (2012) who conducted a critical review of the research, questioning both the data and the analyses used to make the very strong claims put forward by Cingel and Sundar. There is growing evidence that that many students do actually recognize the clear boundaries between formal and informal use of written language and see a clear distinction between digital technology for social and academic activities (e.g., Rosen, Chang, et al., 2010, Underwood & Okubayashi, 2011).

Psychological theories have attempted to explain why text messaging may have such a detrimental effect on students' formal literacy skills, the most common of which relate to the Low-Road/High-Road Theory of Transfer of Learning (Salomon & Perkins, 1989) and models of situated learning (Brown, Collins, & Duguid, 1989). According to Salomon and Perkins, low-road transfer occurs when learned skills are unconsciously and automatically transferred across activities and high-road transfer occurs when previously acquired skills require more conscious effort and thought.

Therefore, if the prevailing media reports are correct, then low-road transfer should be occurring whereby knowledge of these text abbreviations or short-cuts will be unconsciously and automatically transferred from informal contexts to more formal styles of written English. Similarly, Brown et al.'s model of situated learning would also stress the importance of unintentional transfer of skills, or in this case, the transfer of text abbreviations, from one context to another without any deliberate thought or intention. The study by Rosen's team (2010), which examined the impact of text abbreviations on formal and informal styles of writing, found evidence of low-road transfer of learning. They found that the increasing use of linguistic-based text abbreviations (phonological contractions, clippings) was related to poorer levels of formal writing. However for informal styles of writing, sending more text messages was related to better levels of performance. Nevertheless, it is important to note that other studies by Drouin and Davis (2009) and Drouin (2011) found contradictory evidence to the findings of Rosen's team. In their analyses these authors show how students were able to make conscious decisions in their use of abbreviations, applying them only when deemed appropriate (such as in informal settings) thereby suggesting evidence for the high-road theory of learning.

Abbreviations Mediated Through Technology

Changes in the orthographic features of written communication are partially mediated through the type of technology that learners adopt. As evidenced by the literature, the use of informal written abbreviations are not just constrained to mobile phones, but evident in many other media, including Internet chat rooms, social networking sites and IM, all of which are growing in popularity, especially among teenagers and adolescents (Baron, 2010). Drouin (2011) noted how an individual's frequency of adopting short-hand text abbreviations often varies as a function of context, often determined by their choice of communication technology. For instance, as they note in their findings, abbreviations were most frequent when US college students were using SMS text messages but less so when using IM and chat functionalities within social networking sites. This suggests a greater awareness and recognition of the use of appropriate forms of language within different modes of communication.

As far as IM is concerned, some authors have systematically assessed fine-grained changes in the linguistic features of written communication during students' interactions in online chat rooms. Some studies have analysed shifts in the types of contextual cues used to initiate interactions (Merchant,

2001) while others have focussed on the identification of different social identities portrayed through instant messaging (Lewis & Fabos, 2005). Other studies have focussed on exploring individual-level characteristics of age and gender to explain the frequency and type of linguistic features often associated with messaging (e.g., Tagliamonte & Denis, 2008; Valkenburg & Peter, 2009).

As we know, similar types of abbreviations to those found in text messaging can also be found in IM. IM language is simply mirroring the tendency for written forms of language to be more like speech, becoming more colloquial in nature. Research by Varnhagen, et al. (2010) examined this rise in students' use of new abbreviated forms of language through the reliance on acronyms, word combinations and punctuation by analysing the actual content of users' IM communications among 40 adolescents. They highlighted commonalities with text message abbreviations, G *clippings* (e.g., doin for *doing*), acronyms (e.g., bf for *best friend*) and letter/number words (e.g., u r for *you are*) and found fewer cases of using pragmatic devices and misspellings/typographical errors. One of the most striking findings concerned the lack of relationship between students' scores on traditional formal tests of spelling and the reliance on the use of different abbreviation categories, suggesting that this new written language may not have any detrimental effect on formal spelling ability. The data provided by Varnhagen and colleagues, comparable to Driscoll's (2002) earlier analysis of similar short-cuts used in adults' interactions during online gaming, suggest that engagement with this new form of written language is not damaging to traditional literacy skills.

However, one distinction concerns the frequency with which individuals use these abbreviated forms of written language. Unlike the popularity of abbreviations in mobile text messages, abbreviations are used far less within social networking sites or instant messaging (Ling & Baron, 2007). Baron (2004) and Tagliamonte and Denis (2008) suggest there is little evidence that IM language is riddled with abbreviations, shortcuts and symbols, as the popular media would contend. Baron (2004) noted that based on corpus data collected from US students, many forms of communication actually follow traditional forms of written text. Only 0.3 per cent of words contained phonological abbreviations and 0.8 per cent contained initialisms (lol, brb). Similarly, Tagliamonte and Denis analysed over a million and a half words of natural and unmonitored IM discourse from 71 teenagers and found little evidence of new forms of written language. Unlike the fears and scaremongering in the media they found similar types of abbreviations, phonological contractions and short-cuts to those identified in text messages, but these only accounted for 3 per cent of all the naturalistic data on IM that they collected and analysed. Although IM communication may be part of a broader trend towards more informal language use generally, the data suggests that the actual use of this new hybrid language is limited and that students do perhaps demonstrate a tendency to outgrow the stylized form of written communication at a relatively young age. Nonetheless, the actual influence of digital literacy in the classroom and its effect on learners' performance is under-researched. There are growing attempts to examine the hybrid language of digital texts seen in synchronous online communication, emails and text messages and a stronger focus on new digital literacies (Merchant, 2007).

Perhaps in light of current psychological evidence, there is limited support for claims that new abbreviated forms of written communication represent a breakdown of the English language nor does it reflect students lay attitudes towards spelling and grammar. An alternative suggestion is that the use of text message abbreviations represents the evolution of new forms of written communication (Baron, 2010), one that incorporates phonological aspects of our spoken language and prepares students for engaging in new digital literacy practices (Tagliamonte & Denis, 2008).

The Effects of Text Abbreviations on Literacy Skills

So, as the social transfer theory suggests, are individuals simply wasting their time by inventing and playing with new forms of written language at the expense of their academic learning? Perhaps we are all too eager to dismiss text messaging. The evidence from recent psychological research seems to suggest this may not be the case at all and that there is little evidence to suggest that text messaging is threatening traditional standards of literacy. In fact, a growing number of researchers have argued that our engagement with text messaging, and our understanding of text message abbreviations, may actually lead to an improvement in our reading and spelling abilities. In their initial study, Plester, Wood, and Bell (2008) directly examined the relationship between children's understanding of text message abbreviations and their performance on standardized tests of spelling and writing with a group of 10 to 11 year olds. The study incorporated a detailed translation exercise in which the children were asked to translate a sentence from text register language (Hav u cn dose ppl ova dare?) into Standard English and from Standard English (I can't wait to see you later tonight) into text speech. Plester and colleagues also analysed the frequencies of different types of text message abbreviations in students' texting behaviours, including: letter/number homophones (CUL8R), phonological reductions (nite, wot, wuz) and other abbreviations. Correlations revealed that the level of ability on traditional tests of spelling and writing was positively associated with the better translation to text message abbreviations. Further studies by these authors have similarly shown how knowledge of text abbreviations not only predicts gains in both word and non-word reading ability (Plester, Wood, & Joshi, 2009) but also predicts gains in spelling ability when tested a year later (Wood, Meacham, et al., 2011). Overall, the relationship between text use and formal tests of spelling and writing appear promising.

It also seems that many individuals can quickly learn to adopt text message abbreviations even when exposed to abbreviations for the very first time. An interesting study by Wood, Jackson, et al. (2011) used an intervention design with 114 children who had never owned a mobile phone and assessed their ability to learn how to generate text message abbreviations. Half of the students in this sample acted as a control group, while the other half (or the intervention group) was given a mobile phone (for texting only) to use at weekends and over half-term during a 10-week period. While there were no significant differences between the two groups of children in terms of their literacy attainment during that period the findings do not show that this new-found ability to send text abbreviations does in fact lead to any positive gains in spelling ability.

There are caveats, of course, which we should be aware of when reviewing this research (see, e.g., Vosloo, 2009). The effects of socio-economic status, parental education or cultural values have not been taken into account. While Plester and Wood (2009) acknowledge that they have not established a causal link between children's experience and skill with texting and word reading ability, there may be alternative explanations. As Vosloo argues, it is possible that children who are comfortable with writing, particularly those with good literacy skills, may be allocated to the experimental conditions and use textisms more frequently than other less-skilled or less-confident children. However, a further note of caution is perhaps needed. Barks, Searight, and Ratwik (2011) reported negative effects on academic performance with undergraduate students achieving lower exam scores if they were active texters. They found that students exhibiting higher levels of text messaging skill had significantly lower test scores than participants who were less proficient at text messaging. They suggest that their findings question the view, held by many students, that this form of multitasking has little effect on the acquisition of lecture content.

These, some would say counter-intuitive, findings resonate with the findings of Bushnel, Kemp, and Martin (2012) and Drouin (2011). Bushnell's team studied of 227 10 to 12 year olds and found 82 per cent reported sending text-messages using both predictive and multipress entry methods.

The level to which the children used textisms was significantly positively correlated with general spelling ability, which fits with previous findings of positive relationships between children's textism use and literacy. Drouin found that in a sample of US undergraduates there was a significant positive relationship between text messaging frequency and literacy skills such as spelling and reading fluency. He also found significant *negative* relationships between text-speak usage in certain contexts, for example, on social networking sites and in emails to tutors, with such students tending to have lower reading accuracy. Students who do not recognize the inappropriateness of the use of text speak to a tutor are not likely to understand the traditions and etiquette of academia and are likely to struggle in this educational environment.

Additional studies have similarly found that our ability to engage with, and send, text message abbreviations may also lead to a greater reading fluency and reading comprehension scores (Johnson, 2012) although, as we have already discussed, others question whether they hinder the development of grammatical skills (Cingel & Sundar, 2012). While the findings seem promising what is not known is whether the new-found ability to send text abbreviations does, in fact, lead to any positive gains in spelling ability.

The advantages of using text abbreviations extend well beyond young children. Quite recently, evidence has emerged that suggests that using abbreviations in written language may help encourage those with learning difficulties in sustaining online interactions, particularly through IM. New technologies may be providing opportunities that would otherwise impede individuals with learning difficulties. Individuals with Specific Language Impairment (SLI) are a good example, as they often show profound difficulties in language production and comprehending written text. While many do struggle with using online communication, presenting lower uptake in online interaction and fewer text abbreviations (Durkin, Conti-Ramsden, & Walker, 2011), there are many who choose to engage with online interactions to stay in touch with their friends and who use these online features in pretty much the same way as typically developing peers (Durkin, Conti-Ramsden & Walker, 2010). Similarly, as Veater, Plester, and Woods (2010) have highlighted, children with dyslexia also show comparable numbers of text message abbreviations to age-matched controls, the only difference being in a reduction in the use of phonetic types of abbreviations. It is suggested that many individuals, especially those who may struggle in forming face-to-face communications, can form online interactions through emailing, text messaging and communications via social networking sites (Lenhart, Arafeh, et al., 2008). Perhaps this can be explained by the relaxed and informal nature of this new form of written language. Features of IM and text messaging are less stringent: they do not follow conventional rules of English spelling and grammar leading to a much more relaxed and informal communication and interaction. Language and literacy requirements within text messaging and IM are less arduous than more traditional formal modes of online communication and therefore allow greater opportunities for all learners.

Risks, Skills and Opportunities

There is a key concern regarding the use of new digital communication tools and online safety. By moving away from one-to-one towards one-to-many forms of social interactions children are increasing the probabilities of communicating with strangers. Enhanced communication technologies, therefore, raise concerns for not just how we communicate, but also with whom we communicate during our time online. Aside from the media hype around the enhanced risks of communicating with strangers, the evidence appears to suggest that communications are irrevocably changing and adapting and more students are turning to Internet chat rooms and social networking sites, like Facebook, Bebo and Myspace, to establish one-to-many forms of online communication (Ellison, et al., 2007). There is also speculation that this over reliance on the use of digital communication tools, particularly IM, tweeting and texting on mobile phones is having a detrimental effect on traditional features of the English language. However, it may be appropriate to acknowledge that mobile technology is not simply used for social and leisure activities, but can offer a real potential for allowing educational learning to occur beyond the constraints of the classroom. There is an abundance of evidence to suggest that mobile technology can be used to support language learning, especially for those who may have English as a second language (Kukulska-Hulme & Shield, 2008) and new theories of mobile learning are beginning to emerge within the literature (Sharples, Taylor, & Vavoula, 2005). However, despite promising opportunities for mobile technology in education, we may have some way to go before the full benefits of mobile learning are fully integrated into the school curriculum.

Conclusions

There is a growing body of research to suggest that learners' engagement with computer-mediated communications plays a key role in the development of written language. We have focussed on the pragmatics of language use by illustrating changes in the nature of online communications from one-to-one to one-to-many forms of interactions occurring. However, learners' engagement with these new forms of communication tools, such as text messaging, IM and social networking, has given rise to changes in the nature of their online communications and a notable shift in their use of the orthographic features contained within written language. The rise in the use of new informal styles of abbreviated language is most prominent within children and teenagers, and has caused great controversy among teachers, parents and the social media. Learners have begun to play with language in a way that has given rise to a new abbreviated form of written language. This new informal language register is now used worldwide among learners and can be seen as a hybrid between written and spoken English. However, despite ongoing controversies about the detrimental effect on more conventional written forms of language, the empirical evidence on text messaging appears more promising. Perhaps our reliance on a new written orthographic form of language may simply reflect a natural progression in the evolution of language, most generally one that is associated with the youth of our digital age and is transforming our literacy practices as a result.

Chapter Four
E-Books, E-Readers and Tablets, Are they the Way Forward?

Introduction

Computers are transforming the way in which people interact with the written word not just through online communications, like Twitter or Facebook, but also through the accessibility of digitized texts. Learners, and the public in general, now have access to a proliferation of texts online, from e-books to web pages. As a result, the death of the traditional printed text has been heavily discussed (see Birkets, 2006) and these deliberations show no sign of abating. There may be growing substance in this assertion concerning the printed book. For example, Amazon.com reported in April 2011 that for every 100 print books it sold, it sold 105 Kindle books[1]. Reading electronic books on the iPad or tablet device is not just for social pleasure; it can also have an effect on the way in which formal literacy skills are taught within schools, particularly with a growth in computerized educational materials, such as electronic books, e-readers and tablet devices, which offer new and powerful tools for teaching literacy skills.

The ability to read and comprehend textual information remains a crucial skill. It is a core skill underpinning all aspects of education as well as society in general. Reading refers not just to the ability to decode individual words on a written page, but relates to our ability to decipher written text with appropriate speed and expression (fluency) and to understand what is being read (comprehension). In this chapter we explore the extent to which new and exciting forms of computerized and multimedia learning environments can help promote

[1] http://portables.about.com

Learning and the E-Generation, First Edition. Jean D. M. Underwood and Lee Farrington-Flint.
© 2015 Jean D. M. Underwood and Lee Farrington-Flint. Published 2015 by John Wiley & Sons, Ltd.

literacy skills among learners and how the focus on teaching reading skills may be shifting from static formats to more interactive media with the introduction of multimedia electronic books (e-books) and touch-screen tablet devices.

Multiple digital devices, such as e-readers, iPods and iPads, have been described by some as a 'game changer', providing much-needed educational reform especially for equipping the current generation of learners with much needed literacy skills (Falloon, 2013). We are increasingly placing less reliance on printed texts to provide the knowledge and skills required to become proficient readers. Books are being replaced by electronic-texts and rather more depressingly by the worksheet. But is there any hard evidence to support such claims that technological advances in reading instruction can support reading skills? Clearly, e-readers and e-books have become widely accepted with a marked transition to replace paper textbooks with e-textbooks. Despite an overwhelming quantity of research into the benefits of multimedia e-books for supporting emergent reading, there have, as yet, been very few projects focusing on the role of e-readers and tablet devices to support literacy skills within educational settings. As these devices are the way forward is there sufficient evidence to show increased levels of attainment with readers than for print? A number of key issues are addressed with regard to the extent of this e-reading revolution and whether there is sufficient evidence to support the claim that a shift in multimedia reading instruction can be beneficial to young children. We then ask whether there is sufficient evidence to show that reading acquisition differs from traditional paper formats before, finally, asking whether such digital technologies are able to support struggling readers in their communication and acquisition of reading skills within the current digital age.

E-books: Are they Effective Teaching Tools or an Adjunct to Real Reading Activities?

The use of online digital resources to support the acquisition of reading skills is not a new concept. There is a long history of creating online digital resources to support and promote young children's reading skills through the implementation of computerized methods, from CD-ROMs to alternative web-based technologies, with an emphasis on improving letter recognition, phonological skills and sight–word recognition. A series of studies by Savage and colleagues at the University of Montreal have shown the affordances associated with web-based resources for teaching a balanced phonics approach to acquiring phonological skills with kindergarten children using the ABRACADABRA software (Comaskey, Savage, & Abrami, 2009; Savage, Abrami, et al., 2009; Savage, et al., 2013). With a focus on teaching phonics, this software has been shown to increase reading skills on a number of levels, from gains in the development of early phonological skills, to vocabulary and reading comprehension using online web-based resources, although some trials of this software have proved less successful as Harper and colleagues (2012) have found. However, teaching phonological skills out of context may not always promote emergent reading. That is, the focus has been on teaching specific components of reading, usually with a focus on teaching phonological approaches such as onset and rime, and phonemes and graphemes in isolation from story texts. This reduces a learner's reliance on contextual cues and access to story books.

Unlike phonological training programmes, there has been a recent shift towards using interactive multimedia storybooks to support the reading skills of many young children with promising outcomes (see Morgan, 2013). Most e-books are designed to replicate those books that exist in hard copy but have the potential to scaffold literacy through independent reading without any additional adult support. There are a range of terms that appear within the literature to embrace digital story books that includes 'e-books', 'living books', 'talking books' or 'CD-ROM storybooks', all of which contain an element of multimedia to teach reading skills to varying degrees (Shamir & Shlafer, 2011). They can range from simple text with static words and pictures presented in an electronic format to more highly interactive electronic story books that embrace dynamic multimedia elements with narration, background visuals and animations. These may include sounds, moving images, narration and even interactive games (Silverman & Hines, 2012). They provide young readers with the option to hear stories narrated as they follow on screen and allow them to attend to the individual written words, phrases or passages that are being read aloud. E-books sometimes include optional hidden hotspots that can be activated by the user and which elaborate on the illustrations or the text. By clicking on the text the child may hear it read aloud. In line with Mayer's (2003) cognitive theory of multimedia learning, electronic books can offer an array of multimedia content, rather than a relatively static representation found within printed books. These multiple representations (text, voices, pictures and animations) can be highly engaging and can transform the reading experiences of many children who usually read independently or with adult support solely using printed texts. It is now widely accepted that multimedia elements appear engaging and stimulating while offering a motivational aspect to print-based learning. Yet despite difficulties in evaluating electronic books, new media, such as CD-ROM talking books have been found to support young children's print-based literacy development not just for typically developing readers (McKenna, Labbo, et al., 2003) but also among struggling readers (McKenna, Reinking, et al., 1999).

Why are electronic storybooks so appealing to young readers? Davies and O'Sullivan (2002, pp. 106–107) note several potential benefits for using electronic books to support literacy by enabling young children to:

- enjoy a text and interact with events and characters on screen
- read for meaning and enjoy stories with focused talk and joint attention supported by the explicit nature of the text on the screen
- develop their understanding of print through text which is highlighted as it is read
- develop their own narratives linked to what is happening on screen;
- understand aspects of texts on screen, such as icons, navigational features and 'hotspots'
- develop ICT skills such as use of the mouse
- collaborate and negotiate with others.

The term 'edutainment' has been used to characterize the highly interactive playful qualities and educational goals associated with using online resources to help students acquire some of the core skills associated with reading, writing and comprehension (Underwood & Underwood, 1998). It is this combination of education with engaging multimedia qualities that enthuse and engage learners of all ages. However, we need to look beyond the purely entertainment value of technology to assess the true benefits of teaching literacy skills using multimedia devices and digital tools.

New software affects young children's language (e.g., vocabulary and story comprehension) and emergent literacy levels (e.g., word recognition and phonological awareness) and the evidence, at first glance, appears rather encouraging (Reinking, 2005). The use of multimedia electronic storybooks appears to promote the acquisition of verbal knowledge and development of phonological skills, which are two of the emergent literacy skills that have been tested among typically developing children using multimedia educational e-books. For instance, Wood, Pillinger, and Jackson (2010) did research into the role of multimedia storybooks on children's emerging literacy skills and suggest that the use of electronic talking books may not be detrimental to the acquisition of emerging reading skills. In one study, Chera and Wood (2003) assessed improvements in literacy skills in a group of children aged 3 to 6 who were exposed to an e-book intervention during a four-week period compared to a control group. She found that those involved in the intervention did show greater gains, from pre- to post-test, in their phonological awareness when compared to the control group. In a later study, however, Wood (2005) examined differential gains in phonological skills following a short-term intervention using either a phonic-based 'talking book' or one-to-one reading tuition with an adult. In this instance, no substantial differences between the groups were noted, and both groups showed gains from pre- to post-test attainment in phonological skill. Although these findings suggest no substantial differences between printed text and electronic storybook activities, they do at the very least suggest that such e-books can provide a much needed tool that teachers can employ to ease demands on their time in large classes.

Any gains found in e-book interventions may also be susceptible to individual child-level factors, such as socio-economic status (SES) and the lack of opportunities to work with digitized literacy software. Often those from low SES families show poorer levels of literacy within the home environment, especially availability of digitized books or educational games, alongside lower levels of parental mediation compared to higher SES families (see Shamir, Korat, & Fellah, 2013). Yet supporting those from low SES backgrounds appears encouraging, at least through the use of electronic multimedia story books (see for example, Biancarosa & Griffiths, 2012; Korat & Shamir, 2007; Segal-Drori, Korat, et al., 2010). Korat and Shamir examined the effectiveness of electronic books with 128, 5-to-6 year olds from low to middle SES when randomly assigned to one of three subgroups. The two intervention groups comprised children who individually read an electronic book and children who were read the same printed book by an adult. A third control condition incorporated a group of children who simply received the regular classroom literacy programme. In line with other studies Shamir and Shlafe (2011) found significant gains in post-test vocabulary scores for both intervention groups, but no gains in phonological awareness or word recognition when compared to the control group.

Korat and Shamir (2008) in a similar study manipulated the level of support by including three conditions in e-book exposure. Children were exposed to either 'read story only', 'read with dictionary', or 'read and play' during three sessions across low and middle SES groups of 5 to 6 year olds. In comparison to a control group, systematic gains in word meaning were found across all three experimental groups. Moreover, Korat and Shamir found that those children from low SES backgrounds made the greatest gains in word reading across the 'read with dictionary' and 'read with play conditions' indicating how levels of interactivity can support literacy gains.

While there appear to be some advantages in using multimedia e-books for improving phonological skills, there is also growing evidence that e-books can also lead to improvements in children's whole-word/sight-word reading. There is a suggestion that whole-word multimedia software could be a useful classroom aid for supporting early literacy skills in children who are struggling to learn to read. In their initial study, Karemaker, Pitchford, and O'Malley (2010a) carried out a systematic comparison between the multimedia software, Oxford Reading Tree (ORT) for Clicker, and traditional ORT big books, with a group of 61 5-year-old typically develop-ing readers. Both interventions were delivered over five 1-hour sessions over the course of a week. Post-intervention scores found greater gains in word recognition, word naming, rhyme awareness, segmentation skill and graph-eme awareness following the children's exposure to the ORT for Clicker intervention. Similar gains in word-recognition scores at post-test were associated with the Clicker intervention rather than the big books interven-tion can also be found for struggling readers (Karemaker, et al., 2010b).

It remains clear that presenting high-quality children's books on computers with interactive multimedia, such as the text being read aloud expressively with simultaneous highlighting of the words being read, can enable students to acquire vocabulary and phonological skills. E-books are often found to contribute to the enhancement of young children's phonological awareness (Chera & Wood, 2003; Wise, et al., 1989) and their verbal knowledge (Lewin 2000; Segers & Verhoeven 2002) as well as their ability to recall stories (Underwood & Underwood, 1998). Yet the findings are somewhat inconsist-ent at best. For some studies, systematic comparisons in reading ability from pre- to post-test scores between printed texts and e-books show a similar contribution in both contexts (de Jong & Bus, 2002; Korat & Shamir, 2007; Wood, 2005) while for others, there are significant gains in word reading for e-book conditions only (Korat, 2010; Korat & Shamir, 2008). Significant gains can also be found for vocabulary (Korat & Shamir, 2007; Lewin 2000; Segers & Verhoeven, 2002) and phonological skills (Chera & Wood, 2003; Karemaker, et al., 2010a, 2010b). However, caution is needed in interpreting these various findings. There are so many different e-formats that it is diffi-cult to make systematic comparisons about the effectiveness of any interven-tion design (Labbo & Kuhn, 2000). Many researchers have observed that the use of talking books in the course of regular classroom activity is often marginal to the literacy curriculum. This reflects the educational practi-tioners' concerns about their genuine educational potential (Littleton, Wood, & Chera, 2006) and what constitutes effective literacy software still remains unclear (Underwood, 2000).

Promoting Collaboration and Peer-Group Interactions

So far we have considered the student's engagement with multimedia story-books as a way of gaining skills in emerging literacy. It is not simply the promotion of reading skills or the learners' level of interaction with e-books that promotes learning; the use of multimedia e-books can also facilitate different styles of working and encourage collaborative learning. For instance, we know that peer tutoring can be instrumental to literacy development, particularly in the form of paired reading and peer-assisted learning strategies (PALS), both of which have been noted to raise attainment in reading and phonological awareness (Fuchs, et al., 2001). Often this is because, as Topping and Whiteley (1993, p. 58) acknowledge: *peer tutoring promotes more positive social relationships and more independent learning (through co-operation).* But, how are collaboration and peer group interactions influenced when working with more digitized and electronic forms of literacy instruction?

Wood, Littleton, and Chera (2005) explicitly examined the effect of collaboration when working with e-books by comparing the types of interactions that occur between 'equal' pairs, where the children were of equal reading attainment and 'unequal pairs', where there was a disparity between the children's reading attainment. The pairings were less important in determining interactive styles; it was gender that affected collaborative learning with talking books. Wood and colleagues identified strong differences in girls' and boys' use of software with boys showing greater dispute and girls showing greater negotiation and collaboration. These findings echo earlier work by Underwood and Underwood (1998), which also noted similar discrepancies in interaction between boys and girls on multimedia talking books and highlights how interactional styles may well influence the effectiveness of different types of educational software (see also Littleton, Wood, & Chera, 2004, 2006; Underwood & Underwood, 1990).

A further aspect of interaction relates to dialogic reading, which traditionally is an approach found in joint-reading activities. Dialogic reading refers to the strategies used by tutors as they use open-ended questions to prompt a deeper understanding of the story and its narrative during joint reading exercises. There is increasing evidence that dialogic reading interventions can be an effective way to increase receptive and expressive vocabulary scores and develop narrative abilities in pre-school children (Hargrave & Sénéchal, 2000; Hay & Fielding-Barnsley, 2007). Wood, Pillinger, & Jackson (2010) in their initial assessment, looked at the types of interactions on storybook reading among beginning readers by comparing specially designed talking books with one-to-one tuition with an adult using the paper-based versions of the same books. Although there was only a marginal improvement in phonological skills associated with talking-book intervention, they did find different styles of working in pairs and differences in the interactional styles adopted by the children, supporting earlier findings (Wood, Littleton, & Chera, 2005; Underwood & Underwood, 1998) yet no evidence of spontaneous dialogic reading between pairs was identified. As they conclude, evidence of dialogic reading was only found among the adult-led intervention group but not the electronic talking book group, which suggests possible limitations on the use of technology for spontaneous peer collaboration.

Adult Instruction is Still Important

Is electronic storybook software sufficient to promote gains in literacy skills among young readers without any further adult assistance? It is clear that when left to their own devices, electronic storybooks can help to improve children's reading scores, yet the inconsistencies in findings suggest that implementing e-books alone will have varying degrees of success. Further issues concern the role of scaffolding and whether e-books can be instrumental in acquiring reading skills both with and without adult support. There is some suggestion that adult instruction with e-books is still important in order to achieve success, given that adults may help sustain children's attention on task and help to avoid distractions.

The majority of previous studies have simply compared e-books and printed books without considering the gains in the provision of adult support. Experimental work by Korat and colleagues (e.g., Korat, 2010; Korat & Shamir, 2012; Korat, Shami, & Arbiv, 2011) has systematically explored the development of emergent literacy among young children and particularly the role of adult instruction in using traditional versus electronic texts. However, adult instruction still appears to be a crucial factor in determining the success of e-book interventions. For instance, Segal-Drori, et al. (2010) compared the effects of reading electronic and printed books with and without adult instruction with a group of 5 to 6 year olds from low SES backgrounds. They found, consistent with other studies (Korat, Segal-Drori, & Klien, 2009; Korat & Shamir, 2012), that over four sessions, significant gains were only found for phonological awareness, word reading and concepts about print among those who received e-book intervention with adult instruction. This was also true when considering the effects of e-books with adult support on emergent writing skills (see Korat, Shamir, & Arbiv, 2011).

However, using electronic books to support and promote specific literacy skills, such as letter knowledge, decoding, concepts about print and phonological skills, provides only a partial explanation of the skills required to become a proficient reader. The process of acquiring reading skills becomes much more complex once we begin to consider how children learn to comprehend written text. Unlike word reading or decoding, research that has examined the effects of using e-readers, computer screens and paper formats on comprehension scores has often found no significant differences between experimental and control groups. Margolin and colleagues (2013), for example, found that these three different presentation media do not differentially affect the comprehension of text and there are no significant improvements in written comprehension when taking a qualitative analysis of students' written transcripts of text (Connell, Bayliss, & Farmer, 2012). Although, in part, this could be explained by software characteristics and a lack of focus on comprehension skills per se, rather than any lack of improvement.

However, do multimedia storybooks always promote significant gains in children's emergent literacy skills? There is some suggestion that e-books can have detrimental effects on emergent literacy, one that constrains or inhibits the development of reading skills (Labbo & Kuhn, 2000). For example, animated areas of the screen might disrupt children's attention and interfere with their ability to connect scenes, make inferences and follow the story-line: they offer detours and distractions from the main story and impact on the comprehension of narratives and reduce memory capacity (Ricci & Beal, 2002). Furthermore potential inconsistencies between the animations and the storyline can impede reading success and students' comprehension of the text (Labbo & Kuhn, 2000; Underwood & Underwood, 1998). Similar to Labbo and Kuhn, de Jong and Bus (2002, p. 154) found that: *the many attractive options of e-books seem to divert children's attention from text and number of readings of the text in favour of iconic and pictorial explorations.* Similarly, as Underwood (2000) notes, any gains in reading proficiency or instructional style are often mediated by software characteristics rather any other instructional factors.

The quality of the animation, therefore, remains an important factor to the perceived success of e-books. There is a subtle distinction, offered by Labbo and Kuhn (2000) between 'considerate' and 'inconsiderate' types of animations, which are respectively considered to be supportive or distractive. Considerate e-books are those that contain hotspots or activities that are deemed congruent with, and are integrated into, the content of the story. That is, the illustrations, narration, functions and animations need to remain integral to the story narrative for any substantial gains in learning to be found. There is also a strong element of cognitive resourcing: when digital picture books pair text narration with animation, the cognitive load is substantially reduced and the learning capacity markedly improved (Mayer & Moreno, 2003) rather than appearing 'merely amusing' or 'incidental' to the story-line (Korat, et al., 2011).

The Benefits of Kindles and iPads

While there seems to be growing evidence for the implementation of e-books in schools and their effects on learners' emerging literacy skills, considerably less research has considered the presentation of text on newer mobile technologies (Connell, et al., 2012). The increase in tablet devices, particularly iPods and iPads, shows a greater potential for promoting 'anytime, anywhere' learning. The Pew Research Centre Report (Rainie, Smith, & Duggan, 2013) has shown that among US students aged 16 years and over, 35 per cent own tablet computers and 24 per cent own e-readers, such as the Amazon Kindle, Kobo Aura and Nook Simple Touch. In addition the data show that 95 per cent of US students brought mobile phones and 29 per cent brought laptops to class very day (Aguilar-Roca, Williams & O'Dowd, 2012; Tindell & Bohlander, 2012). Furthermore, these technologies have been embraced, not only within the private school sector but also the state sector, with over 1.5 million iPads deployed in educational programmes in the United States, with comparable figures within the United Kingdom (Brian, 2012).

While mobile technologies have been shown to provide new approaches to learning over a number of years (Johnson, Levine, & Smith, 2009), the introduction of the iPad, and other similar tablets, has changed mobile learning possibilities for teachers and students. Neumann and Neumann (2013) describe tablets as an ideal tool for supporting literacy skills through the versatile functions that develop reading and writing as well as downloadable applications (apps) for alphabet matching, phonics games and stories. They can be interactive, easy to use and engaging. A recent analysis of the growth in children's use of educational apps certainly supports this assertion, with nearly 72 per cent of apps aimed at pre-school children, and more than 50 per cent of the top-selling apps targetting primary school children (Shuler, Levine, & Ree, 2012). The evidence, however scant, suggests that touch-screen tablets, like the iPad, have the potential to enhance children's literacy skills, including their alphabet knowledge, print concepts and emergent writing. This raises the question whether touch-screen tablet devices and mobile technologies can be instrumental in supporting reading acquisition in the current young generation? iPads and apps have achieved global popularity among a broad range of users, including pre-school children. As such they offer considerable promise in the educational arena. The iPad was used as an instructional tool to facilitate emergent literacy and seems to be highly engaging, motivating and supportive of literacy acquisition even with pre-school children (Beschorner & Hutchison, 2013). While observational studies, often incorporating qualitative design, show promising and encouraging evidence in support of using iPad apps to transform learners' behaviours (Hutchison, Beschorner, & Schmidt-Crawford, 2012), other quantitative studies, which have compared iPads apps to traditional books, seem to show a negative effect on reading comprehension (Chiong, Ree, & Takuechi, 2012) and story recall ability (Parish-Morris, Mahajan, et al., 2013). As Kucirkova (2013) rightly acknowledges, a more detailed and innovative methodological approach is needed to assess clearly the true educational potential of iPads as a tool for improving children's learning:

> Researchers interested in finding out how novel features of iPad books affect children's learning, need to adopt a theoretical framework which facilitates conceptualizing iPad books as unique, 21st century learning tools. This is closely linked to the need for adopting a detailed and innovative methodology to ascertain the books' value for children's learning.
>
> (Kucirkova, 2013)

However, unlike multimedia e-books, some devices like the Kindle e-reader simply serve as an electronic presentation method, replicating the printed text but on screen. Kindles and other e-readers do not have any additional requirements such as the need to search or problem-solve or to navigate through hyperlinks. Yet despite the lack of multimedia elements, their appeal concerns their portability and ease of access as well as offering a comfortable size and weight, touch-screen, and Wi-Fi data connection for online access to information. The use of tablets, iPads and other mobile devices are beginning to allow literacy activities to occur outside the classroom, and to connect school and home learning activities. This is helped by improvements in the design of the Kindle as it now provides less strain on the eyes and is more akin to 'real-book' reading.

Although there may be a lack of research evidence, there is growing support for the use of iPads and iPods, especially for encouraging early pre-school literacy instruction. We know that parent-child storybook reading can offer early foundations to acquiring literacy skills including enthusiasm for reading and vocabulary skills (Kucirkova, Messer, & Whitelock, 2010, 2012). Early exposure to texts can support children's awareness of print, modulation of joint attention and early vocabulary growth. But how has technology helped to support these literacy skills? One particular study investigated the role of iPads and the use of a personalized 'our story' application with 4- to 5-year-old Spanish children. The 'our story' application was devised to support children's learning through the activity of story-creation and story-sharing (Kucirkova, Messer, et al., 2014). Within this study, Kucirkova and her colleagues found that high-quality engagement often supported joint problem-solving, exploratory talk and collaboration among children using this personalized app in comparison to other available apps. Although little research has been carried out with personalized story apps for pre-school children, the findings appear positive and suggest that early instruction may provide some foundation for acquiring literacy skills later on. Even with older children, iPads have been found to encourage intuitive participation in open-ended literacy-based interactive games (Verenikina & Kervin, 2011) and recent surveys of English teachers in primary and secondary schools are also encouraging in offering a promise of supporting reading skills in alternative formats to traditional print (see Goodwyn, 2013a, 2013b for further details).

Beyond pre-readers, there are very few examples of the successful implementation of iPads or Kindles in the classroom, and at best, the evidence relies on personal anecdotes from teachers or literacy coordinators. However, the trend may be changing: there is some suggestion that incorporating iPads into the curriculum may help to revolutionize students' literacy learning (e.g., McFarlane, 2013; Simpson, Walsh, & Rowsell, 2013) with clear examples of possible structured frameworks for embedding iPads into formal teaching activities (Northrop & Killeen, 2013) even though the evidence for their success remains anecdotal at best.

However, unlike primary or secondary schools, universities do seem to be taking full advantage of electronic texts and digitized materials. Such materials are now part of the mainstream educational practice across most, if not all, higher education institutions. Increasingly undergraduate students are rejecting textbooks as they move to the use of a Kindle, iPad or other tablet devices that allow easy access to online course materials. However, this is perhaps not out of choice: while academics may see the perceived benefits on electronic resources, some undergraduates still need to be convinced. For example, in their own survey of undergraduate students, Olsen, Kleivset, and Langseth (2013) reported that while the iPad received better scores than Kindle DX, 51 per cent of students still showed a strong preference for relying on traditional printed texts, noting how functions such as commenting, highlighting and annotating non-linear texts remains difficult online. The data suggest that promoting a reliance solely on e-books may not provide the most efficient learning experience in higher education. These findings are similar to previous surveys among university-level students with 61 per cent demonstrating a preference for print on paper as the best medium for engaging in academic study (Camacho & Spackman, 2011). Clearly the preference for using e-books and other electronic resources, particularly among undergraduate students remains a contentious issue and the actual benefits beyond using printed texts remains uncertain. Students do report, nonetheless, that e-texts do support affective and psychomotor learning and provide easier access to module resources that rely solely on printed texts (see Rockinson-Szapkiw, Courduff, et al., 2013). It is argued that as students become more and more familiar with e-books and handheld devices or tablets a dramatic increase in student selection of e-texts is expected (Smith & Caruso, 2010).

Mobile Technology and Second Language Learning

Digital technologies are changing the way we engage with text in its written form and this is particularly true in the case of vocabulary acquisition. There is growing evidence to illustrate how mobile phones, in particular text-initiated vocabulary learning as well as interactive gaming, can help to improve language acquisition, particularly among those who are learning a second or additional language. Quite clearly, exposure to abbreviated forms of language is insufficient for this purpose, but how can digital technologies support language development? Although the quantity of previous work on computer-assisted language learning (CALL) is beyond the scope of this chapter, there have been some detailed texts that discuss the affordances of Web 2.0 technologies for promoting language learning (see Reinders, Thomas, & Warschauer, 2012).

Some examples of vocabulary training for second language learners can be seen through the adoption of mobile phone technology. The use of mobile-based technologies for supporting vocabulary developments has been particularly beneficial in second language learning, especially those from less-privileged areas, such as rural India. In one study, Başoğlu and Akdemir (2010) compared vocabulary learning for target words over 6 weeks presented through SMS text messages on mobile phones (experimental group) or presented on paper flash-cards (control group) and found significant improvements in the students' vocabulary when using SMS text message presentation.

Zhang, Song, and Burston (2011) also present compelling data with regard to the effectiveness of vocabulary learning via mobile phones among a group of undergraduate students attending a Chinese University. Through the intervention study, students received vocabulary training on 130 selected word items either through SMS text messages (experimental group) or via traditional paper methods (control group) and the gains in vocabulary knowledge were compared through immediate and delayed post-intervention test scores. The results confirmed that the experimental SMS group made significantly greater gains in vocabulary learning than the control group, although the retention rates are questionable given that delayed post-intervention test scores failed to show any notable differences in vocabulary gains over time. Notwithstanding the questionable long-term gains in vocabulary learning, these authors acknowledge the potential gains in using mobile technologies to support vocabulary acquisition among those who are attempting to learn English as a second language, not simply through SMS text messaging but also through the access to email via mobile phones (see Lu, 2008).

However, it is not simply mobile phones that promote second language learning, but the use of interactive websites. Although social networking sites have been seen largely as non-educational tools to facilitate social interactions, particularly by teachers and parents, they do offer real and valuable learning opportunities. For example, they can facilitate second language acquisition as they offer the possibility to engage in real-time interactions. Examples of interactive websites include Palabea[2] and Babbel[3] which offer online communities that promote synchronous and asynchronous forms of social interaction. A further example is Whyville[4], which was developed primarily for educational purposes allowing learners to interact, discuss, share movies and play educational games, all for the sole purpose of language learning. As the previous studies clearly illustrate, the more productive we are in learning new vocabularies, the greater the gains in retaining this information, so interactive game playing may prove fundamental to learning new languages.

What About Those at Risk of Reading Difficulties?

Given the potential benefits of mobile phones, multimedia e-books and iPads for typically developing children, it is likely that such devices or software programmes may also be supportive for those who struggle, especially those children who experience profound difficulties associated with vocabulary acquisition, phonological awareness and concept of print. In fact, Neuman (2009) notes that children at risk of reading disabilities tend to improve when exposed to more forms of media, such as computers, television and radio, in addition to the printed text supporting the multimodality of digital literacy. Others suggest that the use of film-like digital e-books can be highly beneficial for the most at-risk children as well as those who are learning English as a second language (Bus, Verhallen, & de Jong, 2009; Verhallen, Bus, & de Jong, 2006) as well as the use of assistive technologies to support learning among those children with the most severe risk of developmental disabilities (Reichle, 2011).

[2] http://www.palabea.net
[3] http://www.babbel.com
[4] http://www.whyville.net

There is a long tradition of using computerized tasks to support struggling readers and often these tasks have been found to support literacy skills within many primary classrooms (Lynch, Fawcett, & Nicholson, 2000). But what about those who are diagnosed with specific difficulties in learning to read? Is there any evidence that computerized programmes or e-books can facilitate learning for these children with more extreme difficulties in deciphering written text? Children with dyslexia seem to be an ideal population to benefit from the use of multimedia e-books given their apparent difficulties associated with acquiring emergent literacy skills. Such difficulties relate to decoding skills, manipulation of phoneme-to-grapheme correspondence and short-term memory constraints. The majority of previous computerized intervention programmes have revealed promising results for specific phonological skills training among typically developing children (Savage, et al., 2009; Torgesen, Wagner, Rashotte, et al., 2010) as well as children diagnosed with both dyslexia and a specific language impairment (SLI) (Segers & Verhoeven, 2004). Such interventions have often, though not always, focussed on specific word reading skills, such as a focus on improving phonological skills and teaching grapheme-phoneme conversion (GPC) rules. Yet, until recently, few studies have focused on evaluating the effectiveness of electronic story books or tablet devices for supporting struggling readers (see Shamir & Shlafer, 2011). Verhallen, et al. (2006), for example, make strong claims that those books with multimedia features (e.g., e-books) have a greater potential for stimulating early reading development than those containing static pictures (e.g., printed books) particularly for those younger children who show dyslexic tendencies. Similarly, there is a strong narrative to support the argument that animated story books with spoken text can provide a crucial advantage to improving shared reading and story comprehension among many disadvantaged and at-risk readers (de Jong & Verhallen, 2013). Certainly those few studies that specifically assess the impact of e-learning technologies on children diagnosed with special educational needs appear encouraging (Segers, Nooijen, & de Moor, 2006) but the body of evidence is not currently sufficient to make any substantial claims regarding the overall effectiveness of e-books on emergent literacy skills.

Alongside multimedia e-books, text-to-speech software has been recognized as a valuable tool to support struggling readers including those diagnosed with dyslexia (Balajthy, 2005). Computer-mediated text has focused on simple text-to-speech (TTS), which uses voice synthesis software to provide oral reading of ordinary electronic text files, such as word-processed documents, text on webpages, and e-books. Yet the success rate of text-to-speech is variable at best. Some studies that have analysed the effectiveness of TTS on students' reading acquisition and comprehension skills found significant gains in decoding skills (see Reitsma, 1988); while other studies note that TTS improved comprehension skills particularly among those at risk of developing reading difficulties (Wise and Olson, 1994). Yet other studies have found less favourable outcomes. For instance, in a more recent study, Hecker and colleagues found that results on a formal reading test did not vary across groups exposed to print format versus TTS format for college students with attention-deficit disorder (ADD) (Hecker, Burns, et al., 2002). The research did find, however, that attention to text, as measured by the number of distractions during reading, was improved greatly in the TTS format group as was the time spent reading passages. What remains clear is that while the potential benefits may be found in the use of text-to-speech software, or through the use of e-readers and electronic texts, the choice of software must be aligned to the individual learning needs of the struggling reader for any substantial gains to be made (King-Sears, Swanson, & Mainzer, 2011).

A Multisensory Experience

There is growing evidence concerning the benefits of incorporating tablet devices and iPads into mainstream classrooms to help support the literacy skills development of struggling readers. It is argued that touch-screen tablets do offer a multisensory approach to literacy instruction, which remains a crucial aspect of success for students with dyslexia (Reid, 2011), and new research evidence is beginning to emerge. Assistive technologies, through iPads and personalized apps, are supporting students with dyslexia in higher educational institutions (see Reid, Strnadová, & Cumming, 2013) and can help support struggling readers with literacy skills below age-level expectations to improve motivation, reading comprehension and reading fluency (Elliott, Livengood, & McGlamery, 2012). For example, Schneps, Thomson, et al. (2013) recently used eye-tracking techniques to compare undergraduate students reading on a small-screen e-reader (Apple iPod Touch) with reading on a larger tablet computer (Apple iPad), and found that when students with dyslexia read using the iPod device, oculomotor performance markedly improved over reading using the larger format. In a further study by Schneps, Thomson, et al. (2013) reading on paper was compared with reading on a small handheld e-reader device (Apple iPod Touch) that was formatted to display a few words per line and found that the use of the device significantly improved speed and comprehension, when compared with traditional presentations. A possible argument is that the use of tablet devices, particularly iPads, may provide a more inclusive environment for learning about print, which allows users to regulate the size of text to accommodate their own needs (Langdon & Thimbleby, 2010).

So why would the use of e-readers or iPads lead to such positive outcomes in supporting the literacy skills of students with dyslexia? Unlike the more traditional drill-and-practice reading exercises often found within the school context (Labbo & Reinking, 1999), tablets and e-readers can offer opportunities to increase motivation and engagement for reading (Ciampa, 2012) and also offer greater control over flow of information by containing shorter line widths that reduce extraneous visual demands (Schneps, Thomson, et al., 2013). There is little evidence that touch-screen tablets are being used to support struggling readers within primary-school classrooms, despite positive and encouraging response towards the use of e-readers from primary-school teachers (Goodwyn, 2013a).

However, the affordances of these new technologies in supporting communication and literacy skills extend beyond students with dyslexia. Many students on the autism spectrum disorder face challenges when trying to learn, including problems with attention, lack of motivation and deficits related to word decoding and phonemic awareness as well as difficulties in communication (Yaw, Skinner, et al., 2011). Augmentative and alternative communication (AAC) interventions have been shown to improve both communication and social skills in children and young people with autism spectrum disorders and other developmental disabilities with growing evidence for the use of iPads for teaching social communication skills to children with autism (Bondy & Frost, 1994; Flores, et al., 2012; Kagohara, et al., 2013). AAC is considered to provide a supplementation of natural speech and/or writing through alternate means of communication including speech-generating devices (SGDs) or picture-exchange communication systems (PECS), which have been instrumental in supporting learners in home and educational settings. One example of this is the Grace App[5], which allows the customization of photos and picture galleries on the iPhone or iPad to support communication exchanges and requests. It allows children with autism to build semantic sequences from personalized photographs that can be stored as a book online. Since the introduction of PECS and the exponential growth in educational apps for autism, there have been a growing number of evaluations of the PECS system in supporting and improving communication revealing very encouraging results from both case studies (e.g., Boesch, Wendt, et al., 2013; Greenberg, Tomaino, & Charlop, 2012) and randomized controlled intervention trials (Lerna, Esposito, et al., 2012; Schreibman & Stahmer, 2014).

---

[5] www.graceapp.com

Although these tools have proved a viable option for improving communication in the mainstream population, are touch-screen devices also able to support young children on the autistic spectrum to develop necessary literacy skills? There are some claims that electronic digital tools can be used to support literacy instruction too. Although based on a single case-study design, there is evidence to suggest that computer-assisted sight-word instruction does seem to support emerging reading skills among children with autism. Moreover, the use of computerized support can lead to improvements, not just in vocabulary learning, but also in students' motivation levels and decreases in their observable behaviour problems during their engagement with computer-assisted activities (Moore & Calvert, 2000). Indeed, in their own study of four children with ASD, Chen and Bernard-Opitz (1993) found that despite no overall differential gains in learning rates, those children using computer-based instruction showed fewer behavioural problems compared to those undergoing tutor-led instruction. A systematic review of training studies by Ramdoss and colleagues (2011) found ten studies that involved some form of computer-based instruction to teach communication skills to children with autism spectrum disorders. Although limited in number, all of these studies reported some improvement in communication.

There is encouraging support for the use of digital technologies for reading instruction in other difficult to reach populations including children with ADD (McClanahan, Williams, et al., 2012) and those with Down syndrome. The latter show profound difficulties in expressive language and written forms of communication and clearly benefited from alternative text presentation formats (Black & Wood, 2003). Although as noted by Feng, Lazar, et al. (2010), most of the software, games and websites that children with Down syndrome interact with are aimed at typically developing children and such applications are necessarily less effective and at times inaccessible to such children. In their large survey of over 600 hundred parents of children with Down syndrome, Feng and colleagues report that educational software designers must take into account the age, the specific type of difficulties encountered, as well as related design challenges that are needed to support specific populations.

It appears that there are many affordances for the use of electronic texts in supporting young children's communications, reading and literacy practices, especially among those who struggle with acquiring knowledge of the written text. However, the actual success and outcome of integrating e-books and digital devices to promote easy access to written materials is perhaps an issue that we shall see more and more of in the future.

Risks, Skills and Opportunities

Our access to and engagement with digitized texts seems to be increasing, especially with the growth in touch-screen and tablet devices. There is also some suggestion that such devices can help support literacy teaching in schools. But there are risks. Software that is purchased hastily, without any plan of implementation, will remain less effective in supporting literacy skills. It is pertinent to acknowledge that simply incorporating iPads and tablet devices into the classroom, despite showing motivational effects, will not necessarily lead to any sustained outcome or improvement in literacy skills unless they are embedded into the curriculum in a pedagogical way. The use of e-books, iPads or other digital devices needs to be available to enhance curricular goals and support student learning in new and transformative ways if this is to be at all successful (Hutchison & Reinking, 2011). As Reinking, Labbo, and McKenna (2000) have coherently argued, new technologies are often merely assimilated into existing teaching practices without any pedagogical function. Yet to make full use of its potential, substantial changes to existing structures and practice, including teachers' perceptions and curriculum, is required However, exactly how these tools can be incorporated into existing classroom practices remains an interesting if not perplexing question. We know that multimedia e-books seem to offer a fruitful way to support and develop literacy practices, and there is also some evidence that the same may be true with regard to digital devices like iPads and Kindles (Hutchison, et al., 2012; Northrop & Killeen, 2013). Recent evidence from case studies demonstrates effective ways to embed tablet devices, such as iPads, into the early years literacy curriculum across pre-school and primary-level classrooms to support not just literacy skills but also other cognitive skills connected to reasoning, problem-solving and deciphering text (McClanahan & Stojke, 2013). Software design and requirements need to consider accessibility issues to ensure they are accessible to all students if they are to be effective (see Ramdoss, et al., 2011).

Conclusions

Assistive technologies in the form of touch-screen tablets, iPads and other digital devices can offer innovative tools to promote communication and literacy skills within typically developing children as well as those deemed at risk of learning difficulties. So how have these new technological advances shaped our definition of reading and emerging literacy skills? With the focus on multimedia electronic books as one method for supporting reading skills among typical and atypical populations, the evidence appears to be promising despite contradictory results. There is some evidence to suggest that multimedia e-books may provide a viable resource to support literacy skills in phonological awareness, vocabulary and word reading (e.g., Chera & Wood, 2003; Karemaker, et al., 2010) For others, a reliance on educational books alone remains insufficient to promote gains in reading: adult instruction is still required to ensure that multimedia books work efficiently for improving reading skills (Korat, et al., 2009; Korat & Shamir, 2012). While the evidence in support of other digital devices like e-readers and iPads remains less compelling, there is some suggestion that these tools create personalized child-parent storytelling opportunities in children yet to receive formal school teaching. If the future is with electronic texts what does this mean for our current generation of learners? We are aware that practitioners can support early literacy development across multiple media formats through e-books and touch-screen devices like iPads to support decoding, comprehension and collaborative interaction (Plowman, Stevenson, et al., 2012). However, the optimal use of tablets or touch-screen devices for early literacy learning may be dependent upon the type of scaffolding used by parent or teacher and the availability and quality of tablet applications (Neumann & Neumann, 2013).

Chapter Five
Becoming Digitally Literate

Introduction

It is apparent that digital media and new communication technologies are not only influencing our online interactions and the teaching of literacy skills, but also influencing our written communication. However, the effects of digital technology are far more extensive than just affecting written language: it is also shaping literacy skills in quite innovative ways. If we consider the multimodal features of the digital world, and our ability to extract meaning not just from traditional print (books) but also through visual (photographs, videos, animations) and audio materials (music, audio narration, sound effects), then we can see how literacy skills are being extended. Literacy occurs online through a variety of media including text messaging and social networking sites with tweeting seen as a new literacy practice (Greenhow & Gleason, 2012). So how have these new communication tools shaped our understanding and definition of literacy? In contrast to some of the more traditional definitions of literacy, which focus primarily on reading, spelling and the written exposition of ideas, the term 'digital literacies' is encouraging us to think beyond such narrow definitions and to recognize a broader skill-set that includes acquiring and evaluating information within a multimodal environment. While we have long been surrounded by visual imagery through television, films, videos and computers, images rather than words are increasingly used as a communication tool. Pictures are passed from mobile phone to mobile phone with very little text accompaniment and are easily understood particularly by the young. Indeed an emoticon, voice over or tune may be used to enhance the meaning of the image being

Learning and the E-Generation, First Edition. Jean D. M. Underwood and Lee Farrington-Flint.
© 2015 Jean D. M. Underwood and Lee Farrington-Flint. Published 2015 by John Wiley & Sons, Ltd.

shared rather than a conventional written description of the image. This develops greater confidence and ability in dealing with many of the multimodal aspects of digital environments.

This use of digital technology has clearly influenced our understanding of literacy skills. Given the rise in sales of electronic books, and touch-screen tablets coupled with the digital resources to enhance reading, the traditional definitions of literacy are perhaps outdated and possibly even redundant in the digital age. The term *digital literacy* has been considered, discussed and embraced by many academics and practitioners within recent years leading to extended definitions of digital literacy, visual literacy, television literacy and, within many HEIs, information literacy (see Buckingham, 2006). Yet digital literacy is much more than a functional matter of learning how to perform online searches or to navigate through web pages. It involves a whole new skill set centred around extracting information, evaluating sources and deciphering written and visual representations online. Being digitally literate involves a multidimensional and interactive approach to learning and the ways in which learners are developing new digital and visual literacy skills is the focus of this chapter.

Engaging with New Forms of Literacy

Traditional views of literacy provide the fundamental building blocks of the educated person but Web 2.0 technologies demand more from individuals who would call themselves literate in a twenty-first century world. We have previously seen how the nature of online communication is rapidly changing, with an increase in one-to-one and one-to-many types of online interactions, and a growth in the participatory media culture that is now emerging – in the form of blogging, social networking, podcasting and texting (Jenkins, 2006).

Engagement with digital technologies has therefore produced a new, lively community of readers and writers engaged with new tools for digital communication. The digital divide between literacy as an 'academic' practice and literacy as a 'social' practice remains evident (Lankshear & Knobel, 2003). Yet digital literacy is not a new concept, and the ability to assess, retrieve and comprehend information within a digital landscape has intrigued academics for the past 20 years. However, education has still focused on teaching literacy skills using traditional methods and has shown a reliance on print rather than screen.

Traditional views of literacy focus primarily on text-based reading and writing activities within an educational context, thus emphasizing the importance of those basics skills or building blocks commonly associated with print-based text. In the case of more traditional alphabetic skills, literacy still consists of the mastery of letters and phonemes so that a person is able to encode and decode print. Yet learners need to demonstrate certain skills in: *deciphering complex images and sounds as well as the syntactical subtleties of words* (Lanham, 1995, p. 200). One argument is that a focus simply on the acquisition of alphab etic skills alone remains insufficient for providing the current school cohort with essential literacy skills. Teaching traditional literacy skills and a reliance on printed texts may be outdated and restrictive, a point clearly articulated in the following argument:

> Literacy is wider than reading and writing in traditional print genres … the ability to decode information in various orthographic formats, including digital media, to make and take meaning from it and to encode information into those formats to communicate ideas to others.
>
> (Plester and Wood, 2009, p. 1109)

This argument is further emphasized in a quote by Krause (2013) who clearly advocates how the focus on relying on traditional print as a means for literacy instruction can often restrict and marginalize learners:

> Traditional conceptualizations of literacy as reliant on print forms of text are outdated and unresponsive to the dynamic changes of the 21st century, thus, creating a potentially marginalized group of learners.
>
> (Krause, 2013, p. 237)

Rather than marginalize different groups of learners, as Krause suggests, we need to teach students a much broader range of literacy skills beyond those simply provided by traditional printed texts. That is, our current teaching practices need to acknowledge how literacy is embedded not simply within textbooks but across a growing range of media texts, including print (books), visual (photographs, videos, animations) and audio (music, audio narration, sound effects). Our society is saturated with different forms of digital media and knowing how to access, evaluate and apply information is necessary for success in the workplace and at school and this requires learning a new literacy skill set. In essence we need to reskill the current generation of learners.

So Which Literacy Skills are Required to Become a Digital Native?

Changes in literacy practices appear synonymous with the introduction of new digital technologies. For example, our early engagement with the Internet, often defined as Web 1.0 technology, required us to use a version of the web containing static and often linear forms of information, that is material to be downloaded or delivered to the Internet user. Within this context, literacy skills often relied on our ability to read, identify and select material online within a fairly structured and linear way. Often skills required for online literacy appear analogous to those required for reading printed text. With the introduction of Web 2.0 technologies, these skills have changed and information is available in a more participatory, dynamic and social place with an emphasis on uploading information for communication, collaboration and discussion as well as on reading information in a non-linear, and highly interactive way (Sharples, 2010). Accessing digital information, especially within the context of Web 2.0 formats, now requires a greater reliance on interactivity, collaboration and communication rather than simply deciphering written texts online (Greenhow & Gleason, 2012). For example, children using the Internet need to learn how to locate and select appropriate material. In essence, this involves learning how to use browsers, hyperlinks and search engines, and to read information effectively online. While the reading and comprehension of written material still applies, the way in which this information is retrieved, interpreted and delivered to others is changing as a result of the rapid increase in our engagement with these digital technologies (Buckingham, 2007). There is an implicit expectation that learners will embrace a wide range of skills, including cognitive, motor, sociological and emotional skills, in order to function most effectively within this new highly interactive digital landscape (Kress, 2010).

Contrasts between the characteristics of written communication on the page and on screen have been carefully explored (Kress, 2003, 2010; Merchant, 2007). Arguably, using new forms of digital technology to assist with promoting online communication with a remote audience provides a further dimension to conceptualising literacy work in the classroom, opening up new possibilities for young writers (Merchant, 2005, 2007). Some researchers (Gee, 2003; Jenkins, 2006; Lankshear & Knobel, 2003; Lankshear, Knobel, & Curran, 2013) contend that any social activity that involves the use of digital technology, such as browsing the Internet, transferring images or playing video games, promotes some literacy practices that are often ignored by teachers or educators.

There is also some recognition that technologies are changing how writing is produced, received and delivered to an often much wider range of audiences. Many popular literacy practices show a commitment to more inclusive, collaborative and participative forms of written communication. Written information plays a central part in many screen-based forms and some of the most popular of these, such as email, texting and blogs, are conducted predominantly through the written expression of ideas where traditional conventions are often ignored or adapted for convenience. The previous chapter has shown how text message abbreviations succeed admirably in promoting new conventions for written language. As learners engage within a broad spectrum of applications such as social networking sites (SNSs), collaborative authoring, information sharing and multiplayer games, they are using their written language to exchange ideas and communicate effectively. There are claims that students' text-based interactivities on social networking sites, such as Facebook, represent a new dimension of social literacy practices (Davies, 2012; Gee, 2003). There is much educational potential and some suggestion that practices involving digital literacy can fruitfully bridge gaps between people's home and school learning lives (Davies & Merchant, 2009; Willett, Robinson, & Marsh, 2009).

The Multimodal Landscape

The ability to function within a multimodal environment is a crucial aspect of becoming a digital native. Paivio's (1986) dual-route model is often used to explain issues of transfer and integration of meaning between words, images and other symbol systems. In this model verbal and non-verbal information is held in the dual-coding system, which suggests that the two systems are intricately connected. However, this surfeit of images does not necessarily lead to deeper understanding. Eye-movement studies of primary school children's abilities to integrate text and images have shown that this does not take place automatically and the higher the prior knowledge of the topic, the more able the children were to integrate material from different modalities. Mason, Tornatora, and Pluchino (2013) assumed that such prior knowledge allowed the child to exhibit more strategic behaviour and integrate verbal and pictorial information. This ability to integrate material or information across different modalities has been associated with improved academic performance. Students assume that they are able to comprehend images well since they can be processed so much faster than written or audio text (Schroeder, et al., 2011). This is demonstrated by the following quote from a middle-school pupil: *Seeing is beeter [better] than hearing, seeing is believing* (Hibbing & Rankin-Erikson, 2003, p. 765). This is a dangerous assumption on every level. For example, Hibbing and Rankin-Erikson have demonstrated that children with low-reading ability have difficulty in creating and using images because they are so focused on their attempts to decode words. The cognitive load of such decoding for a poor reader does not leave spare cognitive capacity to integrate the pictorial and textual information.

So while the multimodal textual landscape of digital literacy is widely established (Kress, 2010) extracting meaning from a range of different representations can be a highly complex process. This involves the conversion of information between one form of representation to another, which requires understanding of relationships between the different external representations (Mayer, 2003). This ability has been termed 'representational competence' (Kozma & Russell, 1997). Without such competence, like the young readers in Hibbing and Rankin-Erikson's study, learners will fail to stitch together the information available to them in these multiple representations. Learners need to be familiar with the visual conventions used in such representations, which are prerequisite for extracting the idea that is being represented (Ainsworth, 2006).

However, this shift towards digital literacy is not without its critics. Concerns are raised about learners being so immersed in web-based technologies in their broader lives that they have difficulties engaging in more conventional forms of study and educational practices, such as academic reading and writing essays (Lea & Jones, 2011). The complex inter-relationship between literacy and technology may well have the potential to disrupt traditional academic practices, especially among those teachers who are less familiar with digital literacies and feel that literacy should be confined solely to the realm of writing (Barton, 1994; Kress, 1997). Despite concerns about the threat to conventional standards of literacy, the major shift in the use of digital technologies to enhance reading and writing practices raises important questions about our conventional definitions of literacy, and more importantly, its current role within education, society and culture.

Visual Literacy and Visual Representations

While digital literacy skills are almost second nature to many of those considered to be digital natives (Prensky, 2001), the ability to extract written information online, as we have alluded to above, is just one aspect of this skill set. Educators are recognizing the importance of helping students develop visual literacies in order to survive and communicate within a highly complex visual world. A key skill is the learner's ability to read intuitively and freely read and interpret information in visual-graphical forms by deciphering and interpreting symbols and other visual representations. Much can be gained from understanding how individuals use these visual representations, particularly for the purpose of promoting collaboration, discussion and problem-solving (Salomon & Perkins, 1989).

Visual literacy is often defined as the ability to evaluate, apply or create conceptual visual representations using digital formats. One way in which we can help support learning and aid digital literacy is through the use of visual-based external representations. Diagrams, graphs, and pictures are a few typical types of these external representations. But external representations are much more than memory aids. External representations are so intrinsic to the tasks, that they guide, constrain and even determine the pattern of cognition. Arguably, external representations may facilitate not just inference or problem-solving but also enhance learners' conceptual understanding within a given domain (Suwa & Tversky, 2001). These representations may be static forms of representations (e.g., diagrams) or more advanced dynamic forms of representations that display pictures, animations and sounds graphs simultaneously.

How do these visual representations work? External visual representations capture and structure knowledge using: *physical symbols, objects or dimensions (e.g., beads of abacuses, dimensions of a graph) which have a physical configuration (e.g., spatial relations of written digits, visual and spatial layouts of diagrams, physical constraints in abacuses)* (Zhang, 1997, p. 179). We use these representations to support many of our day-to-day tasks from the mundane grocery shopping list, assessing changes in the popularity of political parties through graphs and tables, or driving to an unfamiliar destination with the help of a road map or, more often these days, an audio voice-over from our satellite navigation system. However, it is their role as powerful representational aids to understanding, problem-solving and learning, that is the focus here (see, for example, Larkin & Simon, 1987; Novak, 1990; Zhang, 1997). There is also some suggestion than encouraging the use of more than one single visual representation can support students' learning because they will: *capture a learner's interest and, in so doing, play an important role in promoting conditions for effective learning* (Ainsworth, 1999, p. 131). The use of multiple forms of representations can often be found within the classroom, particularly in supporting students' leaning of complex concepts in mathematics, science and geometry. For instance, using a combination of graphs, equations and tables to develop students' understanding of complex arithmetical functions can often aid learning and deepen understanding (see Ainsworth & Van Labeke, 2004).

These visual representations can be identified, analysed and interpreted through our perceptual systems and integrated into a range of different learning activities across many subject areas. This encourages, and may promote, active learning and a deeper level of processing academic information. Certainly, access to these representations can support students' academic performance, especially when attempting to solve difficult cognitive tasks.

For instance, Larkin and Simon (1987) argue that diagrammatic representations often aid learning because learners can recognize features easily and make inferences based on those diagrams while Stenning and Oberlander (1995) argue that diagrammatic representations such as Euler circles can help learners to make inferences in logical reasoning tasks. Therefore, our ability to use representations as another form of literacy can have a crucial impact on other aspects of the learning process.

Why should the use of these, often highly complex, visual representations support learning? The argument for the value of external representations for cognitive learning is that they reduce working memory load. By acting as an external memory store such representations leave spare working memory capacity to conduct those mental operations often considered essential for problem-solving (Newell & Simon, 1972; Tversky, 2001). They also serve as visuo-spatial retrieval cues for long-term memory. In addition to providing working memory capacity external representations facilitate higher order thinking skills by making the problem both external and visible. The manipulation of symbols and objects in space allows judgements and inferences to take place when solving problems. The use of symbols and objects lies at the heart of pedagogical practice, for example, early years mathematics teachers used simple counters and more complex representational objects such as Dienne's rods to instil the wonders of number into their young charges' minds. If we consider the task of calculating, counting or solving simple arithmetic problems, learners often perform better if they have access to these external representations (such as an abacus) to help support mental calculations. Even on more difficult scientific problems, such as interpreting velocity and speed, students can often draw a velocity–time graph to help aid or scaffold their understanding. Having access to such physical representations reduces memory load and provides concrete representations to aid performance. In this instance, the choice of representation can influence an individual's conception of a problem and hence the ease of finding a solution (Suthers & Hundhausen, 2003)

How Can Visual Representations Support Learning?

In order to assess how external representations may impact on students' thinking and learning it is important to address how these visual representations are being used. Much of what we do inside and outside the classroom involves us fitting our thinking to a standard format even when we create the representation. For example, there is standard format for representing data in a graph, particularly within science or geography which all students are expected to follow. The creation of individual personal representations is seldom called for, particularly in formal education, although cognitive or mind maps are one such example.

Using a preformed visual representation may help to support learning. When learners are asked to work through a task using the prestructure of an external representation, as a background for extending their own thinking, they need to integrate their own externalizations into the given prestructure. In such cases, the structure of the representation can act as a cognitive tool to help guide students through their own intuitive learning process (e.g., Baker & Lund, 1997, Pfister & Mühlpfordt, 2002). The key issue for education is to ensure that the type of representation is matched to the demands of the situation because it is only then that performance and understanding improve. If the type of external representation appears vague or difficult to interpret, then its value as an education tool remains somewhat limited. Identifying the correct type of representation is therefore crucial for learning success. Ainsworth (2006) identified a number of cognitive prerequisites for ensuring that external representations can support and improve learning. She suggests that learners need to:

1. understand the representation
2. understand the relation between the representation and the task
3. understand how to select the most appropriate representations
4. recognize how to, when appropriate, construct their own form of external representation of any given task.

As we know: *learning complicated scientific concepts, interacting with multiple forms of representation such as diagrams, graphs and equations can bring unique benefit* (Ainsworth, 2008, p. 191). Yet relying solely on pre-existing representations may have its limitations. As Ainsworth (2006) argues, it is not simply the ability to interpret and understand any given representation that remains important but the ability to generate our own form of visual representation. Scientists themselves do not simply use words to express complex scientific ideas but also rely heavily on diagrams, graphs, videos and photographs to make important discoveries and explain their, often highly complex, findings. Students can also benefit from a similar process (Ainsworth, Prain, & Tytler, 2011). There is growing evidence to suggest that encouraging learners to construct their own set of representations, such as creating diagrams or graphs, can aid their conceptual understanding. However, as Ainsworth, Prain, and Tytler note, students are often asked to interpret other visualizations and rarely rely on generating their own visual representations while solving scientific problems. Yet, it is suggested that allowing students to generate their own representations may in fact lead to a deeper and more conceptual level of understanding and will help them to translate difficult concepts into more explicit forms of knowledge. For example, Grossen and Carnine (1990) explored learners' ability to solve logic problems and found that problems were solved much more effectively when they were asked to develop their own form of representation rather than relying on a pre-existing representation devised by another. Furthermore, modelling through pictorial representations can provide a really useful structure to support the scientific discovery and learning of many students who find scientific concepts difficult to grasp (Leenaars, van Joolingen, & Bollen, 2013).

Such metacognitive processes, that is 'thinking about your own thinking', are supported by drawing diagrams or developing representations, allowing learners to constantly monitor their own progress in what they are learning and ensure that the representation is closely tied to the task domain. Drawing pictorial representations is thought to support thinking and reasoning processes. One example for the effective use of external visual representations within education is that of learning about complex scientific concepts. If we consider the complexities involved in grasping concepts, such as velocity, time, speed and distance, particularly within physics, these can often cause great difficulty without the use of external representations to guide learners' understanding.

A further way of developing our own representations is through our ability to generate self-explanations while attempting to solve problems. Ainsworth and Loizou (2003), for example, found that being presented with a diagram rather than text promotes a greater level of self-explanation leading to a greater incidence of students' learning. Those in the text condition produced significantly fewer self-explanations and showed limited benefits to their overall learning when compared to those who were encouraged to generate self-explanations when presented with visual representations or diagrams.

While representations may facilitate learning in some instances they may inhibit the learning process especially if these representations are inconsistent with the demands of the task (Ainsworth, Bibby, & Wood, 2002). While certain representations, for example, graphs, diagrams or even animations may work for one person, they may not work for another, so recognizing how individual learner characteristics may constrain or facilitate the use of representations is crucial. We also know from research on perception that such visuo-spatial displays, especially vague and ambiguous ones, can be interpreted and reinterpreted in many different ways. Familiarity with the representation is crucial for learning – a learner who fails to understand the relevance of any representation will undoubtedly fail to use this to support their learning activity. Similarly, if learners misinterpret representations, then their ability to solve any given task may suffer as a result because the representation will act as a further distraction from the task in hand.

While visual representations remain an important aspect of digital literacy, particularly within the current digital landscape, these skills need to be embedded firmly into our digital lives. As Friere (1994) asserts, the development of any literacy takes off when it speaks to the needs of the individual and is clearly exemplified by the rapid assimilation of digital technologies into the fabric of the lives of those of us that are less than 25 years of age. These skills are not encapsulated in an older generation of teachers but they are being developed in the digitally literate younger generation and we would argue Internet users and gamers are at the forefront of these new literacy practices (Gee, 2003; Underwood, 2007). Prensky (2005) sums this up when he expresses his amazement that the debate on education standards in the United States has not taken into account the fundamental fact that in a digital world the students themselves have changed. According to Prensky, the younger generation are digital natives while we, the teachers, are mere tourists. It was further argued that digital natives' brains are likely to be physically different from those of digital tourists as a result of the digital input they received while growing up.

Risks, Skills and Opportunities

Although the evidence suggests digital literacy skills are an important aspect of our student's education, particularly how they extract information from a range of digital resources from images, graphs and text, there are potential risks in promoting digital literacy within the classroom. As we have seen, there is a lack of a clear definition of the exact skill set required to become digitally literate. Neither is there any clear advice of how digital literacy skills should be embedded within classroom practices. Nonetheless, learners need to be taught how to navigate effectively within a multimodal digital environment and to extract information from visual representations. The ability to read information through visual forms is crucial for learning within this digital age, and visual representations can act as a cognitive tool to help guide students through their own intuitive learning process. However, students need to be taught how to interpret visual representations effectively. This may have a small impact on the able but, without explicit teaching, for the less able there is a very real possibility of the digital divide becoming an unbridgeable chasm. There are some encouraging examples of embedding digital literacy into the curriculum. For instance, there are clear examples of the use of blogs to promote digital literacy activities and peer-collaboration within the classroom context (Huffaker, 2005; Mullen & Wedwick, 2008) and some suggestion that these digital literacy skills can fruitfully bridge gaps between people's home and school learning lives (Davies & Merchant, 2009).

Conclusions

The need for the ability to work within a multimodal digital landscape remains clear (Kress, 2010) and we are aware that many children deal with written and visual representations prior to receiving any formal training or education. They are highly experienced in surfing the net, using images and audio to share and express ideas as well as interpreting visual pictures or diagrams. For many, these skills are second nature. Their engagement with new technologies is having a profound effect on their developing literacy skills. To be digitally literate, students' need to embrace the multimodality of their digital environments and such skills embrace much more than simply reading or decoding text on a digital screen. The required skill set often goes beyond the more traditional values of functional literacy to include collaboration, communication and synthesizing ideas in a structured and often non-linear fashion. This can involve using hyperlinks or web pages to identify written information and creating and authoring digital resources through video, multimedia, and audio recordings – core literacy skills needed within a rapidly changing and highly digital world. Using written texts online, while still an essential skill, represents just one aspect of digital literacy and learners need to be taught how to incorporate visual representations to support their learning activities and to work with multimodal representations beyond that of the written word.

Chapter Six
Social Networking as
an Educational Tool

Introduction

We have already established that participation in contemporary society is increasingly reliant on digital technologies. This is a trend that shows no sign of abating and it is the communication function of these technologies that is driving this trend. The Ofcom survey of 2012 shows that, in the United Kingdom, young people spend on average 17.1 hours per week engaged in online activity. A large proportion of this time is spent developing their social relationships and online identity through social networking sites (Livingstone, 2008; Manago, Taylor, & Greenfield, 2012). Social networking has arisen from our transition to more collaborative digital forms of technology. The early Internet often thought of as Web 1.0 technology, was used primarily for static information: material to be downloaded or delivered to the Internet user. Web 2.0 is more participatory and interactive and this has seen an increase in our use of computer-mediated communication (CMC) allowing interchanges to occur through the use of two or more networked computers. From its beginnings in email, bulletin boards and list servers, CMC technology has increased in complexity and diversity to cover a broad spectrum of applications such as social networking sites (SNSs), e-communities, collaborative authoring, information sharing and multiplayer games. As Borland (2007, p. 1) clearly acknowledges:

> Web 1.0 refers to the first generation of the commercial Internet, dominated by content that was only marginally interactive. Web 2.0, characterized by

Learning and the E-Generation, First Edition. Jean D. M. Underwood and Lee Farrington-Flint.
© 2015 Jean D. M. Underwood and Lee Farrington-Flint. Published 2015 by John Wiley & Sons, Ltd.

features such as tagging, social networks, and user-created taxonomies of content called folksonomies, added a new layer of interactivity.

Such technologies are simply the most recent manifestations in a long line of communication media (see Fidler, 1997). Unlike most of these technologies, even email and social networking appears to be omnipresent and routinely embedded within the daily lives of millions of people worldwide (Boyd & Ellison, 2007; Valkenburg & Peter, 2009). SNSs comprise of bundles of information coupled with communication tools that allow individuals to accomplish multiple goals. In an SNS such as Facebook users share common interests, photos, music and videos and generally socialize online. Facebook along with other social networking tools are collectively referred to as Web 2.0 applications. SNSs are increasingly popular. More than 700 million people worldwide now have an SNS profile, on sites such as Myspace and Facebook attracting over 1.2 billion members worldwide (Statistic Brain, 2012). The nature of SNSs and the perceived educational benefits of promoting new Web 2.0 technologies for communication and collaboration is the focus of this chapter.

Facebook as a Popular Networking Tool

Although initially we would assume that SNSs are akin to the types of attributes we use in everyday social interactions, they often share many features with computer-mediated communication (CMC). Walther (2007) argues that computer-mediated communication has four key features that distinguish it from face-to-face interactions. These are editability, time flexibility, physical isolation from the receiver and loss of visual cues, which results in reduced cognitive load allowing greater concentration on the intended message. This perspective suggests that CMC can lead to equal or even more socially desirable interactions than do face-to-face interactions (Walther, 1996). This positive interpretation of the loss of visual cues is possibly the most contentious, as they have been shown to affect communication processes, the social judgements individuals make about each other and also task performance (Burgoon, et al., 2002; Sia, Tan, & Wei, 2002).

Facebook, the most prevalent SNS, has two of the four CMC features. However, its multimodality reduces physical isolation and allows the cues and subsequent biases prominent in face-to-face interaction to re-emerge, providing an online equivalent of physical or face-to-face social networks. SNSs then are social mediating technologies that provide multiple means of interacting and socializing so distinguishing them from more restricted CMC of simple communication in email, chat and instant messaging into applications. SNSs allow individuals to select to connect with others in either a semi-public space with close friends or relatives within a 'close' bounded system or a public space with relative strangers, who may have nothing more in common than 'latent ties'. Either way individuals are not necessarily looking to meet new people; they primarily communicate with people who are already part of their extended social network (Boyd & Ellison, 2007).

An individual's SNS profile is a projection of their identity (Selwyn, 2009) and is comprised of personal information created from a blank template, which can be publicly displayed or suppressed by enacting privacy settings. In addition to the individual's name and age, a user may supply personal information on date of birth, residence, sexual preference, contact information as well as work and leisure activities (Tong, Van Der Heide, et al., 2008). Message boards, known variously as The Wall, Testimonials, and Comments, are public spaces located on profiles on which friends are encouraged to leave messages, which can be read by interested third parties who are granted access to the profile (Granovetter, 1973). SNSs have quite clearly revolutionized how we promote ourselves and communicate with others online, providing a wealth of opportunities to keep in touch with people.

Social Capital

The rich platforms that compose the current generation of SNSs are designed to connect people with both those in their own circle of friends and family and with extended and new groups of individuals known only through the virtual world. Such linkage can have a strong influence on an individual's social capital or social support and hence on their psychological wellbeing. Social capital is the benefit derived from an individual's position in a social network, both in terms of the number and character of the ties and the resources those ties themselves possess. A characteristic of all forms of capital (social, financial, human, intellectual) is that they are convertible to another form of capital. In the case of social capital this might, for example, be favours from another member of the group or, in the case of a SNS, the network itself (Resnick, 2001). Although across the social disciplines different aspects of social capital are emphasized, there is a measure of agreement that social networks have value and that people derive benefits from their interpersonal relationships and the groups they belong to, ranging from improved health to access to expertise and financial resources (Coleman, 1988). More recent conceptualizations of social capital acknowledge the importance of community to build generalized trust but also recognize the importance of individual choice in order to create a more cohesive society (Ferragina, 2012).

Two constructs, bonding and bridging, are central to our understanding of social capital (Katz & Aspden, 1997). While close relationships such as those with family or good friends provide bonding social capital, a large number of weaker ties lacking the specific reciprocity, emotional support and companionship of the family generate bridging social capital. The value of bridging social capital is that an individual often gains novel information from these diverse links whereas the close ties of friends and family tend to furnish known, redundant information (Granovetter, 1973). However, the external groups are less likely to provide emotional support. Bridging and bonding are not mutually exclusive, but rather different dimensions of the resources in a social network.

Facebook's features appear to be particularly well suited to the development of bridging social capital, with studies showing a stronger relationship between Facebook use and bridging than with bonding (Ellison, et al., 2007). Manago and colleagues' (2012) survey results show that Facebook facilitates more expansive social networks in which there is significant growth of the network through less intimate relationships with acquaintances or activity connections. This does not preclude the expansion of the number of close relationships or indeed stranger relationships, but these take place at slower rates. Longitudinal surveys have shown that receiving messages from friends is associated with increases in bridging social capital, but that this is not the case for other forms of social interactions. However, individuals with lower social fluency who are passive consumers do draw value from their connections as demonstrated by the number of followers of various celebrities' sites. The value of those connections differs depending on the demographics and social resources of individuals and individual differences are apparent in its use (Bessière, Kiesler, et al., 2008; McKenna & Bargh, 1998). For example, some users focus on one-on-one or one-to-few communication while others openly broadcast to a much wider audience (Burke, Kraut, & Marlow, 2011, Underwood, et al., 2011). As with other potentially interactive media there are also passive consumers of social news who find interest in following others without the need to broadcast.

One study, which at first seems counter-intuitive, gives pause for thought. In a study by Weiser (2001), which explored the reasons and goals for using the technology, two types of use were identified. Weiser termed these goal and reasons *socio-affective regulation* (that is a social orientation toward Internet use) and the *goods-and-information acquisition* (a utilitarian or practical orientation toward Internet use). He found that when users' goals appeared to be related to *socio-affective regulation* then their reported psychological wellbeing tended to be negative, which resulted in reduced social integration. However, Internet use motivated principally by *goods-and-information acquisition* appeared to have a favourable effect on reported psychological wellbeing and an increase in social integration.

What should we make of this study, which suggests that those looking for social contact may be damaged by the digital world? Perhaps those reaching out are already more vulnerable than those who see a more utilitarian use for the Internet. This muddies the waters in our understanding of SNS use but a possible explanation lies in Underwood, et al.'s, (2011) broadcaster–communicator dichotomy. Communicators have a clear utilitarian reason for using Facebook, the maintenance of their group, while broadcasters have a less focused goal or perhaps less coherent goal of 'being out there'. There are no clear findings to substantiate this claim but it has a level of plausibility.

Since an SNS provides a number of ways for users to interact and constantly create connections among users, it has a broad appeal. Facebook in particular has captivated many students who then spend large amounts of time using it. It is no surprise, therefore, that those hard-pressed educational institutions are attracted to tools that students find alluring as a pedagogical device. However, despite some reports of success (McCarroll & Curran, 2013), the evidence for engaging with SNS as a potential tool for improving educational performance is not always compelling.

Social Networking in Educational Contexts

There is no doubt that SNSs are seen as having great educational potential and a number of commercial companies are exploiting the opportunities they afford. For example, Connectivity Learning are using Facebook as they are inspired by collaboration, co-teaching and global connections within a twenty-first century community. The Facebook organization itself has its own dedicated page to education applications that shares the experiences of teachers and provides examples of effective practice. The European Union funded SVEA project[1] also explores the educational use of Facebook. It provides a useful starter guide for those educators who are relatively new to social networking. Facebook provides an easy-to-use and familiar technology for learners to leverage social networking to share and generate tacit knowledge between each other within the small group environment.

One characteristic of SNSs that can be exploited for educational purposes is the function that allows the creation of special interest groups. It is clear that an online site designed for people with similar interests to communicate and collaborate would have great potential for group work,

[1]www.svea-project.eu

collaborative assignments and other class-based activities. A Facebook Group has the overall look and feel of an individual Facebook page but its use can be restricted to an invited membership and it is intended for group communications and resource sharing. The key features of the group are that there is a closed membership managed by the person who has set up the group. Students and tutors in such a group can communicate and share resources, post messages and comment on those of others. Documents can be collectively created and shared. There is also a group chat facility for real-time discussions and a notification facility. Group members can also choose to be automatically informed by email of all activities happening on the group page.

Within Web 2.0 technologies, the interactive sites and facilities that can be found in cyberspace allow learners to share, create and broadcast information relatively easily. An example of the power of this approach is a facility created for teachers of psychology. For example, Psychexchange[2] is an interactive site, which allows teachers to upload and comment on teaching resources, ideas, videos and material. Since it was created in 2008 it has developed into a large and active community of psychology teachers. Psychexchange provides a valuable repository for storing teaching materials and provides a strong community network for the sharing of good practice. It had over 21,700 users of which 5,000 have been active in the last month (as of May 2010). There were 3,700 files uploaded and these have been downloaded over 800,000 times. A community of practice, that is a group of people who share a concern or a passion for something they do and who learn how to do it better as they interact regularly, has been created within a short time that allows teachers to share resources and good practice (Banyard, Underwood, et al., 2011). This site is now part of an amalgamated set of sites supporting open learning[3].

A second key use of SNS is as a tool for social support. Learners enjoy and appreciate both the social learning experience afforded by the online social network and the reciprocal support of their learning, enhancing their own and other students' experiences. The notion of online learning communities is not new (see, for example, Fontana, 1997). Buckingham, Shum and Ferguson (2010) acknowledge the impact of technology in facilitating the growth of online learning communities. They also cite shifts in social values, problems that require social knowledge to address, and changes to institutional views as contributing factors. Selwyn's (2009) indepth qualitative

[2] http://www.resourcd.com/@psychexchange
[3] www.resourcd.com/

analysis of contributions to Facebook walls by 909 UK undergraduates found that five main education-related interactions emerged:

- recounting and reflecting on the university experience
- exchange of practical information
- exchange of academic information
- displays of supplication and/or disengagement
- humour.

Selwyn's (2009) study showed that Facebook walls were certainly a valuable means of exchange for those students primarily maintaining strong links between people on a course, that is individuals already closely linked in offline relationships. The technology tended not to be used to create new contacts in other courses or institutions, but rather activity was confined to a geographically-bounded campus community (Ellison, et al., 2007).

Status updates can be viewed as a restricted form of microblogging, that is the exchange of small elements of content such as short sentences, individual images, or video links. In Facebook News Feed these short messages are posted to the individual's own welcome page to all Facebook Friends of the user as well as the user's own profile page. In this way users receive a constantly updated list of their friends' Facebook activity.

A more recent and interesting manipulation of student use of Facebook has been conducted by Deters and Mehl (2013). In this experiment they investigated the value of undergraduate students posting regular status updates on Facebook. Some 100 regular users of Facebook were randomly divided between a target and control group. The target group was then asked to increase their rate of message posting for a week, while the control group received no instructions on use. Deters and Mehl were interested to find out whether status updates as a means of communication were both an impoverished form of communication and also undermined quality face-to-face contact, as has been argued elsewhere (see, for example, Moody, 2001). Although, as Ryan and Xenos (2009) found, Facebook activity was linked to personality type, we should be careful in assigning a causal link between engagement with any SNS and loneliness. They found that Facebook users were more extrovert and narcissistic than non-users, while the latter were more conscientious and socially lonely than users. In the Manago, et al. (2012) study those users with larger networks self-reported that larger numbers of contacts in their networks were observing their status updates. Such users were keen to demonstrate others' interest in their activities, a finding that resonates with that of Deters and Mehl. Further Manago and colleagues found that larger networks and larger estimated audiences predicted higher levels of life satisfaction and perceived social support on Facebook. They argue that the findings show the psychological importance of audience in the Facebook environment and this appears to be the case for high-users. However, as with many activities, we need to recognize that users are a self-selecting group and the opportunity to communicate with many is naturally sought out by the extroverts but not the shy or withdrawn.

The key finding from Deters and Mehl's (2013) study was that increased status updating reduced loneliness in the target group while there was no change in self-reported loneliness for the control group. Those students who regularly updated their status updates felt more connected and in touch with friends as they shared the highs and lows of their daily experiences with them. Possibly worth noting is that the level to which an individual received responses to their postings was not found to be an important factor is reducing loneliness, as the very act of communicating with an audience appeared to be sufficient to bring about the feeling of connectedness. This finding is consistent with studies that show psychological benefits, including improved social functioning, when individuals simply write about personally important topics (Pennebaker & Chung, 2011). Although, in Deters and Mehl's study, the finding should be viewed with some circumspection as the majority (79%) of posts did elicit responses and could simply represent a ceiling effect.

A number of studies have shown that higher wellbeing is associated with spending less time alone and more time talking to others but that the talk should be substantive rather than small talk (Diener & Seligman, 2002; Mehl, Vazire, et al., 2010). Deters and Mehl (2013) argue that the benefits seen from postings online might well be because increased contact led to more substantive exchanges in which individuals showed interest in the comings and goings of their fellow students, showing awareness of their activities and soliciting information, and in so doing fostered feelings of social inclusion.

Exploiting social media to improve student engagement, but also their health and wellbeing, is a central reason why educators have an interest in this tool. While Selwyn found positive but limited educational use of Facebook, Wise, Skues, and Williams (2011) present a less positive picture. In their study of Facebook use in a group of first year psychology students they found that 94 per cent of the students had Facebook accounts that they used predominantly for personal activity. Such activities occupied a social land that was inhabited by students for an average of an hour a day. However, as with many studies, this average hid significant variance between the students with more conscientious students tending to use Facebook less than less conscientious ones. As a consequence they argued that Facebook was a distracting influence rather than a way of increasing academic engagement, a tool to socialize with rather than one supporting the students' own learning. While it is self-evident that student engagement is important for positive learning outcomes, they argue that simply increasing the metrics associated with student engagement does not necessarily create good students. So an effort to promote social engagement, through social media, does not necessarily result in the improved cognitive engagement that is required for successful learning. Engagement needs to promote the behavioural and cognitive activities required for learning to occur (Fredericks, Blumenfeld, & Paris, 2004).

So Why is the Educational Use of an SNS Different from Using a Virtual Learning Environment (VLE)?

Phipps, Cormier, and Stiles (2008) argue that while the VLE has an important role in enhancing the student experience making it a safe and sensible option from the perspective of the institution, it is a solution to an old problem, which may have lost its relevance in a world of continuous change that requires commensurate reskilling of the population. In particular they question the appropriateness of the VLE as a tool to encapsulate the full sum of a student's educational experiences: in so doing they are highlighting the need for enhanced e-portfolios that may be held across a range of interactive tools, devices and platforms.

The VLE is able to provide access to a range of learning resources and activities as well as providing the most basic types of information about courses and assessments (see Weller 2010; Sclater 2010, for an in depth discussion). It is also able to facilitate interaction between users but this facility does not appear to be well developed or used. Many learners are ambivalent towards the VLE. Learners and teachers prefer to use facilities outside the VLE and outside school. Even the humble data-stick can be a tool of choice because it gives an element of privacy while the VLE allows the learner to be tracked (Underwood, et al., 2009). We have found a number of teachers have rejected VLEs because of this perceived bias towards teachers rather than students.

Good news stories abound concerning the transformational nature of a VLE (Banyard, et al., 2011). On the other hand there are numerous stories of abortive attempts to install a working VLE that illustrate the frustration of embedding large-scale technology innovations into an institution (Underwood, et al., 2010). With emerging ways of working with the technology provided by the potentialities of Web 2.0, Ofsted (2009a, pp. 34–35) has questioned whether this technology may become redundant even before it is fully embedded as it is unable to meet people's expectations. They found no direct correlation between computer expertise and VLE development. However, more skilled and confident teachers and tutors were able to deploy them effectively as just another tool in a good teacher's repertoire, not an end in itself (Ofsted, 2009b, p. 12).

The VLE appears self-evidently to be a good idea but does it deliver as much as it promises? What are the key benefits and also the key barriers to success? One perceived benefit is the possibility of predicting student performance from the large body of log file and other data concerning student activity through the application of data mining methods to discover hidden patterns, associations and anomalies (Nagi, Suesawaluk, & U-Lan, 2008; Superby, Vandamme, & Meskens, 2006). However, this function requires greater technical skills and as such is not extensively used. The VLE is currently used to store content and to communicate with students and so has extensive overlap with the functions available on any SNS. Therefore individuals deemed 'technologically savvy' are already looking elsewhere for increased functionality by using facilities outside the VLE, such as blogs and other Web 2.0 tools to increase their knowledge and identify resources. This frustration is mirrored by many of our digital natives, those who have grown up in a digital society, who show a preference for Google to their library interface in their attempts to seek out appropriate learning resources. Nonetheless, care should be taken not to overhype the value of Web 2.0 software. Underwood and Stiller (2013) have shown in recent studies that the rhetoric does not always match actual usage.

Where Does This Leave Us?

If we go back to the digital divide, then the rise of social software means that learners are able to personalize their learning outside the structures of their schools and colleges (McLoughlin & Lee, 2007). The technological affordances offered by Web 2.0 technology have been grasped by many learners and also some teachers as they find new ways to excite and encourage their students. However, a 2009 comparison of staff and student responses to Facebook showed that students were much more likely than faculty to use Facebook and were significantly more open to the possibility of using Facebook and similar technologies to support classroom work. Faculty members were more likely to use more 'traditional' technologies such as email (Roblyer, McDaniel, et al., 2010). Staff members are also more responsive to the VLE although this might in part be due to the need to follow institutional policy (Underwood & Stiller, 2013)

While the school VLE provides a valuable data resource for teachers and managers, the utility of these data is enhanced though the activities of a dedicated data manager. Teachers are confident with this aspect of the network and appreciative of the gains it provides. The usefulness of network facilities as an aid to pedagogy is less developed, which is a common observation in schools. Could it be that the VLE provides a basic resource for teachers for them to build their teaching on? This can work well for teachers who can use it as foundation for their teaching, but the perceived value of the VLE is such that many teachers and managers see it as a sufficient teaching resource rather than a starting point.

However, is this simply a case of information overload? How is the information flow in social networking best managed? Many of us who are Facebook users find that it can become overwhelming very quickly. Much of the information seems like 'noise'. In the face-to-face classroom, both students and tutors generally know how to deal with such 'noise'. This may not be the case in the online environment. Social Learn[4], a platform for online open learning at The Open University, utilizes open educational resources with the goal of improving the quality of material available to online learners (Buckingham, Shum & Ferguson, 2010). It is based on the premise that the understanding of content is socially constructed through conversations and interactions with others (Brown & Adler, 2008). However, there have been significant problems for students with information overload, which has left learners struggling to identify what represents useful material, or to understand how to build connections between concepts or even to recognize solutions when they find them. We tend to lose sight of the learning process in providing a wealth of resources to students online.

The Need to Establish Rules of the Game: Netiquette

The idea of 'netiquette' was a concept established during the early adoption of the Internet and described a set of social norms that govern proper decorum in using online computer-mediated interactions (Shea, 1994). Although Internet users no longer embrace netiquette, the utility of social norms is not lost within online communities (Yee, Bailenson, et al., 2007). Social norms unique to SNSs are learned through other users and cues available in the environment. However, some newer media, such as SNSs, have loosely articulated social or interactional norms dictating appropriate actions and behaviours.

[4] http://sociallearn.open.ac.uk/public

One further issue concerning the use of new Web 2.0 technologies is how best to allay parental concerns of risk. There are of course concerns about the use of social media in schools although this is less prevalent within higher education institutions. Guarding the safety of the student and protecting the reputation of the institution make these two groups very wary. Some are concerned that the students might encounter inappropriate content or be exposed to bullying online. Others are just as concerned about students wasting valuable learning time and overloading technical resources. Wolak, Finkelhor, et al. (2008) argue that society's perception of these dangers is distorted. They argue that the belief that there are online 'predators' who prey on naive children using trickery and violence is erroneous. They argue that Internet sex crimes involving adults and juveniles better fit a model of underage seduction than one of forcible assault. While this does frame the issue in a different way, lowering the level of violence, it does not take away the gravity of such acts. Wolak, et al. (2008) and Wolak, Finkelhor, and Mitchell (2007) suggest that what is needed is not an excessive reaction to the problem but to equip students with the necessary skills and awareness to protect themselves. Our own research has shown that schools that discuss these difficult issues with the students in the context of open but monitored Internet access tend to produce more risk aware and therefore potentially safer cohorts of pupils (Underwood, et al., 2008). While Facebook has a set of tools that allow reporting of anti-social online behaviour, these often appear cumbersome but, by encouraging students to use these tools as well as informing relevant adults, a less frightening environment is possible.

Risks, Skills and Opportunities

There is a growing awareness around the potential risks of embedding Web 2.0 technologies within educational contexts. This is not simply the view that SNS often work as a distraction from academic learning, but a recognition about the potential bullying, victimization and access to unsolicited information, which cannot be dismissed or simply ignored. For example, Ybarra, Boyd, et al. (2012) recently noted that Internet harassment, bullying and victimisation is a growing concern, one that may often lead to serious psychological consequences for the individual involved. That it is not recognized as bullying by those submitting their peers to abuse, is perhaps the most worrying finding from current research. For example, Palasinski (2012) has shown that 'happy slapping', using a mobile phone to record a physical assault on an unsuspecting victim and then making the act public via the Internet, is perceived by many adolescents as a form of entertainment and not abuse. Her young interviewees distinguished between harmless 'happy slapping' and injury inflicting 'unhappy slapping', the former being viewed as a comedic prank showing an individual's creativity. Recording the event is portrayed, by Plasinski's interviewees, as a safety measure to prevent things going too far. Similar findings were identified in a subsequent study in which students were interviewed about harmless pranks and happy slapping (Palasinski, 2013).

Nonetheless, there is a recognition that Internet dangers are perhaps no worse than real-life equivalents (Dooley, Pyżalski, & Cross, 2009) and, as we have seen in the case of bullying, this often occurs more within traditional face-to-face arenas than online. Although bullying and similar behaviours do not require the use of technology, the technology does add two new dimensions to the problem (see Sugarman & Willoughby, 2013). The first dimension is that abuse can occur at any time and in any place. The second is the level to which the abuse becomes a very public act again leaving little respite for the victim. Perhaps the way forward is to raise individuals' awareness of the potential risks involved in negotiating interactions online and to build up their resilience to trust in their maturity and judgement to deal with the matter appropriately (a theme we return to in Chapter 10). Once we see beyond the risks, Web 2.0 technologies have a great deal of benefits for the learner. More importantly, once these risks have been identified and addressed, then there is real scope for the pedagogic advantage of fully embracing digital technologies, particularly SNSs such as Facebook, into the curriculum (McCarroll & Curran, 2013).

Conclusions

The activities and interactions encouraged through SNSs will no doubt produce more informed citizens of the digital age. Social networking is hugely popular, with more than 700 million people worldwide known to have access to their own networking profile. However, there is still no clear decision as to whether social networking can actually support and enhance students' engagement within the context of their formal learning. We are aware that even within formal learning settings, such as lectures or tutorials, many students use laptops, iPads and smartphones to access course materials or related resources and do so easily and effectively (Kraushaar & Novak, 2010). However, while exploiting social media may help to improve student engagement, and to promote the behavioural and cognitive activities required for learning to occur (Fredericks, et al., 2004), this does not always translate into effective learning. Many aspects of these tools can be distractions rather than facilitating features and care must be taken to identify what aspects of these social networking tools are relevant or pedagogically useful to students before they can be fully implemented (Gehlen-Baum & Weinberger, 2012). In part, this lack of successful integration into the educational contexts is perhaps fuelled by teachers' perceptions of social networking. Teachers' reluctance to embrace SNSs could be due to the perceived risks associated with cyber-bullying and exposure to online 'predators' or simply by their own negative perceptions that SNS, will detract students from the very principle of learning, seeing SNSs as a distraction at best. Whatever the reason, there is at least some evidence to suggest the SNSs can offer skills to learners that cannot be found within VLEs and the difficulty remains in the affordances that can be instilled within the classroom context.

Chapter Seven
Absorbed by Technology

Introduction

Previous chapters have provided evidence of the impact of digital technologies on young people's lives, particularly the way in which they communicate with their peer group and develop new and highly complex digital literacy skills. Ofcom's (2010) UK-wide survey showed a tipping point when adolescents and young adults preferred use of digital technology. For the first time 16 to 24 year olds declared their mobile phones and the Internet more important than television, although the majority of post-24 year olds remained wedded to the television. Similarly, Carrier, Cheever, et al. (2009) in their cross-generational study in the United States found that those born between 1982 and 2001 were spending more time than previous generations on media-related activities such as web surfing, texting and video games. So are there any benefits for education of all this tech-time? The evidence at first sight is equivocal. While Davies and Good (2009), for example, have found a positive relationship between personal access to the Internet and the extent to which learners use the technology for their school or college work, students are acutely aware of the clear boundaries between technology for school and technology for leisure activities.

Returning to the Ofcom survey, it found that in 2009 almost half of young people aged between 8 and 17 have a profile on a social networking site such as Facebook. Social media are now integral to most young people's everyday behaviours. This is not confined to the university sector, as the Ofcom data show some pre-adolescents are using adolescent and adult

Learning and the E-Generation, First Edition. Jean D. M. Underwood and Lee Farrington-Flint.
© 2015 Jean D. M. Underwood and Lee Farrington-Flint. Published 2015 by John Wiley & Sons, Ltd.

social networking sites despite an age embargo. The question remains to what extent engagement with digital technology affects learning and whether those impacts are largely positive or detrimental? The shift to interactive digital technologies by the young has both increased opportunities and raised concerns and, because of the extensive adoption of social media by students across a wide age-range, there is a great deal of interest in how these media activities impact on academic performance. In this chapter we look at what is different about the way in which we interact in a digitally rich world and how those changes affect cognitive abilities. At the heart of most definitions of cognitive abilities is the perception of the potential of the individual's mind but Salomon has argued that once those abilities are coupled with 'intelligent technologies', then it is the performance of the joint system on which an assessment of performance should be based (Salomon, Perkins, & Globerson, 1991). Whether systems such as Facebook should be classified as 'intelligent technologies' in a Salomonesque way, they do nevertheless impact on cognition and behaviours – although they are not necessarily an enhancement of human abilities. This is a point that Salomon also makes when he if can technology can do too much, thus rendering the human input to a subsidiary role resulting in loss of performance without technology. Children's declining performance in mental arithmetic following the introduction of the calculator is an example of abilities that have atrophied. A key theme of this chapter is the relationship between technology use and cognitive skills: in particular we explore in some depth the effect of multitasking on performance. However, first we turn to the relationship between technology use and the users' health and wellbeing. Much has been written on the ills of technology but here we focus on the emotive issue of technology addiction and the less sensitive issue of time wasting.

Addiction and Wellbeing

There are many scare stories in the media about technology addiction particularly in relation to smart phones and video games. So we find headlines in the media such as 'Student addiction' to technology 'similar to drug cravings'[1] and magazine articles reporting the damaging effects of addiction (Codey, 2011). For some the fact that many young people text while driving, even though they know it is dangerous, is seen as an example of their inability to control their technological urges, although personal observation

---

[1] http://www.telegraph.co.uk/technology/news/8436831/Student-addiction-to-technology-similar-to-drug-cravings-study-finds.html

suggests that the use of mobile phones while driving is not confined to the young. While there is, currently, evidence of a weak link between heavy electronic media use and mild attention problems the anticipated link to more serious attention deficits, such as ADHD, is not established (Schmidt & Vandewater, 2008; Schnabel, 2009). Indeed, when students with ADHD played a computer game that they enjoyed they exhibited similar positive behaviours, such as fewer errors, less impulsive responses and an increased ability to stay on task, performing in a similar way to their typically developing peers (Shaw, Grayson, & Lewis, 2005).

Nevertheless, 'Internet addiction disorder' is already accepted as a psychological diagnosis in China, Taiwan and South Korea and it is included in the fifth edition of the Diagnostic and Statistical Manual for Mental Disorders (DSM-V). However, we need to question whether addiction to the Internet is a real condition that needs to be treated just like any other addiction, with care and caution, or is it an obsession? Montag, Kirsch, et al. (2012) have argued not only that Internet addiction exists but also that it has the same genetic cause as smoking addiction. His comparative study of 132 problem Internet users and controls showed that a gene mutation, which promotes addictive behaviour, was more prevalent in those participants in the study who scored highly on the Internet Addiction Test Questionnaire. However, the gene variant was largely confined to female problematic Internet users, rather than male users described as having online addiction.

Work on Facebook shows some corroborating evidence that this addiction is a real phenomenon and that females are a particularly vulnerable group. A Swedish survey of 1,000 adults aged 17 to 73 years, found that 85 per cent of the respondents use Facebook as part of their daily routine (Denti, et al., 2012). Further there was an inverse relationship between the level of Facebook use and general wellbeing. This negative correlation only held for a subset of high users comprising females with low incomes or less highly educated individuals in general. Both groups rated themselves as feeling less happy and less content with their lives than their more affluent and well-educated peers. In addition individuals who compared themselves to other Facebook users also felt less happy. Indeed, students who spend more time on Facebook are more inclined to perceive others as living happier lives in comparison to their own life (Chou & Edge, 2012). One partial explanation for these findings is that engagement with Facebook is habit forming. So is our engagement with digital technology nothing more than Internet addiction to which females are more vulnerable than males? As we saw in the previous chapter, SNS may have a detrimental effect on educational learning (Hew, 2011), but is the extensive engagement with SNSs also having a negative impact on our general wellbeing?

Montag and colleagues (2012) acknowledge that previous research has tended to show males as more prone to problematic Internet use than females, so the link to genetics in his own study is, as he freely admits, puzzling. It could be argued that only females are affected by their biology but perhaps a more straightforward explanation, one that is well established in the social psychology literature, is that perhaps females are more assiduous in filling out questionnaires and therein lies the potential bias. There has been some unease in the research community about the level of reliance on questionnaire data in the absence of any corroborating evidence. Other information gathering techniques are available and have been widely used in studies of decision-making and reasoning. Atchley and Warden (2012) borrowed one such technique from the decision-making literature to explore young people's addiction to texting, which was measured by the ability of the young person to resist answering a text from a significant person in their lives. They offered cash rewards to induce the young people to delay their response to the text. The longer they delayed the higher the monetary reward. Thirty-five students answered a series of questions based on scenarios, such as: *You receive a text from a significant other. You can have $5.00 now if you choose to reply immediately, or you can have $100 in 60 minutes if you wait and reply then.* The waiting time varied between 1 minute and 480 minutes (8 hours). Such choices have been used to demonstrate the impulsivity of people addicted to alcohol or drugs. Those deemed addicted tended to choose an immediate response over a delayed but highly rewarded response, addicts showing a massively skewed preference for smaller cash plus immediate rewards.

Atchley and Warden (2012) found no such immediacy effect: the students were able to delay their responses to achieve a financial gain. However, the lure of money in the future was tempered by the desire to respond to a text. While in a control condition receiving $100 after a two-week delay was valued at 25 per cent lower than receiving $100 instantly, when money was combined with texts, this discounting speeded up. It took just a 10 minute wait for $100 plus text to lose 25 per cent of its value and the students seemed to view the reward of texting in the same way as the financial reward of money, offsetting one against the other. However, the need for an immediate reward was not overwhelming, as one would expect to find if the individual was addicted. This contradicts the notion that students make decisions about texting in the way an addict makes decisions about drugs.

When the importance of the individual trying to make contact was varied, that is when the text was from someone less significant, a friend or a casual acquaintance, then the willingness to delay the response and reap the money also varied. Only when receiving a text from a significant other did the students agree to forgo the cash incentive and respond quickly. Again this suggests that their text-based decision-making was thoughtful rather than impulsive. This research supports the conclusion that young people are not addicted to their phones like an addict is to a drug although, as with the questionnaire studies, the findings here are based on self-reported behaviour and are not corroborated in any way. Is the students' engagement with digital technology here better described as a thoughtful rather than an addictionive or impulsive behaviour?

Time Wasting

So addiction may not be the issue but obsessive behaviour leading to wasted time could be a downside of digital activity. At a simplistic level there is a pervading view that the digital technologies are leading to non-productive activity: they are distractions for the Internet users. There can be very few lecturers who have not had the experience of their students deeply focused, not on what they are saying, but on a small screen tucked under the desk by the shy or waved around in the air by the brazen. This is shown by one unattributable student's response on an open discussion forum to the question: 'Why text when you can talk on the phone?': *If you are texting or IMing, you can do it in places where you shouldn't be talking. Library, meeting, class, work.*

An extensive set of surveys has led to researchers at the Kaiser Family Foundation to conclude that although computers have educational potential, they are largely used for pure entertainment rather than meaningful content creation. Moreover, their recent study has shown that those children in lower socio-economic groups spend more time in such activities. The 2010 Kaiser Family Foundation Youth Lifestyle Study (YLS) found that children and adolescents whose parents do not have a college degree used digital media for 90 minutes more per day than children from higher socio-economic families. This media-use gap was only 19 minutes in 1988 (Dunedin Multidisciplinary Health and Development Study, DMHDS, 1998; Robertson, McAnally, & Hancox, 2013). So the use of technology is widening the time-wasting gap (Rideout, Ulla, et al., 2010). It is anticipated that this in turn will lead to a wider achievement gap with children from low socio-economic families falling further behind.

The entry into the digital world, either passively through television or more actively through online exploration, has been found to impact on real-world relationships. For example, more time spent television viewing and less time spent reading and doing homework was associated with low attachment to parents for both cohorts. In these two Kaiser surveys taken 16 years apart, among the YLS cohort, more time spent playing on a computer was also associated with low attachment to parents. Among the DMHDS cohort, more time spent television viewing was associated with low attachment to peers (Richards, McGee, et al., 2010). This is a global phenomenon. Students in China reported difficulty controlling the amount of time they spent online blaming the Internet for diminished face-to-face communications and message misinterpretations. However, enlightened employers argue that a little downtime, either shopping or watching YouTube, leads to a more productive workforce. There is a cultural shift promoting a 'work–life balance' as opposed to a work culture in which employees increasingly answer work emails outside office time. Such employees see a little downtime during the workday as simply part of the general flow (Salary.com. 2012).

However, one study looks at the time issue and its impact on core educational skills using a randomized controlled trial of the effects of video-game ownership on the academic and behavioural functioning of young boys (Weis & Cerankosky, 2010). Encouraged participation in the study was achieved by offering boys (elementary/middle school) who did not have a video-game system in their home access to a machine loaded with interesting games. Half of the sample of 64 young adolescents was rewarded immediately with a machine while the control group received the reward of a game system 4 months later after the final assessment. Overall, boys who received the video-game system at the beginning of the study showed relatively stable and somewhat below average reading and writing achievement while the control group showed increased reading and writing achievement across the duration of the study. The lower academic achievement scores displayed by boys in the experimental condition were observable by teachers: boys who received the video-game system earned significantly higher Learning Problems scores, which reflect delays in reading, writing, spelling and other academic tasks; boys in the experimental condition spent more time playing video games and less time engaged in after-school academic activities than boys in the control group. Their time was absorbed by the technology resulting in a lack of improvement in core educational skills. Consistent with those of Roberts, Foehr, and Rideout (2005), the authors conclude that video-game ownership may impair academic achievement for some boys in a manner that has real-world significance.

Driven by the Fear of Missing Out (FOMO)

There is an increasing awareness in the literature that engagement in digital worlds may not be a manifestation of addiction to the technology per se but by social anxiety termed FOMO (the fear of missing out) (Przybylski,

Murayama, et al., 2013). Przybylski and colleagues found that the condition was most common in those who had unsatisfied psychological needs such as wanting to be loved and respected. The condition is particularly associated with SNSs that provide constant opportunity for comparison of one's status. It manifests itself in repetitive behaviours, for example, as continual mobile phone checking. He found that from his sample of 500 undergraduates, 38 per cent reported that they were unable to last more than 10 minutes before checking their laptop, smartphone, tablet or e-reader. Rosen, Carrier, and Cheever (2013) have similar findings for adolescents and undergraduates endeavouring to complete their work in the home environment. The average length of time the participants stayed on task before switching was less than six minutes and this loss of focus was most often due to technological distractions including social media and texting. Students who switched tasks most frequently had more distracting technologies available in the form of open desktop windows and the mobile to hand. While having a positive attitude toward technology did not affect being on-task during studying, those students with multiple technologies available were more likely to be off-task than peers who limited their distractions.

FOMO has been linked to the fear of being ostracized from the group. William's (2009) needs–threat model of ostracism resonates with the concept of FOMO as it suggests that the fear of social exclusion, whether perceived or real, will result in an individual exhibiting an innate need to increase his or her sense of belonging and control in order to compensate for decreases in life-satisfaction and self-esteem. Ostracizm is life-threatening (Williams & Zadro, 2005) as has been clearly demonstrated by the tragic cases of adolescent suicides in the United Kingdom and elsewhere. Przybylski and colleagues (2013) suggest that in the context of online social networking use, FOMO results in individuals seeking to reaffirm their identity by spending more and more time online, leading in turn to further fears of missing out, and an increased capacity for exposure to risk through self-disclosing and friending behaviours.

The Interplay of Cognition and Internet Activity

Zhong, Hardin, and Sun (2011) have posed questions about cognitive behaviours associated with SNS use. For example, they have questioned the quality of thinking associated with high SNS use. Specifically they asked whether effortful thinking, that is seeking out and finding enjoyment in cognitively demanding tasks, was compatible with high SNS use. At the same time they asked whether innovativeness, defined as openness to new experiences and novelty is associated with SNS use (Agarwal & Prasad, 1998). Their work suggests that those individuals who actively seek out cognitive stimulation through demanding tasks (that is show a high 'need for cognition') tend to be lower users of SNS than their peers. Such individuals were also significantly less likely to add anyone to their SNS accounts than low NFC individuals. However, there was no difference between types of thinkers in terms of maintaining several SNS accounts or sharing information through these sites. In this case the variation in use was due to a desire for cognitive stimulation. So why should different types of thinkers respond in such diverse ways to digital technologies? Is there something inherently different in the nature of the interactions promoted by the use of such media? A behaviour frequently commented upon is the propensity of users to multitask when working with and through technology. Multitasking has become part of the media routine in the lives of Internet users. Media multitasking, or the involvement in several concurrent activities at least one of which is related to media use, increased significantly during the 2000s (Foehr, 2006). The younger generation of media users tend to multitask more than older generations such as the 'Baby Boomers' (Carrier, et al., 2009). So multitasking is often the norm when using digital technologies. Our students listen to their iPods while surfing the net and texting or messaging their friends or peers.

A study by Pew International (2012) has shown that the active use of the mobile (cell) phone is common while watching TV. These 'connected viewers' used their mobile phones for a wide range of activities, for example over one-fifth exchange text messages about the programme with friends who were watching the same programme in a different location, while 11 per cent check what others are saying about the programme. Television viewing has become interactive and connected. While some view this requirement to multitask as a strength of such activities, others argue that multitasking necessarily leads to sub-standard, shallow learning. Davies and Good (2009) report that a substantial proportion of learners multitask while engaged in homework activities, in ways that are likely to be distracting for some and constructive for others. It is also clear that multitasking, often using Facebook, can have a detrimental effect on the quality of students' learning, both within formal and informal contexts (Hew, 2011). So multitasking is an essential aspect of technology use but it comes with both benefits and costs. To understand the source of those costs we turn to studies in cognitive psychology and neuroscience.

What are the relationships, if any between SNS use, media multitasking and behavioural factors, such as total Internet time and online time for work or study? Zhong, et al. (2011) found little difference between low, medium and high 'need for cognition' groups as far as media multitasking was concerned, indicating that it is now both pervasive and routine behaviour among the young. We should remember that Holmes (2011) has found a substantial number of young people are not engaged with digital technology, although whether they simply refuse to engage or have a lack of access to technology is unknown. In fact, new data within the United Kingdom has shown that as many as a third of young people are only partially engaged with the Internet, while the reaming two-thirds are engaged but do not present an homogenous group, but rather a number of different groups each pursuing a number of different online activities (see Holmes, 2011).

Does multitasking require a qualitatively different type of attention and if so what are the implications for cognitive skills in both development and learning? William James, in *The Principles of Psychology* (1890), identified qualitatively different forms of attention. He considered steady attention to be the default condition of a mature mind. Mature attention, he argued, was in large part the result of personal mastery and discipline, a sense of discipline that we seem to find increasingly elusive. This seems a world away from the buzz of a multitasking adult in the modern world. James's solution to the buzzing cacophony of the modern world was to advocate 'acquired inattention'. In modern parlance that is to treat texts, tweets, emails, and the call of the mobile phone or mp3/4 player as background noise or distraction. So for the younger generation of multitaskers, the multitasking behaviour is an expected part of their everyday life.

When the brain is forced to respond to several stimuli at once, as happens when multitasking, then task-switching behaviour occurs. Functional magnetic resonance imaging (fMRI) scans of people engaged in task switching have found evidence of a bottleneck when the brain is forced to respond to several stimuli at once. As a result, task switching leads to time lost as the brain determines which task to perform. Our ability to perform simultaneous tasks is limited and we can only successfully perform multiple tasks when these tasks are automated (Broadbent 1957; Fisch 2000). If a task requires focused attention, as is the case for any academic work, the learning of students engaging in multiple activities will be impaired (Kirschner & Karpinski, 2010). So, as the brain cannot fully focus when multitasking, people take longer to complete tasks and are predisposed to errors.

Further, Foerde, Knowlton, and Poldrack (2006) have shown that while people can and do learn things while multitasking, the learning is less flexible, more specialized and hence more difficult to recall when needed. The state of constant intentional self-distraction, it is argued, is detrimental to individuals as their attention is split among many competing tasks.

As individuals attempt to learn new things while multitasking they compromise the quality of that learning. In addition, the more the task requires attention and concentration, such as learning a new subject, the more the learning will be negatively affected by multitasking and therefore represents a poor long-term strategy for learning.

Is multitasking always detrimental? Studies are now appearing that show that this shift in activity is having deleterious effects on young people's academic performance. While multitasking is not new, it is a characteristic feature of the younger generation, particularly in association with the use of communication technologies. The question asked by many researchers is whether this spread of attention leads to more rounded learning or whether attentional switching leads to a loss of performance. In one study over half the students surveyed agreed that their high level of instant messaging while engaged in academic activities had a detrimental effect on their schoolwork and resulted in a failure to complete essential learning tasks (Junco & Cotten, 2011).

Fox, Rosen, and Crawford (2009) addressed the issue of multitasking by investigating the impact of instant messaging (IM) on student performance in a reading task. The students completed a reading comprehension task uninterrupted or while holding an IM conversation. Participants in the latter condition took significantly longer to complete the reading task, indicating that concurrent IM use negatively affects efficiency. However, there was no decrement in performance and IM use did not affect reading comprehension scores. Those students self-reporting extensive time spent messaging had lower reading comprehension scores and lower self-reported performance in US national tests.

Lee, Lin, and Robertson's (2012) study at first sight offers a more complex picture of the multitasking behaviour in learning environments. Their findings supported the assertion that we retain less information when we perform more than one task at a time. In this case reading a text versus simultaneously reading the text and watching a related video on which they would also be tested, lead to a decrement in recall from the reading task when the students were presented with multiple rather than single information sources. However, when not told that the video would be part of the post-test, there was no loss of performance on the reading task, although the students retained little information from the video when presented with a surprise test on its contents.

Lee and colleagues (2012) argue that the observed differences in performance are related to the differences in the cognitive load of the tasks. If the video was treated as background noise – the TV in the corner of the room or music playing down the headphones – then there is less need to focus their attention on that material. What we find interesting about their study is the ease with which students could tune out irrelevant information to focus on the task in hand. The study tells us less about multitasking and more about students' abilities to selectively attend when the need arises – a very encouraging message for all educators.

So attentional switching has limited affect if going from an unfamiliar to familiar task that makes very limited cognitive demands. Moving from the familiar to the unfamiliar takes additional processing capacity that is increased if the unfamiliar task is not simple (Rubenstein, Meyer, and Evans, 2001). However, learners can focus their attention and block-out unwanted 'noise' when they need to. Meyer and colleagues (1995) have long argued that rather than causing a bottleneck in the brain a process of adaptive executive control takes place when prioritizing task processing. While this is not a controversial stance, Meyer has argued that, with training, the brain can learn to task-switch more effectively, and there is some evidence that certain simple tasks are amenable to such practice. Again the picture is not all positive, as research has also found that multitasking contributes to the release of stress hormones and adrenaline, which can cause long-term health problems.

Are Multitaskers Always at a Disadvantage?

The question as to whether heavy multitaskers are always at a disadvantage is taken up by Lui and Wong (2012). Multitaskers have been shown to perform poorly in certain cognitive tasks involving task switching, selective attention and working memory, possibly because they tend to pay superficial attention to lots of information without paying sufficient focus on the information that is most relevant to the task at hand. However, there is evidence that this cognitive style may not detrimentally affect performance in all tasks. Lui and Wong found heavy media multitaskers performed better in a multisensory integration task than others due to their extensive experience in integrating information from different modalities.

A number of studies have shown positive effects of playing video games as they have found that games can promote divided attention skills, the perceptual foundation for multitasking. A more recent study employed a tool that measures how effectively a participant performs on four tasks carried out simultaneously (Dye & Bavelier, 2010; Dye, Green, & Bavelier, 2009; Green & Bavelier, 2003). One study showed that participants who played two hours of a shooting game called Counter-Strike had higher multitasking scores than those in a control group who did not play the game. There was a potential facilitation of development of attentional skills in children who were avid players of action video games. Playing video games improved visual attention in youths aged 7 to 22, in terms of allocating attention and filtering out irrelevant information. Other research teams have also shown positive impacts of playing video games as they enhance the ability to divide visual attention in college students (Greenfield, deWinstanley, et al., 1994). While the use of electronic visual media may enhance skills of visual attention and visual–spatial processing, it may not adequately cultivate higher-order cognitive processing skills (Greenfield, 2009).

Video gaming requires multitasking and gamers have been shown to be highly effective on tasks such as driving while using a hands-free mobile phone. Testing gamers and non-gamers in a driving simulator, Telner, Wiesenthal, et al. (2008) showed the standard decrement in driving performance for non-gamers when using a mobile, whereas, gamers were significantly less impaired by the dual task challenge presented by driving and using their mobile. So video games promote skills in multitasking, but many parents, educators and researchers are left asking whether multitasking is fundamentally a good thing. Recent studies have investigated whether someone performs better or processes a task more deeply if it is executed alone rather than in a multitasking environment.

Going with the Flow

Game playing leads us to a consideration of flow theory. A state of flow, a phenomenon first articulated by Csikszentmihalyi and Csikszentmihalyi (1975) in their study of individuals involved in activities such as rock climbing and chess, has been shown to enhance student learning. Flow is characterized by the complete absorption or engagement in an activity and refers to an optimal experience (Csikszentmihalyi, 1990, 2002): a state of consciousness that is sometimes experienced by individuals who are deeply involved in an enjoyable activity to the exclusion of everything around them (Inal & Cagiltay, 2007; Kiili, 2005). To achieve a state of flow an individual must be involved in an activity with a clear set of goals and progress that has appropriate and immediate feedback. In addition there must be a balance between the *perceived* challenges of the task and the individual's own *perceived* skills. So an individual going with the flow or 'in the zone' has an optimal experience in which they are so involved in the activity that it becomes spontaneous with a level of automaticity and as a result they stop being aware of themselves as separate from the actions they are performing.

Why should we be interested in flow theory? Csikszentmihalyi (1990) suggests that enhancing the time spent in flow makes our lives happier and more successful and it has been shown to be associated with states of enjoyment, positive affect and psychological wellbeing (Bryce & Haworth, 2002). Studies of video gamers have found that flow is associated with gaming enjoyment and positive affect (Klimmt, Hartmann, & Frey, 2007; Smith, 2012). Sweetser and Wyeth's (2005) GameFlow model identifies eight elements that result in an enhanced game enjoyment: concentration, challenge, skills, immersion, control, clear goals, feedback and social interaction. This evidence suggests that gaming is intrinsically motivating and provides positive experiences for those who engage in the activity.

However, flow experiences have been shown to foster addiction and it has been argued that it is related to an increase in engaging in risky behaviours such as rock climbing (Schüler, 2012). While Keller, Bless, et al. (2011) have shown that even during pleasurable flow experience, maintaining a balance of personal skills versus task demands results in reduced heart rate variability indicating enhanced mental workload, and this is accompanied by stress as indicated by relatively high levels of salivary cortisol. These findings are consistent with those of Meyer, et al. (1995). Reaching a state of flow then is hard and demanding work, yet individuals seek out this state and it might be argued this is how we move forward as a species, testing ourselves on the edge.

So What are Young People Learning?

Young people spend a considerable amount of time in their technologically-rich world but does this have any academic spin-off? There are those that will point to young dot-com millionaires and say of course the hours spent 'playing' in the digital world are of value. The expertise literature at first sight would seem to support this assertion: '10,000 hours' practice is required to acquire expertise is now well evidenced and widely accepted. However, simple time spent 'doing' an activity is not enough to take command of a skill. Ericsson, Charness, et al. (2006) point out that time spent on any activity must be quality hours of 'deliberate practise'. Practising already acquired skills quickly leads to a learning plateau. To advance you need to push the limits of your understanding and target weaknesses as this allows you to broaden your skill set. The question then is not a simple one of what young people are failing to learn when engaged with social networks but what they are learning and, as a consequence of this refocusing of their endeavours, what skill and abilities valued by society are not being honed? This leads to a further question that we have yet to answer as a society: whether those valued skills are still relevant and, if so, how do we encourage their development when there is no realistic chance of weaning the young off their enthusiasm for digital technologies?

Risks, Skills and Opportunities

Risks are often associated with the dangers of multitasking and becoming immersed within the digital world of technology. Many parents, educators and researchers are left asking whether multitasking is fundamentally a good thing? Not only can multitasking have negative influences on family relations and attachment to parents (Richards, et al., 2010), but this can also have a detrimental effect on the quality of students' learning both within and outside formal educational contexts. There are concerns that students are being absorbed by this technology, which is resulting in a detrimental effect on their health and psychological wellbeing and leads them to engage in non-productive, time-wasting activities. Of course, the media hype regarding the use of mobile phones while driving warns us about the inherent risks of multitasking and road safety. We know that texting while driving can be a regular source of distraction and this is most problematic for young drivers who are more often attracted to and more ready to adopt new communication technologies (Lee, et al., 2011). But there are real opportunities too and the pros may outweigh the costs. Practising the skills associated with multitasking may surely allow individuals to become better at attentional-switching, visual-spatial processing and other quite advanced higher-order cognitive skills.

Conclusions

Learners are enticed by the range of technological tools available and often find themselves immersed within the range of tools available to them, whether these tools facilitate social networking, downloading music or instant messaging. What we do know is that within the current net generation, people are not always content on doing one thing at a time. Frequently, they multitask: they engage in multiple tasks aimed at attaining multiple goals simultaneously. Given that people rapidly switch their attention back and forth across tasks, they falsely believe that they can 'multitask' but in reality, they cannot, and, by trying to do so, neither task receives optimal attention or focus. This is because multitasking is both cognitively and physically demanding, requiring the refinement of cognitive skills involving task switching, selective attention and placing additional constraints on working memory capacity. We often find that those individuals who do prefer to multitask are those who are impulsive, have low behavioural inhibitions and are often sensation seekers (see Sanbonmatsu, et al., 2013). However, we do know that multitasking is not detrimental to all individuals as it can allow the development of multisensory integration and a better awareness of flexible task-switching. As discussed in the next chapter, multitasking through video game playing can have real benefits and promote divided attention skills, and a refinement of behavioural, cognitive and affective skills that are needed to engage within a digitally rich social environment.

Chapter Eight
Games, Learning and Education

Introduction

There is little doubt that we are a nation addicted to gaming, in one sense or another. Whether it is Angry Birds on the iPhone, interacting with the Sims on the laptop or indulging in mayhem in Massively Multiplayer Online Role-Playing Games (MMORPGs) such as World of Warcraft, gaming is hugely popular with a substantial proportion of the global population. This growth has been possible as a result of wider access to broadband connectivity, advances in technology and relative reductions in costs. In 2008, in the United States, the Pew Internet and American Life Project surveyed 1,102 12 and 17 year olds and found that that 97 per cent – both boys (99%) and girls (94%) – played some type of digital game (Lenhart, Kahne, et al., 2008). De Freitas and Liarokapis (2011) showed that the video-game industry sold 84.64 million Nintendo Wii consoles, 50 million Microsoft Xbox 360s and 50 million Sony PlayStation 3s. In 2006 the income of the global online gaming market had reached $4.5 million; this amount tripled in the following 5 years and is predicted to reach $82 billion by 2017 (see de Freitas & Liarokapis, 2011). While the economic benefits of this thriving industry are there for all to see, the psychosocial benefits, particularly within educational contexts, are hotly disputed.

Video games have gone from being seen as irrelevant or dangerous, to being the darlings of the media and educational industries. There is often a generational divide in our perceptions of video games. For many parents and teachers, the perception of learners sat for hours in front of a television screen or laptop playing on games is rather negative and damaging to

Learning and the E-Generation, First Edition. Jean D. M. Underwood and Lee Farrington-Flint.
© 2015 Jean D. M. Underwood and Lee Farrington-Flint. Published 2015 by John Wiley & Sons, Ltd.

their educational development. For many, the stereotypical video gamer player conjures up an image of a reclusive individual who spends hours in his or her bedroom because of an inability to operate in the real world. However, this does not match gamers' perceptions of themselves as highly socialized individuals. Pejorative terms such as nerd (passionately pursues intellectual or esoteric knowledge) and geek (inordinately dedicated to and involved with technology) are often used to describe such individuals. The perceived link between such obsessive behaviour and the manifest popularity of technology-based games for students of all ages is a nightmare scenario for many and it places game playing at the forefront of the debate on the ills of Internet and technology in general. Is gaming being falsely accused? Is there little or no merit in an activity that so many of our children enjoy? It is becoming increasingly apparent, despite anecdotes of aggressive and violent behaviours, that video games do provide opportunities for learning and development that often go unrecognized (Ferguson & Olson, 2013). It is these positive impacts on learning and the potential ways in which games can shape education that we focus on in this chapter.

The Nature of Games

Technology-based games are highly varied and difficult to classify with any precision. Over the years, gaming has taken on a range of different formats, ranging from Atari's ping-pong, which dominated the scene in the 1970s, to the best-selling Mortal Combat, rated the top game in 1993, to the more recent MMORPGs such as World of Warcraft and the virtual worlds of Second Life. Many of the early games were mini-games in Prensky's (2001) parlance, as are the majority of educational games currently available on the Internet. In contrast the virtual worlds epitomized by the MMORPGs are complex games. These too have their parallels in the education world, for example, Economics 201[1]. Prensky (2006) argues that mini-games are not 'bad' for learning although they tend to be restricted to single skills while the learning from complex games is multifaceted. Such virtual worlds, it is argued, present exciting new opportunities to education (Gee, 2003). In these rich virtual environments learning is inherently social. However, the experience of playing a game like the Sims or Civilization III, which requires a cerebral blend of planning, building, managing, and competing with other civilizations, is very different from playing games, such as World of Warcraft,

[1]http://gamepolitics.com/2007/07/11/economics-201-the-online-game

which require rhythm and timing as they encourage participants to immerse themselves in complex virtual societies.

> Non-gamers usually imagine that mastering a game is largely a matter of learning to push buttons faster, which no doubt accounts for all the 'hand-eye coordination' clichés. But for many popular games, the ultimate key to success lies in deciphering the rules, and not manipulating joysticks:
>
> (Johnson, 2005, pp. 42–43)

The proficiency required for playing video games is more than the physical coordination of pressing buttons on a keypad: it requires the development of quite sophisticated cognitive skills, which include strategic planning, reasoning and sophisticated problem solving.

Simply Addicted to Games?

As alluded to in the previous chapter, addiction to technology is a real concern and this is most apparent when we consider the nature of gaming. Some behaviour patterns do give cause for concern. For example, in a sample of over 7,000 gamers just fewer than 12 per cent fulfilled the diagnostic criteria of addiction in relation to their gaming behaviour, although in this study there was only weak evidence of a link between aggressive behaviour and excessive gaming in general (Grüsser, Thalemann, & Griffiths, 2006). A study of over 4,000 gamers ranging from 14 to 40+ years old, using Gaming Addiction Short Scale (GAS) that covers seven criteria including salience, withdrawal and conflicts, found only 3.7 per cent of gamers could be considered problematic users, that is met at least half of the seven conditions. The percentage of problematic gamers among adolescents was higher at 7.6 per cent. High GAS scores were associated with aggression, low sociability and self-efficacy, and lower satisfaction with life. Additionally, these scores correspond with intensive use and preferences for certain gaming genres across all age groups (Festl, Scharkow, & Quandt, 2012).

However, the research is beginning to show just how complex the situation can be between video games and aggression. In fact the claim that video games cause real-life aggression may be seen as a gross oversimplification. For example, Adachi and Willoughby (2011) assert that only one of the many investigations into the links between violent and aggressive behaviour and the playing of violent video game used an unambiguous measure of aggressive behaviour. The overwhelming majority of experimental studies have used a measure of aggression that may also serve to measure competitiveness and so from these studies it is not possible to establish with any certainty whether the games are engendering aggression or competitiveness. Of course it is important to measure what you say you are measuring but a further criticism of this body of research is that if competitiveness is what is actually being measured then why was this not controlled for when selecting test games? Another claim by Adachi and Willoughby (2012) is that there is no study to date that has equated the violent and non-violent video games on competitiveness, difficulty and pace of action and this is crucial given the research instruments that are being used. Their study is a telling indictment of a body of research that is having considerable influence over policy makers and, through the media attention, parent groups. Unsurprisingly, following the tenor of their argument, in a later study Adachi and Willoughby (2011) suggest that video game play may meet, or may be related to, positive outcomes such as flow, cooperation, problem-solving and reduced in-group bias, that is, that gaming engenders the twenty-first century skills deemed so essential by Larson (2000) for the cultivation of positive youth development (see Chapter 1 for an extended review of Larson's theory and intrinsic motivation).

Although media speculation has suggested that specific features of game play may be associated with problematic behaviour including addiction and a propensity for aggressive and violent behaviour, new evidence undermines these claims. A meta-analysis by Johnson, Jones, and Burns (2013) shows an emerging body of research focusing on the potential positive influences of video games. While admitting that excessive engagement is not good for mental health and can be associated with negative outcomes, such as anxiety and insomnia, they found that game playing can have a positive influence on young people's emotional state and is associated with higher self-esteem, resilience and well-functioning social relationships. They argue that video games can help the young to manage their own mental health, wellbeing and psychological distress with little evidence of the adverse effects from video games often found within the social media (Ferguson & Olson, 2013).

Russoniello, Fish, and O'Brien (2013) add further support to this therapeutic view of game playing. They conducted a randomized controlled clinical study of the impact of casual game playing on individuals' suffering both mild and severe depression. Depression is a debilitating illness usually treated with expensive pharmaceuticals or behavioural techniques such as cognitive behavioural therapy, which are often stigmatized. Their study asked whether a prescribed regimen of casual video gaming would reduce symptoms associated with depression, a question answered in the affirmative. They demonstrated that such game playing resulted in a significant decrease in depression both in the short and long term and was equally effective for both mild and severe cases of depression. They also recorded no negative or adverse effects during game playing and so argued that the use of games in this manner provided a safe therapeutic experience. While these results may seem surprising at first sight and no explanations were provided by the researchers as to why these effects occurred there is a simple possible explanation. Depression tends to narrow an individual's perspective and sustains that situation. Game playing is absorbing and if an individual is to be a game winner they must focus outward on the game and not on the negative aspects of their life that have led to their depression. So a simple refocusing of attention may be an effective clinical treatment. This might be of some assurance to parents concerned about their child and they may be keen to see moderate game playing as an adolescent stress buster.

Another recent study further highlights some of the complexity of the impact of gaming (Happ, Melzer, & Steffgen, 2013). Students were asked to play Midway Games' Mortal Combat versus DC Universe on the Playstation 3: a fighting game in which the player controls an on-screen character and engages in close combat with an opponent. The game scenario is built around known fantasy characters. The 'good guys' Raiden (Earthrealm's god of Thunder) and Superman (protector of the Earth) repel invaders from their worlds but a consequence of their actions is that there is a merging of *Mortal Kombat* and DC villains. Inevitably these heroes and anti-heroes clash and screens full of gratuitous violence ensue. This is the type of game that causes consternation among parents and those charged with developing the next generation.

To return to Happ, Melzer, and Steffgen's study (2013) that had a two-by-two design in which students either played as the morally good character Superman or as the Joker, one of the arch-villains in the Batman films. The two groups were further divided with half of the participants acting as Superman or as the Joker reading a bogus Wikipedia article about their character. In the first case it was designed to encourage the player to empathize with Superman while the Joker brief described how he had suffered abuse in his childhood. Apart from these differences, the game experience was the same for all participants. In all four groups players spent their time in hand-to-hand combat against a variety of other computer-controlled game characters.

After the game, the participants were asked to rate a number of faces on how hostile they looked. There were both angry and neutral faces, but participants who had played the Joker were more likely to perceive hostility in neutral faces (a marker of an aggressive mindset), as compared with the participants who played Superman. For Superman, empathy led participants to interpret neutral faces as less aggressive. When playing the evil Joker, however, empathy was seen to encourage hostile perceptions. Happ and colleagues (2013) interpret this as showing that empathy may not be positive per se and that it may backfire depending on the interaction of game characters and the empathy players feel for them. So, while media violence is suspected of leading to a violent and desensitized personality this analysis shows individuals with this type of character are affected differentially depending on the level of empathy they have for that character. No bonding with the character or playing the 'good guy' protects the individual from aggressive perceptions.

Games and Learning

As we know all too well, many students are disengaged from the academic and social aspects of school life. Student engagement, the interaction between the time, effort and other relevant resources invested by both students and their institution, is central to effective schooling. Engagement in learning has been identified as a valuable indicator of students' academic performance (Appleton, Christenson, & Furlong, 2008; Hancock & Betts, 2002; Underwood, 2009). Specific aspects of engagement, such as involvement, time on task and quality of effort, have repeatedly been linked to positive outcomes. One explanation that has been put forward for the reported benefit of video games is that they can serve to enhance arousal levels, which in turn boosts motivation and interest levels to maintain focus on a task (Slusarek, Velling, et al., 2001). Engagement and motivation are often perceived as interchangeable. Maehr and Meyer (1997) suggest that motivation answers the question, 'Why am I doing this?', while engagement reflects a person's active involvement in the activity. Students who are engaged are attracted to their work, persist in their academic activities despite challenges and obstacles, and take visible delight in accomplishing them. It is unsurprising, therefore, that different approaches have been developed and evaluated to foster students' engagement with games and these offer great potential for educational learning (see Shaffer, 2006).

Such engagement is apparent in the majority of, if not all, video-game players. Indeed game designers build their products to ensure such engagement as it then results in customer loyalty. Engagement can be at the behavioural, cognitive or emotional level. *Behavioural engagement* is essentially a willingness to take part and is expressed through effort, persistence, attention and the absence of disruptive behaviours (Appleton, 2008; Fredericks, et al., 2004). *Cognitive engagement* requires an investment on the part of the individual, whether pupil or game player, to achieve deep understanding and expertise. It implies a desire to go beyond the basic requirements of a task, and to relish challenges (Connell & Wellborn, 1991). *Emotional engagement* occurs with enjoyment and positive attitudes about learning (Appleton).

There are a wide variety of reasons as to why individuals are involved in gaming. People engage in gaming, in general, in order to socialize, as a distraction from the stresses of everyday life, to develop new skills and because gaming is associated with highly positive psychological experiences as proposed in entertainment theory. Player enjoyment is key to game playing and is often used as a measure of intrinsic motivation. Entertainment theory (Vorderer, Klimmt, & Ritterfeld, 2004) posits that media users actively work on their enjoyment experience. Establishing a link between performance and enjoyment, results in players using the game complexity to maximum enjoyment. If a player is experiencing failure, frustration increases and self-esteem declines but task completion leads to growing self-esteem and a highly enjoyable experience. This sense of enjoyment then reduces anxiety and helps the player feel confident about their success. Learning though games can then lead to higher levels of enjoyment, lower task anxiety and better performance, that is, effective learning.

Over the past 10 years serious, educational or persuasive games have emerged to fulfil a range of non-entertainment purposes, such as training and education, advertising, awareness-raising, intercultural empathy, therapy and business and manufacturing support (see, for example, Vannini, et al., 2011). Why should game playing be an effective mode of learning? According to Chatfield (2013), during his TED Global 2010 talk, '7 ways games reward the brain', games are highly rewarding and he cites seven ways that gaming rewards the player:

1. Games provide 'experience bars' to measure continual progress or a profile of the avatar showing continual progress. Every time the player takes action the experience bar, or avatar profile, is updated by the reward so the player is able to visualize the progress being made. This should lead to more reflective learning and motivation, as players are able to make immediate links between their actions and consequences.
2. Games provide multiple long- and short-term aims and having multiple tasks provides the motivation for the player to break things down and make choices, which, it can be argued, will lead to more tactical decision-making.
3. Games reinforce effort and attempt to encourage the player to keep on trying.
4. Games give rapid and clear feedback. Effective learning develops because players are able to make immediate links between their actions and consequences.
5. Chatfield talks about the 'neurological goldmine' that is generated by the element of uncertainty in games, which while a known reward

excites people, the uncertainty of reward increases in the level of the neurotransmitter dopamine that is associated with pleasure, learning and with reward-seeking behaviour. There are increases in confidence and pleasure and decreases in stress and anxiety – developed when increases in dopamine create an emotional feeling of wellbeing.

6. Games that add controlled elements of uncertainty can predict learning and enhanced engagement because when dopamine levels increase, confidence levels increase, and players become braver, more willing to take risks and are more motivated.

7. Games often add 'other people' and peer and group collaboration is a powerful tool in increasing human motivation and as such can lead to increased team skills and increased empathy for members of a group.

Chatfield also recognizes the neurological rewards for game playing, that is, how the uncertainty of reward increases the level of the neurotransmitter dopamine, which is associated with pleasure, learning and with reward-seeking behaviour. More broadly, we can see how digital games may have elements in common with many features that we associate with effective learning. They offer the opportunity to personalize learning, include scaffolding, provide flags for navigation, and incorporate the main components of flow: clear goals, direct and immediate feedback, balance between ability level and challenge, and sense of control (Csikszentmihalyi, 1990; Malone & Lepper, 1987). Challenge has been shown to be central to engagement but also to many digital games, suggesting that the latter are potentially engaging learning experiences for students (Connolly, Boyle, et al., 2012; Prensky, 2001). Finally, games can help promote automaticity of cognitive skills (Underwood & Everatt, 1996).

Discussion of games allows us to explore many of the more important factors affecting the learning process such as motivation and the role of feedback. Games can stimulate content-specific skills, that is, understanding and problem-solving as well as content-independent skills including collaboration, communication and self-regulation. Depending on the characteristics of the game, gaming will potentially result in affective communicative, cognitive and kinetic skills-learning outcomes (van den Bos, van Dijk, et al., 2009). This means they may promote skills-based learning including technical and motor skills, cognitive outcomes including declarative, procedural and strategic knowledge, or change players' attitudes, beliefs or emotions (affective learning) (Egenfeldt-Nielsen, Smith, & Tosca, 2008; Garris, Ahlers, & Driskell, 2002).

Learners as game players inevitably start with failure – errors lead to learning – testing the rules of a game system like Civilization III, with tens of thousands of interacting variables, results in a deeper-level conceptual development. This learning cycle is critical to both intellectually engaging gameplay and academic learning, which illustrates the potential of educational games. Squire (2003, 2005) offers a warning: this testing of the system is in fact a test of the learner also. This act of failing or elicitation of rules as Johnson (2005) might put it, was a critical precondition for learning as students found themselves confronting gaps or flaws in their current understandings through cycles of recursive play accommodating new information with old. Students who become comfortable with this very testing form of learning develop a deeper understanding of the subject in hand along with a range of high-order cognitive skills. However, for other students the lack of certainty and the demands for intellectual rigour proved too onerous and the reading class became a safe and familiar haven. However, once over the hurdle and into the game, effective learning can take place.

Obviously intrinsic motivation is a key factor here but the level of interactivity in the game plays a crucial role. The learner is placed within the role of decision-maker and is pushed through increasingly difficult challenges that allow learning to occur through trial and error procedures, each of which are equally important factors to consider. Decisions are often supported by rapid feedback that is beneficial. Educational games will be effective because knowledge or skills practised through gaming are more likely to be transferred than when practised on a single kind of problem. Once mastered, the knowledge and skills are practised further to provide overlearning (Paraskeva, Mysirlaki, & Papagianni, 2010). As a result knowledge and skills become automatized and consolidated in memory so that the learner can begin to focus consciously on comprehending and applying new information (Gentile & Gentile, 2008).

The potential advantages of video gaming extend beyond cognitive explanations. Egenfeldt-Nielsen (2006), for instance, argues that from a sociocultural perspective, video games are the tools for constructing a viable, authentic learning experience. Video games mediate discussion, reflection, facts and analysis facilitated by individuals within and outside the classroom. Thus, video games are interesting not for their content but for the way in which new explorations initiate negotiations, and turn constructions and journeys into knowledge (Gee, 2003; Paraskeva, et al., 2010). This is not a comfortable mode of operating for some teachers or indeed learners.

There are psychological models that offer further support to the potential benefits of games for learning and education. The appeal of games has been summarized in Mayer's (2005) Cognitive Theory of Multimedia Learning (CTML), which is based on two major theories in cognitive psychology. The first is Paivio's (1986) dual-coding theory, which postulates that a learner's cognitive system uses both visual and verbal cues to represent information and that these two types of information are processed along distinct channels in the human mind, creating separate representations for information processed in each channel. The second theory is Baddley and Hitch's (1974) working memory model, which states that working memory has two largely independent subcomponents that tend to work in parallel – one visual and one verbal–acoustic. Presenting information that exploits these dual systems allows a learner to construct a better understanding of the material by integrating information from both channels. While the dual-coding theory has its limitations, it provides support for the efficacy of multimedia as a learning medium. It is not difficult to see why games, as a specific case of multimedia presentation, could and should enhance student performance. Furthermore, Green and Bavelier's (2006, 2007) series of experiments suggest that action video game play may enhance some aspects of visual working memory and there is supporting evidence concerning the efficacy of game playing, much of which has been conducted using Tetris (e.g., Underwood, 2007).

The research evidence shows that gaming is a powerful tool that supports understanding and learning but that the nature of that learning can be constrained and is not always guaranteed. Griffith, Voloschin, et al. (1983) found that video-game users had better eye–hand coordination as measured by a pursuit rotor task. Drew and Waters (1986) also showed a relationship between increased video-game playing and improvements of eye–hand coordination, as well as manual dexterity and reaction time. As Southwell and Doyle (2004) point out, however, these studies have not identified a causal link and we are debating whether playing such games leads to skills development or whether players with the requisite skills are drawn to games.

Is Gaming a Panacea for Educational Ills?

The use of Tetris, and other video games, to explore problem-solving is a response to arguments about the artificiality of many earlier laboratory studies of learning, which it is argued fail to capture the superior performance of experts because such fixed tasks constrain the expert performer. On the other hand, sitting in front of a computer screen is the natural environment for the video-game player and so studying game playing not only provides a window on the expertise in context but also provides a learning environment in which engagement by the learner is generally ensured.

The recognition that games can engage the learner as well as having the potential to provide concrete learning experiences has resulted in both trials of commercial games in the classroom as well as the development and use of specially designed educational games (Sandford & Williamson, 2006). Studies, such as that by Annetta, Minogue, et al. (2009), show that games can increase student engagement during instruction, academic achievement in different domains, and skills, knowledge and attitudes, especially in the right environment and context. For example, Shaffer (2006) has shown that role-playing educational games using concrete examples of abstract mathematical concepts can be effective learning tools. So should we capture all that motivation, engagement and challenge inherent in games and make education fun and solve the learning crisis in our schools through the use of video games? If only it was so easy! Despite such innovations and potential educational benefits, the emphasis on using games to support learning within the classroom still remains highly contested.

So we ask why does this focused attention not lead to effective learning? This is the wrong question because it is based on a false premise. Game players, if they engage, will learn but not necessarily the knowledge and skills valued by educators. For example, Age of Empires is a series of games that focus on historical events from the Stone Age to the Classical Period. Each game has a historically relevant setting and the task is to manage resources and beat the opponent. However, gaining resources to win becomes the prime goal not running a successful culture. In Squires' (2003, 2005) studies of Civilization those pupils that became immersed in the game did develop a deep conceptual understanding of a culture but they were a minority. Three decades ago we investigated the use of word processors as a tool to promote Lunzer and Gardner's (1979) active reading approach to literacy acquisition (see Underwood & Underwood, 1990). This was a simple exercise in rejoining the first half of a sentence (top) with its tail (second half), and then ordering the reconstructed sentences to make a sensible historical statement. The learners, in this case children in years 7 and 8 (ages 12 to 13) in a UK school, were very adept at using the pick and put functions of the word processor to complete the task; however, a number were less adept at producing the coherent paragraph and when questioned were surprised that this was the objective of the exercise. They saw the technology skills as the goal not the reconstruction of the history. This focus on the technology or the game is seen elsewhere. Math Blaster, a game to teach algebra, involves shooting down asteroids, the consequence of which is the release of algebraic questions, which have to be answered. While the skills of algebra are practised, it has been argued that swiftness and shooting skills take up much space and sometimes work against really thinking about the algebra (see Koirala & Goodwin, 2000). On this basis, perhaps many teachers and educationalists are right to raise concerns over the pedagogic value of games for education.

A number of commercial off-the-shelf games have been applied in educational settings. For example Squire (2003, 2005) reported experiences where Civilization III was used to promote the historical understanding of 17 and 18 year olds. This trial was not an unmitigated success and is a clear example of horses for courses. Less-motivated or less-able students found the time required to get into the game very off-putting and elected to go to reading classes instead of game playing. There are, therefore, individual differences in how learners engage with different types of games, so 'one size' does not fit all.

More recent examples of games for educational learning include the use of games like the Sims 2: Open for Business (Panoutsopoulos & Sampson, 2012), Delta Force adapted for military training (Fong, 2006) or multiplayer role games as World of Warcraft (Dickey, 2005). It is no easy matter to link game objectives and content with those presented in the curriculum not least because it is difficult to identify the learning outcomes in commercial video games (McFarlane, Sparrowhawk & Heald, 2002). As a consequence, the skills and knowledge acquired by students may differ from educators' planned learning outcomes and goals (Sandford & Williamson, 2006). However, Panoutsopoulos and Sampson's (2012) study of the development of mathematical skills using Sims 2: Open for Business, for example, found no benefit of game-supported over non-computer-supported problem-based curricula as far as improving attitudes to mathematics or mathematical performance. However, students involved in the game-supported activities were more effective in meeting general educational objectives, such as formulating and testing their own hypotheses, observing the outcomes of their actions, comparing and contrasting data available from the game, and justifying and evaluating outcomes of performed actions.

However, whether a game will be successful in promoting desired attitudes and behaviours depends on the degree to which the game is tailored, not just to pedagogy and the learning outcome, but also to the individual learner. Orji, Mandryk, et al. (2013) have raised doubts about the effectiveness of such games, arguing that many are based on intuition rather than on a theoretically sound model of what is known to motivate change to more healthy behaviours, and also contend that many programmes have a one-size-fits-all approach. Using the gamer typology identified by BrainHex, which specifies seven gamer types (achiever, conqueror, daredevil, mastermind, seeker, socializer and survivor), they show the difference in their response to determining factors of healthy behaviours as defined under the

Health Belief Model, that is, perceived susceptibility, perceived severity, perceived benefit, perceived barrier, cue to action and self-efficacy (Rosenstock, 1974). While perceived susceptibility, that is risk of any behaviour, has long been assumed to be central to behavioural change, Orji, Mandryk, et al. showed that only achievers, daredevils and socializers were influenced by this factor and that it had no effect on conquerors and masterminds. More surprising therefore was a negative effect on seekers and survivors that prevented these two groups from exhibiting the promoted healthy behaviour. While programmes which promote self-efficacy have been found to have a positive effect on achievers, masterminds, seekers and socializers, it had a neutral effect on other gamer types. So the integration of games for educational purposes needs to address not just potential learning outcomes, but also to cater for different groups of learners with various attitudes and perceptions towards gaming.

This need to match the game to the individual and not simply to the subject at hand requires a deeper understanding of a game than is held by many teachers. Many teachers show a reluctance in the use of games for educational learning and this, in part, may stem from their lack of engagement with games in general. If we consider the generational divide, teachers and parents often have negative opinions about video games. But successful integration into educational curricula requires teacher involvement. Changes to curriculum design require teachers not only to know what subjects and skills can benefit from a games-based approach, but when to use and how to manage such an approach, for the benefit of the disparate learners within the classroom. So teachers need to know the game well, propose specific learning paths, verify their effectiveness and most importantly set the gaming experience in a sound educational framework, which can be achieved via debriefing activities (de Freitas & Oliver, 2006).

Evidence of the discontinuity between the world of games and those within the teaching profession is presented in a FutureLab survey, which found a significant majority of teachers (72%) do not play games for leisure (Sandford, Uiksak, et al., 2006). The digital divide between teacher and student appears to be more a lifestyle choice than a generational gap, that is, many teachers choose not to play games, while peers in other occupations do. Both Sandford's teachers and students agreed that games were motivating, resulting in increased student engagement; however, motivation was higher when playing leisure rather than educational games and when the students had a degree of autonomy in playing the game. In this study neither students nor teachers saw an educational benefit to gaming, which raises very real questions about whether gaming can contribute to formal learning.

Here we can pose one additional question. What happens when gaming takes place in a non-game situation? This problem is exemplified by a system that has proved to be an effective way of improving reading comprehension (Meyer, et al., 2010; Meyer, Wijekumar, & Lin, 2011; Wijekumar, Meyer, & Lei, 2013). While the reading comprehension programme delivers a set of learning objectives, some students treat the system as a game rather than as a tool to develop their reading. Such behaviour can be detrimental as key concepts or skills are not learned (Muldner, Burleson, et al., 2010). This has been called 'gaming the system' and has been shown to result in lower scores on learning measures than for students who do not game the system (Baker, Corbett, et al., 2004).

The Future of Games for Learning

Learning through game playing, either through serious games developed with educational intent or video games designed for leisure, may hold the key to a more effective educational system. Prensky (2006) argues that the move to student-driven learning will generate a demand for educational games, as they are natural environments for the digital natives now in our schools. Rather than being part of the problem, he argues that games are a powerful tool in any school's armoury when dealing with adolescents who necessarily pass through a state of personal identity exploration when wandering attention comes to the fore. By providing problem-focused learning, games not only motivate but also provide the increasing complexity sought by such learners to develop psychologically.

There is considerable evidence that games promote thinking and learning. But why should game playing be an effective mode of learning? It is argued that games may promote skills-based learning including technical and motor skills, cognitive outcomes including declarative, procedural and strategic knowledge, or change players' attitudes, beliefs or emotions. Through the process of trial-and-error, it promotes effective learning, problem-solving and processes of acquiring knowledge and new skills. However, the relevance of games for education and learning are less clear-cut and many teachers and parents fail to see how games can promote educational skills within the classroom.

So if there is to be an effective use of digital games for educational purposes then we cannot simply rely on the enticing power of gaming, and the thrill and excitement that this may offer. There must be alignment between the game features and the intended learning outcomes: selecting an appropriate pedagogical approach for framing game activities is highly important. There also needs to be a greater awareness by teachers regarding the perceived pedagogic value of games and their potential value in promoting educational skills and learning. As discussed within this chapter, while there are quite clearly potential benefits of integrating games into the context of learning, with notable benefits in the refinement of cognitive, linguistic, affective and social skills, the affordances are not recognized within educational settings. The way in which games can be effectively implemented into the school curriculum is an issue for more detailed consideration.

There is, however, a counterargument that says that the alignment between the game and the intended learning outcomes is not what we are about. Shute and Ventura (2013) make the case that an alignment with perceived current educational needs might actually be a false trail as it does not fit the needs of a generation growing up and working in the twenty-first century. As others before them, they point out that the developed world, our world, now relies on individuals who are able:

> to deal with an array of complex problems, many with global ramifications (e.g., climate change or renewable energy sources). When confronted by such problems, tomorrow's workers need to be able to think systemically, creatively, and critically.
>
> (Shute and Ventura, 2013, p.13)

You might ask why we raise this issue here. It is because Shute and Ventura (2013) argue that well-designed games have the added potential of being an effective vehicle to assess learning. They argue that games can provide dynamic and ongoing measures of learning and offer students opportunities to apply complex competencies such as creativity, problem-solving, persistence and collaboration while at the same time helping to combat students' growing disengagement with school. Shute and Ventura argue that current assessments are unable to capture deep learning or the acquisition of complex competencies or individual disposition that lead to effective learning, such as conscientiousness or related persistence (Underwood, et al., 2010). Embedding assessment in games allows multiple behaviours to become measurable. Exemplar measures would be how long a person spends on a difficult problem (where length of time is seen as a measure of persistence), the number of failures and retries before success, and returning to a hard problem after skipping it. All of these measures can be captured. So embedding assessments within games provides a way to monitor players' progress toward targeted competencies and to use that information to support learning.

Risks, Skills and Opportunities

Games are an increasingly important part of our culture and afford many opportunities for the gamer, whether simply as an escape from everyday tensions or the immersion into alternative worlds. Despite strong evidence in support of the intrinsic motivation of games, and an engagement with multimodal learning (Gee, 2003), there are risks associated with game playing that need to be acknowledged (see Guan & Subrahmanyam, 2009) including not only aggression and violence but a feeling that computer games are responsible for eroding young people's social lives. However, by contrast, it could be argued that games provide a safe environment for learners to take risks and to release tensions and arousal in a socially acceptable way. Opportunities for the use of games can be found: a game might be used in a motivational capacity as a reward for good behaviour or excellent performance. On another level, games can help disenfranchised individuals back into education through recognition of their role as expert gamers (Sandford & Williamson, 2006). Games can also provide learners with real-world, authentic contexts in which to learn; they can be challenging and adaptable while at the same time absorbing and highly immersive. However, learning in school is quite different from learning in less formal contexts, and the constraints imposed by the institution often make introducing games as potential learning tools much more challenging than is commonly assumed.

Conclusions

Despite the negative connotations and media hype concerning Internet addictions and gaming addictions, engaging with games can provide a wealth of positive experiences for the learner (Johnson, Jones, & Burns, 2013). These often include positive psychological (flow-like phenomena) and social (collaboration and social interaction) experiences and a general uplift in psychological mood associated with gaming achievements. Gaming is thought to provide the necessary skills required for the twentieth-century individual and games impact on the many essential processes that underpin learning, which include, among others: finely-attuned attentional skills, increased problem-solving and sophisticated reasoning skills (Shin, Sutherland, et al., 2012). Studies indicate that playing video games gives learners a 'mental workout', and the structure of activities embedded in such games develops a number of highly attuned cognitive skills (Johnson, 2007).

However, despite these affordances, focused attention and game playing may not necessarily lead to overall effective learning. There is a need for educators to focus not just on the potential learning outcomes, but also on how video games can help to cater for different groups of learners. It is likely that video games can become a valued addition to classroom practice and, if we can develop games that are pedagogically driven, this may have unprecedented effects on the cognitive, behavioural and effective outcomes for the learner.

Chapter Nine
Misbehaviour or Merely Misunderstanding?

Introduction

Many see the rise in new digital technologies as a catalyst for change, one that provides new and innovative ways for enhancing learning and online collaboration, with the Internet providing access to an unprecedented amount of information across a variety of sources. However, there are growing concerns that a reliance on technology and the easy access to information may lead to the misappropriation of material and the promotion of academic malpractice, especially among undergraduate university students (Underwood & Szabo, 2004). Undoubtedly, technologically-rich environments promoting a wealth of information can help students to copy, share and paste material without any consideration towards academic integrity and originality of their own work. There is no doubt technology makes plagiarism easier but it also facilitates other malpractices as in the case of mobile phone support in the examination hall (Umarji, 2005). Indeed there are now websites giving helpful instructions on how to commit such a felony and advice on how to beat the system to achieve better grades in assessments.

Exploiting the Internet and online resources to plagiarize or to gain access to materials, whether these are off-the-shelf essays or simply bespoke products, presents only a partial picture (for a fuller review see Underwood, 2006). Technology also provides tools to detect malpractice of course: *If plagiarism is easier to commit because of the Internet, it is also easier to catch because of the Internet* (Purdy, 2005, p. 276). Many universities offer, indeed insist, that their students use text-comparison software partly as a means of engendering a strong sense of academic integrity across the student

Learning and the E-Generation, First Edition. Jean D. M. Underwood and Lee Farrington-Flint.
© 2015 Jean D. M. Underwood and Lee Farrington-Flint. Published 2015 by John Wiley & Sons, Ltd.

community. However, we know that the use of anti-plagiarism software does not always work and students can often cheat the system (White, Owens, & Nguyen, 2012). Research has focused on the institution's use of such software and not what benefits the students may take from the experience. It appears that we are in a game of cat and mouse played by some tech-savvy students, aided by 'free spirits' against the educators and regulators, but who are the winners and who the losers? The key issue is whether the prevalence of academic malpractice represents students' misunderstanding or misbehaviour, which is the key focus of this chapter.

What is Academic Dishonesty?

Defining academic dishonesty is easy but interpreting that definition has proved far more contentious. Let us start with a definition. Academic dishonesty is any action carried out to gain an undue advantage and includes cheating in examinations, colluding with other students and plagiarizing another person's work. It is an intentional act of fraud, in which a student seeks to claim credit for the work or efforts of another without authorization, to use unauthorized materials or fabricate information in any academic exercise. Forgery of academic documents, intentionally impeding or damaging the academic work of others, or assisting other students in acts of dishonesty also fall under this definition and are considered to be misdemeanours (Gehring & Pavela, 1994). There are great variations in the types of academic dishonesty: simply 'cutting and pasting' online materials; using a few attributable sentences; purchasing or downloading articles from the Internet; engaging in discussion forums for the sole purpose of copying and pasting other people's responses for inclusion in an essay; purchasing a ghost-written essay from an online provider (Selwyn, 2008); or stealing another student's work online (Austin & Brown, 1999). These types of academic dishonesty, all indicative of misbehaviour or deliberate plagiarism, have become more prominent in recent years and are receiving a high level of media attention (Hughes & McCabe, 2006; Sendag, Duran, & Fraser, 2012).

One example of the media attention around open-access online resources concerns the software Grade.Guru.com, which was originally developed and promoted by McGraw Hill as a free knowledge-sharing network to facilitate the practice of collaboration, peer review and online study forums within the United Kingdom[1]. However, despite winning an Effective Practice award in

[1] http://www.killerstartups.com/user-gen-content/gradeguru-com-get-your-study-notes/

2010 from the Sloan Consortium (Sloan-C) for *revolutionizing digital ways of learning*, the site was closed down in April 2010 for reasons that were not specified. The assumption within the educational community was that McGraw Hill felt their reputation would be in danger if it was seen to be promoting, albeit inadvertently, higher incidences of academic malpractice.

It is often perceived that plagiarism occurs when the writer deliberately uses someone else's language, ideas or other original material without any clear acknowledgement of its source. The use of the word 'deliberately', however, causes much confusion. How do we know an act is deliberate? Who is to judge? These are two crucial but contentious questions that arise from the use of the term: whether this act is deliberate and whether our response as educators to issues of plagiarism significantly affects our response to such student misbehaviour and creates additional issues that continue to cause ongoing difficulties.

Prevalence Rates of Academic Malpractice

There is clear research evidence revealing an increase in student engagement with academic malpractice. There is no doubt that academic malpractice has become a significant problem within many higher educational institutions (e.g., Hart & Friesner, 2004; Hughes & McCabe, 2006; Moon, 1999; Sendag, Duran, & Fraser, 2012; Underwood & Szabo, 2004). While identified as a significant problem within many higher educational institutions as also prevalent in schools, although the research here is less extensive (McCabe, Trevino & Butterfield, 2001). Ofqual, the regulatory authority for national examinations in England and Northern Ireland has banned a range of technical devices such reading pens, mobile telephones, iPods and MP3/4 players from the examination hall. The Authority caught nearly four-and-a-half thousand students cheating in the 2009 GCSEs and A-levels examinations. According to Ofqual (2011): *more than 1,300 penalties were issued to students during the summer 2010 examination series after they were found with a mobile phone or other banned device.*

This is a global phenomenon cutting across cultures and education systems. For example, Moon (1999) found that 60 per cent of UK and US undergraduate students confess to some kind of academic malpractice. Findings corroborated by Underwood and Szabo (2004) who in their manuscript cite a number of studies, including work by McCabe (2005), who found a further indication of the extent to online academic misconduct within 4,500 schools. Among this sample, 74 per cent admitted to serious test cheating, 72 per cent serious cheating with written work, 97 per cent admitted copying homework while 15 per cent admitted taking term papers from the Internet and finally, 52 per cent admitted the deliberate copying of sentences from external web pages.

More recently, Akbulut, Uysal, et al. (2008) conducted two large-scale factor analyses to identify both the types of academic dishonesty and the reasons for students' engagement in a representative sample of 249 undergraduate Turkish students. The first factor analysis identified five distinctive types of academic dishonesty (i.e., fraudulence, plagiarism, falsification, delinquency, and unauthorized help), while their second factor analysis revealed three issues that explain the reasons for students' engagement in academic malpractice: individual, institutional pressures and peer pressure. In another study, Gulli, Kohler, and Patriquin (2007) quote figures of 54 per cent of students at the University of Guelph admitting to being involved in cheating. Further evidence comes from a large-scale US survey which found that 51 per cent of high school students admitted to cheating at least once in the previous year (Josephson Institute of Ethics, 2012). Measures of verifiable, rather than self-reported, behaviour show a lower but still disturbing prevalence of academic misconduct. In the United Kingdom some 15,000 undergraduates have actually been assessed as cheating in each of the three previous academic years (Brady & Dutta, 2012). In a New Zealand study, Walker (2010) found over 25 per cent of 1,000 undergraduate course scripts contained a measurable level of plagiarism, with 10 per cent of the scripts showing extensive copying of material.

The prevalence rates of academic dishonesty have increased over time. For example, the Center for Academic Integrity recorded a four-fold increase over a 5-year period in the number of undergraduates who used unattributed text excerpts from Internet sources to construct assignments (McCabe, et al., 2001). While Brown, Weible, and Olmosk (2010) note there is a shift from 49 per cent of undergraduate marketing students reporting academic dishonesty in 1998 to 100 per cent of undergraduate management students in 2000. Admittedly, this increase in online academic malpractice needs to reflect changes in subject area, but nonetheless this evidence provides a clear indication with regard to increases in academic dishonesty over time. This is not the whole story and there are findings that present a far more positive picture. Cases have been recorded of declining rates of malpractice and a growing student awareness of the serious nature of such behaviours. The Josephson Institute of Ethics (2012) similarly recorded a decline in students admitting to copying from 34 per cent to 32 per cent between the two academic years of 2010 and 2012. What message should we take from this conflicting evidence? The answer is one of hope. While cases of malpractice will continue to rise if no action is taken, there are steps that can be taken to halt the escalation of unacceptable behaviour. We will return to this shortly but first let us look at why such behaviours occur at all.

Why do Students Take the Risk?

There appears to be a general consensus around an increase in prevalence rates, but what about the students' rationale, motivation and reasoning behind such engagement in dishonest academic practices? Is it all about the student or are we creating structures that encourage cheating? It is clear that some students are more resistant to poor behaviours than others and individual student characteristics may be central to encouraging or discouraging malpractice. Many authors have argued that students engagement in, for example, misuse of the Internet can be explained by a range of individual and personal backgrounds as well as other demographic variables, such as age, gender, and motivation (Seifert, Pascarella, et al., 2010). For instance, Internet-based plagiarism seems to be most prevalent among male students, who are relatively proficient in Internet searching (Selwyn, 2008; Sendag, et al., 2012; Underwood, 2006; Underwood & Szabo, 2004). This is certainly the case in Selwyn's study, which surveyed 1,222 undergraduate students attending a UK institution and found that while at least three-fifths engaged in 'moderate' levels of online plagiarism, this was mediated by gender, subject discipline, and the student's educational background. Gender is a key factor, with males being more likely to cheat than females (Jensen, Arnett & Feldman 2002; Underwood & Szabo, 2004) and academic ability another, with students achieving lower grade point scores being more likely to cheat (Straw, 2002). These are the more unequivocal findings in this rather confused area of research.

Students with high emotional stability and conscientiousness tend not to be involved in academic dishonesty (Etter, Cramer, & Finn, 2006) but a lack of self-control and an overall propensity to engage in deviant behaviour or risk-taking has been shown to lead to impulsive cheating (Underwood, 2003; Underwood & Szabo, 2004). We know that impulsivity, an individual's inclination to act without forethought, coming to a decision very fast and having a low boredom threshold, (Barrett & Patton, 1983) has long been associated with problem behaviours such as cheating and gambling. An erroneous conclusion of this research would be to assume that malpractice is chaotic. There is evidence that self-control may lead to deliberate forms of cheating, particularly if the student assesses the risk of detection as being low and the rewards being high (Bolin, 2004). On the other hand, students who view such behaviours as serious breaches tend to have an ethical principle of doing no harm to others, and typically see themselves as idealistic and disapprove of engaging in high sensation-seeking activities involving alcohol, drugs and sex (Etter, Cramer, & Finn, 2006).

As well as self-control, there has been a link between individual personality factors and engagement in online cheating (Sendag, Duran, & Fraser, 2012; Williams, Nathanson & Paulhus, 2010). More recently, there has been an established link between narcissism and increased levels of engagement with academic dishonest practices. For example, it has been noted that narcissistic tendencies can encourage students to cheat (Menon & Sharland, 2011) leading to more rationalized cheating to secure higher grades (Brown, Budzek, & Tamborski, 2009). More specifically, having exploitative attitudes mediates the link between narcissism and academic dishonesty and one particular dimension of exhibitionism (Brunell, Staats, & Hupp, 2010; Menon & Sharland).

However, it is not simply personality factors, but also performance and time pressures, especially when poor organization is coupled with the desire to achieve irrespective of the consequences, which are potent drivers of academic dishonesty. In a recent study, Jones (2011) surveyed 48 undergraduates enrolled on a US online business communications course to assess their views on cheating and online plagiarism. He noted that while 92 per cent of these undergraduates either actually reported online plagiarism or were aware of someone who had committed the act, the most prominent reasons for plagiarism were to improve grades (92%), the result of procrastination (83%) and a lack of time to complete assignments (75%). Whitley (1998) argues that social norms that allow cheating and an individual's own favourable attitudes towards cheating act together to encourage malpractice.

Many background factors have been found to influence students' engagement in academic malpractice. If we start first with the subject discipline, then Gerdeman (2000) found that subject areas perceived as being of low relevance are more susceptible to cheating behaviour because of a lack of motivation to study. However, it is not simply motivational aspects that influence cheating, there are notable subject-level effects in the extent to which students report committing some form of academic malpractice or cheating (e.g., Sendag, et al., 2012; Underwood & Szabo, 2004). High status vocational subjects such as Law and Business Studies are particularly vulnerable (Hendershott, Drina, & Cross, 2000).

Perceptions of teachers and academic institutions lay attitudes towards plagiarism and academic malpractice, often influencing students' engagement in plagiarism or academic cheating (Gerdeman, 2000; Murdock, Beauchamp, & Hinton 2008), which reduces the potential risk of being caught out

(McCabe, 2005; Simon, et al., 2003; Underwood & Szabo, 2004). Moreover, the research also suggests that performance and time pressures may affect engagement with academic malpractice. The conclusions of a 2004 pan-European study confirms this low-risk assessment in that students do not believe tutors will detect their plagiarism and so they commit the act even when there are dire warnings of punitive penalties. It appears that when good grades are critical and competition is high, some students bow to the pressure to achieve and will use any route possible to ensure high grades (Bolin, 2004).

A final area is the social milieu, the context in which the students find themselves. This has profound effects on students' behaviours as they seek social approval, respond to peer pressure to support a friend or simply join the crowd. For many, the benefits of using other people's work through either copying from discussion forums or pasting from original research articles seem too appealing (Gerdeman, 2000; McCabe & Trevino, 1997). Anderman and Murdock (2007) have argued that competition is a toxic ingredient that fuels academic cheating and undermines intrinsic motivation. However, Orosz, Farkas, and Roland-Lévy (2013) have shown that acceptance of cheating and the degree to which the individual feels guilt have significant and direct effects on the propensity to cheat, while others have confirmed that feelings of guilt are the most effective deterrent of cheating (Diekhoff, LaBeff, et al., 1999). Perhaps a suitable step forward is to raise awareness of the principles of academic dishonesty and focus on the moral integrity of students.

Do they Know What they are Doing?

It has been argued that Internet facilitated plagiarism is so easy that students are unaware that they are cheating even when they express disapproval of such unethical actions (Kraus, 2002; Stevens, Young, & Calabrese, 2007). This inability to realistically self-evaluate their actions raises questions about our students' understanding of right and wrong. Olson and Shaw (2011) conducted two studies with 4 and 5 years olds designed by to assess whether at this early age children have any understanding of the concept of ownership of ideas and the associated concept of plagiarism. They found that by 5 years of age children do show an awareness of the ownership of ideas by others and a dislike of the copying of those ideas. These studies suggest that 5 year olds have a moral compass that will guide them towards academic integrity so where and why do they lose that compass? Sadly there are many examples of the great and the good showing a cavalier attitude to another's intellectual property not just within students but also among those receiving professional training (see for example, Jump, 2013). High profile and successful people including politicians, members of religious orders or members of the medical profession, all of whom have been caught cheating, are disturbing role models as they give a face-validity to unethical behaviour. There are many examples of the significant harm that is caused when individuals forget or ignore the effects of their dishonesty. A recent study of pharmacy and medical students has shown that this behaviour may not be confined to the classroom. In this study students who self-reported their cheating were also more likely to suggest unlawful solutions to a series of ethical dilemmas (Henning, et al., 2013).

To complicate the matter even further, there are academic disputes as to what counts as plagiarism. For some copying is not plagiarism but considered to be the careful accumulation of a body of knowledge. This cultural perspective is more prevalent in hierarchical educational environments where learning the 'master's' thoughts is seen as an essential part of scholarship. In many, but not all, Western educational cultures the concept of the guru has largely disappeared but even here there is not a single response to malpractice. For some Western tutors plagiarism is an unintentional act resulting from students' lack of knowledge and understanding of the required behaviour, while for others it is a deliberate act of malpractice designed to gain an advantage.

Many tutors show this ambivalence towards plagiarism. One grey area concerns responses by staff to intentional, as opposed to unintentional, plagiarism. Sutherland-Smith's (2003) qualitative study found that there was a consensus among tutors that downloading texts from commercial sites or from a friend or another college was indefensible and needed to be penalized. However, there was a much more lenient view of unintentional plagiarism, although what this term actually meant to those staff members contributing to this research was somewhat vague. Coren's (2011) findings on staff members' responses to academic dishonesty are more disturbing as they are not a simple matter of setting clearer boundaries. Of faculty members, 40 per cent of those sampled admitted to ignoring student cheating on at least one occasion. While student reluctance to report malpractice is both known and possibly understood (Bilic-Zulle, Frkovic, et al., 2005; Underwood, 2003) the reluctance of individual staff members to highlight malpractice is far more disturbing as it hits at the heart of academic integrity. Coren went on to ask the obvious but necessary question as to why these staff members were exhibiting such reluctance? While a number of staff cited reasons such as insufficient evidence, low level of infringement or that it was a time-consuming activity, a more telling reason was that many tutors found the whole experience of dealing with acts of plagiarism unsettling as a result of the heightened emotional level and stress involved when confronting the student.

And the Solution Is?

Plagiarism is a major challenge for academia but also the wider world. So how do we stop it or more realistically reduce such activity? In a more detailed report Underwood (2006) suggested the three E's approach to cheating and plagiarism: enlightenment, engineering and enforcement (after Hinman, 2002).

- Enlightenment: develop students who do not want to cheat. The rational and moral approach should always be the first line of defence against maladaptive behaviours. Work to foster students' love of learning and understanding of their responsibilities as learners and members of the academic community For example, honour codes and contracts between students and schools have proved effective in reducing cheating.
- Engineering: the prevention approach reduces the opportunities to cheat and reduces the pressure to cheat. One simple solution is being innovative in the assignments set for students.
- Enforcement: the policeman approach in which behaviour is monitored to diagnose those at risk and also those indulging in malbehaviour.

A study at the University of Sydney found that a purely deterrent approach to reducing student plagiarism such as the use of detection software had relatively little effect (White, et al., 2012). However, a new approach, which helped students to understand what constituted plagiarism, proved to be far more effective. Their approach was to ask incoming students, some 1,300 participants, to read some text and construct from that text an appropriate paragraph in relation to a designated research question. Responses were tested using plagiarism detection software and were also assessed according to writing style, referencing and use of quotations. Examples of good and poor summaries fully annotated with comments were posted on the virtual learning platform along with a guide as to what constitutes plagiarism, a demonstration of the frequency of plagiarism, the ease of plagiarism detection and the penalties for plagiarism. In comparison to the year prior to this intervention, the subsequent formal assessments showed a significant fall in the number of 'severe' plagiarism cases following this holistic approach.

While plagiarism software fulfils the policeman role acting as a deterrent, designed to reduce the number of cases that require some level of formal action by the institution, Hunter (2012) argues it can also be a tool to aid student understanding of appropriate behaviour. We can encourage students to view the software as a formative learning tool that will engage them in a meaningful discussion about their understanding of key concepts such as intellectual property rights but also what makes a good piece of writing. Some argue that allowing students access to plagiarism detection software encourages them to defeat the system. There is a level of cynicism here but that does not mean these colleagues are wrong. Their views, even if in a minority, do support our argument that the policing of bad behaviour, while important, should not be a main form of defence against malbehaviour.

There is little doubt that academic dishonesty is a real, non-trivial issue and to ameliorate potential problems we need to have:

- Clear and transparent rules and regulations governing academic dishonesty. All interested parties need to have an agreed perception of what constitutes cheating. This agreement should not just be between teaching staff and students but also between tutors and the executive at all levels.
- Develop a culture of academic integrity that uses peer pressure for good rather nefarious purposes. Honour codes have proved to be highly effective in reducing malpractice.
- Design assessments that reduce the opportunity for malpractice.
- Policies must be practical and workable. Overly bureaucratic procedures will deter staff from taking action.
- Staff's willingness to treat academic dishonesty as a serious but resolvable problem is the key to the successful implementation of any policy. Operating policies at the centre level, with a view to raising standards in centres, is less contentious than operating at an individual level.
- Support staff when they question student integrity but at the same time recognize that students have rights too. So the burden of proof must be necessarily high when dealing with individual student cases.

The way forward is necessarily a holistic approach which fosters and re-engages students and tutors with a love for the value of learning while excluding those conditions in which plagiarism has been allowed to flourish. We must also show less tolerance of malpractice by high profile societal role models. While cheating is seen as a low risk road to success some of our students will remain immune to our entreaties to take the ethical road.

Risks, Skills and Opportunities

The Internet provides access to a wealth of information, from e-books, journals, web pages to Wikipedia, and students are consistently moving beyond printed texts to online resources in order to support their learning activities. This provides a real opportunity for improving and sustaining learning and helps improve access to resources and information that can then support classroom learning. However, access to such material may not be wholly accurate and students have increased access to mistakes, misinformation and unreliable sources. This misinformation and inaccurate information is making its way into the classroom through students' schoolwork. The prevalence rates of academic misconduct show no signs of abating and this can cause a real tension for teachers, educators and educational institutions. But the situation is not too dire. Despite a lack of teaching about how to judge the reliability of information online and insufficient knowledge about plagiarism and academic integrity (Bartlett & Miller, 2011), there are real possibilities to reduce academic dishonesty or acts of deliberate plagiarism. By developing a culture of academic integrity and providing clear transparent rules, the problem can be tackled head on. We know that plagiarism detection software, on many occasions, has relatively little effect so punishment may not be the best deterrent. Raising awareness of good academic values and the direct teaching about plagiarism through quizzes, reflective writing and tutorials are strategies that may show promise (Owens & White, 2013). As Flint, Clegg, and Macdonald (2006, p. 147) clearly suggest: *staff, student and institutional perspectives on plagiarism should not be seen as three alternative and mutually exclusive categories* but instead there is a growing need to change student, staff and institutional views about plagiarism, in a way which provides an integrated focus on informing students of the values and principles of good academic practice.

Conclusions

The current chapter has addressed a prominent issue within education, one that questions whether academic dishonesty is seen as a misbehaviour or merely a misunderstanding of what is required on the part of students. It is recognized that the Internet provides an incredible resource for teaching and learning, one that allows students access to materials far beyond those offered within the constraints of the classroom. However, this has presented a significant shift in education because it provides access to education for anyone who has Internet access. With this increased access to online resources, and often open access to inappropriate, misinformed and on occasion unreliable information, presents a real challenge to educators and institutions, not only in teaching students to become digitally literate but also in ensuring they do not use this material for ill-gotten gains. As we have seen, an individual's propensity to cheat, whether this relates to their gender, academic background or personality factors, is highly influenced by environmental factors that can either encourage or surpass poor behaviours (Whitley, 1998). Many teachers themselves acknowledge their own lack of awareness about plagiarism and show reluctance to penalize students directly (Coren, 2011). This of course presents a complex issue with no easy answers. Any attempts to reduce or ameliorate academic dishonesty require a more focused, institutional-led approach that addresses not just the students' own perceptions and intentions, but those of teachers and educators. Institutions also need to focus on teaching students about the values and principles of good honest academic practice. So any attempts to reduce academic dishonesty require a more focused approach that addresses not just the individual student's perceptions and intentions but also those of staff members and the institution as a whole.

Chapter Ten
Being Emotionally Intelligent and Risk Resilient

Introduction

Digital technologies have the potential to revolutionize learning in a number of different ways, and as such they can be a vehicle for implementing changes in educational contexts. Even those researchers who have raised serious concerns about the participation of the young in the online world accept that the virtual world offers many opportunities for information gathering, entertainment and social interaction (e.g., Whitaker & Bushman, 2009). However, it is appropriate to at least consider some of the dark matters associated with technology use such as Internet addiction, sexting, cyber bullying, child exploitation and identity formation. We are aware that there are real risks around cyber bullying. These include insults and sexual abuse/harassment towards individuals on social networks. The perpetrators tend to be of a similar age to the victim (Katzer, Fetchenhauer, & Belschak, 2009; Staude-Müller, Hansen, & Voss, 2012). We also know that as adults we may find it inconceivable that our own child is involved in bullying (Dehue, Bolman, & Völlink, 2008). Aside from this, there are growing concerns about child exploitation and addiction to the Internet, especially among those who create avatars or net personas that provide alternative realities to escape the real world (McKenna & Bargh, 2000).

So there are dark sides to technology use and there is a real requirement to balance the need to maintain student safety without inhibiting access to the resources of the digital world, while at the same time protecting the reputation of the institution. Until now we have deliberately avoided extensive discussions regarding risks and harm, as the focus of this book concerns

Learning and the E-Generation, First Edition. Jean D. M. Underwood and Lee Farrington-Flint.
© 2015 Jean D. M. Underwood and Lee Farrington-Flint. Published 2015 by John Wiley & Sons, Ltd.

the positive aspects of using technology to support and enhance students' learning. This largely remains our position but as we write the final chapters of this book we are met with the news that Google and Microsoft are to block access to pornographic images of children and that the Child Exploitation and Online Protection Centre (CEOP) wants to recruit tech-savvy individuals to act in tracking down malbehaviour before children can be damaged (CEOP, 2012). These are positive moves but there are seemingly less urgent and frightening concerns that we should be aware of and which we can do something about as parents and as educators.

So what is the answer? We are all aware of the potential dangers or risks associated with online access (Crook, 2008) and the initial reaction from some parents and many teachers is to restrict children's access to digital technology thereby removing potential risks completely. While these reactions are perfectly understandable they may not be the most productive in the long run. In the current chapter we examine the need to focus on educating children and adolescents to be more aware of the potential risks rather than simply putting up defensive barriers (Wolak, Mitchell, & Finkelhor, 2007; Wolak, et al., 2008). These measures revolve round helping children and adolescents to be more savvy users of the technology and encouraging the development of greater emotional intelligence and risk resilience in the young. Before exploring the concepts of emotional intelligence and risk resilience, however, we present an example of the downside of technology and a more encouraging story of the development of a more streetwise approach to technology, which is reducing risk in the online world. Here we argue that a better option would be to help learners become Internet savvy, where this term covers not only the 'how to' do things but 'why' and the 'when to get involved', and then to trust their maturity and judgment to deal with risks appropriately.

Shades of Light and Dark

In Chapter 7 we questioned whether the time spent engaged with digital technology should be viewed as an issue. Often social media hype focuses on the risks associated with multitasking and becoming immersed with the digital world of technology. But is this really so clear-cut? New research suggests that time per se spent surfing the net or being engaged in similar activities may not be entirely detrimental, although health workers might question that conclusion. A generation swopping physical activity for a more sedentary life in the virtual world has done little to combat the obesity crisis here within the United Kingdom and elsewhere in the developed world. Putting that issue aside we look first at the rising concern about the intensity of technology use and physical health.

Punamäki and colleagues in a survey of 7,292 Finnish students between the ages of 12 and 18 years found that boys played digital games and used the Internet more often than girls, but that the girls' mobile phone use was more intensive (Punamäki, Wallenius, et al., 2007). These are unsurprising findings but the study also showed that such intensive ICT-use was associated with poor perceived health if it impacted on sleeping habits, which in turn was associated with increased waking-time tiredness. The associations were gender-specific, especially among older adolescents (16 and 18 year olds). Intensive computer usage was a risk factor for boys, while intensive mobile phone use for girls was a perceived health risk. A Japanese study found a more limited effect of technology use in that length of time spent asleep was negatively associated with the mobile phone use only in early adolescents (Oshima, et al., 2012). Nocturnal mobile phone use was particularly damaging. In this study it was linked to poor mental health, suicidal feelings and self-injury among young adolescents in analyses that looked at sleep length and other confounding variables. These subtle differences in results from the Finnish and Japanese studies might be a consequence of the lower personal space available to Japanese adolescents in their homes, which would render covert computer use more difficult and so that boys' phone use was similar of that of their female peers.

The significance of young peoples' unmonitored personal space became apparent in a recent Finnish study (Nuutinen, Rayr, & Roos, 2013). This longitudinal study of the sleep patterns of 10 and 11 year olds found that using computers and watching television predicted both shorter sleep duration and later bedtimes. More specifically children who had a media presence in the bedroom tended to have irregular sleep habits. A computer in the bedroom predicted irregular sleep habits among boys but not girls, the latter being adversely affected by a television presence, which was not the case for boys. The researchers reached the conclusion, with some justification, that electronic media devices should not be placed in a child's bedroom. They argue that children need more not less sleep as they go through puberty and that media viewing habits need reviewing for any child who appears tired and struggling to concentrate, or who is having behavioural problems. The concerns about lack of sleep are confirmed by Vriend and colleagues (2013) who found that even modest differences in sleep duration over just a few nights could have significant negative consequences for children's daytime functioning including their memory, attention, emotional state and wellbeing.

A related point around this immersion by technology concerns the amount of time spent using the Internet and constructing alternative net personas as a way of escaping the pressures of the real world. Constructing a net persona, possibly by developing an avatar, raises issues concerning identity formation and protection in children and adolescents. Individuals have such a range of alternatives available when designing their avatars that they do not have to reveal the true identity of a person (Lee & Shin, 2004). Bessière, Fleming et al. (2007), investigating game players' assessment of their real and virtual selves, found that while individuals rated their virtual character as being more conscientious, extroverted and less neurotic than their real selves, for those who self-reported higher levels of wellbeing this discrepancy was not large. These are not unexpected findings. Self-discrepancy theory posits a close link between psychological wellbeing and a person's actual self as compared to his or her ideal self and consequently those with larger discrepancies between the real- and the ideal-self tend to have higher rates of depression and lower self-esteem (Higgins, 1987). Those uncomfortable with the 'real me' engage in virtual self-enhancement through their virtual persona. Some evidence suggests that those with a more marginalized self-identity sought affirmation in their use of the Internet and those scoring higher in depression were more likely to use the Internet for escape (McKenna & Bargh, 2000). There is a positive to this invention of a 'better' self as it offers the former group a means to escape poor self-evaluation by deleting negative or unwanted characteristics and enacting a better virtual self. As we can see, although there may be increasing risks or concerns, especially from parents, regarding the time spent using digital technology, there are also positive outcomes that can be found.

Overcoming Risks and Building Resilience

Rather than simply restricting children's access to technology, another possible solution is to carefully monitor their media use. But monitoring alone may not provide changes in behaviours and can give rise to feelings of resentment on the child's behalf. Research has shown that parental monitoring of children's media use can reduce the negative effects of media exposure on children. That monitoring can take the form of:

- active mediation – instructive guidance, discussion and explanation (Livingstone & Helsper, 2008)
- restrictive mediation – setting rules or limits on children's media exposure (Chakroff & Nathanson, 2008)
- co-viewing – by the child and the parent or guardian.

Working with the young person is surely the way forward here, supporting them to become informed citizens, which brings us back to the need to develop both emotional intelligence and risk resilience. However, before entering that discussion it is cheering to note that there are positive behaviours emerging in our use of the technology, as is shown by the changing behaviours of Facebook users. The relationship between privacy and a person's social network is complex. Some information about ourselves is to be shared with a small circle of close friends but not with strangers, while in other instances we are willing to reveal information to anonymous strangers, but this is data that we are loath to tell to those close to us. A 2005 survey of over 4,000 US university students showed that that this population of Facebook users appeared quite oblivious, unconcerned or just pragmatic about their personal privacy (Gross & Aquisti, 2005). However, a study 6 years later showed that awareness of privacy issues has grown and that even over a short period of 15 months the individuals in the study sought greater privacy. They do, however, point out the knowledgeable can reconstruct more of the hidden data than we might suspect should they so wish. Bonds-Raacke and Raacke (2010) have also seen this growing awareness of risk prevention. In their 2010 study students were more likely to set

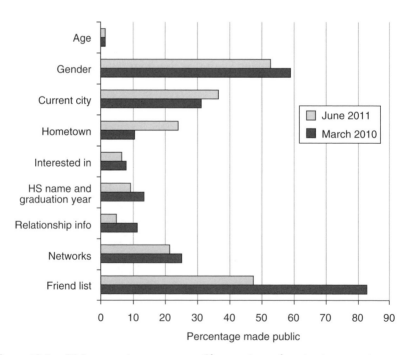

Figure 10.1. Rising security awareness: Changes in students' privacy settings between 2010 and 2011 for a range of Facebook attributes (from Dey et al., 2012).

their profiles to private and less likely to post their daily schedules compared to a study undertaken 2 years earlier.

The study by Dey, Jelveh, and Ross (2012) captured the activity of more than one and a half million New York Facebook users. Data were collected at two time periods 15 months apart, in March 2010 and June 2011. The team was given permission to trawl through the public and full profile pages of these users in order to establish trends in privacy awareness, as exhibited by changed Facebook settings. The results showed that many of the sample had become more circumspect about the personal data they were willing to reveal to the world, as is clearly shown in Figure 10.1. Material that could identify the user such as year of graduation and their relationship data were less available. Of particular significance is the shift from 17.2 per cent of users hiding their friends list in 2010 to 52.6 per cent of the sample doing so only 15 months later. Of course this still leaves nearly half of the sample operating an open list policy but it is nevertheless an important reduction in risk. As Dey, et al. 2012 point out there are a number of studies that show how the friends list can be exploited to reveal seemingly hidden information about an individual including sexual orientation (see, e.g. Jernigan & Mistree, 2009; Thomas, Grier, & Nicol, 2010). This growing awareness is exemplified by a quote from an 18-year-old student:

> So honestly, the only time I've ever deleted for a picture is because I'm apply-ing for colleges. You know what? Colleges might actually see my pictures and I have pictures like with my fingers up, my middle fingers up. Like me and my friends have pictures, innocent fun. We're not doing anything bad, but inno-cent fun. But at the same time, maybe I'm applying for college now. Possibly an admission officer's like, you know, this kid's accepted. Let's see what his everyday life is like. They're like, um–
>
> (Pew Internet, May 2013)

Livingstone and Haddon's (2009) European EU Kids Online survey of 10,000 children between 9 and 16 years old from 25 European countries reported that over half the children who responded to the question, 'What things on the Internet would bother people about your age?' spontaneously included a plat-form or technology in their answer. Video sharing websites such as YouTube (32%) was the most commonly mentioned in terms of risk followed by websites (29%), social networking sites (13%) and games (10%). YouTube content was potentially upsetting because it showed real or highly realistic moving images that could be readily shared among the peer group. Video-sharing websites in general were associated with violent (30%) and pornographic (27%) content, along with a range of other content-related risks.

Further content-related risks highlighted included viewing unwanted, scary or hateful content and content harmful to self-esteem. Fear was most often expressed in relation to scary content. Of those who mentioned scary content 23 per cent also expressed fear. Only 5 per cent of those who mentioned pornographic content expressed disgust, but a rephrasing of the question showed that, of those who expressed disgust in response to online risks, 28 per cent linked this to pornography. Overall, the EU Kids Online survey mostly described commercial content as 'annoying' rather than threatening or invasive.

Self-Disclosure and Social Networking

Can we breathe a collective sigh of relief over the perceptiveness of the young then? Trepte and Reinecke's (2013) work suggest not. They asked whether Facebook itself stimulated the disclosure of personal information and questioned whether SNS use and the psychological disposition for self-disclosure interact reciprocally and as such feed off each other? If this is the case then individuals who have a strong tendency to self-disclose will also prove to be highly active SNS users, the so-called self-selection effect. At the same time, frequent SNS use should increase the wish to self-disclose online, because self-disclosing behaviours are reinforced through social capital within the SNS environment, that is, there is a socialization effect. Their study of 488 SNS users who were surveyed twice over a six-month period confirmed both the self-selection and socialization effects. The disposition for online self-disclosure increased SNS use, which in turn encouraged further online self-disclosure. Both effects were moderated by the amount of social capital, that is, reinforcement from the group users received as a consequence of their SNS use.

One should not conclude that risk necessarily involves harm. Exposure to online risks does not necessarily result in harm. Another report published by EU Kids Online (Vandoninck, d'Haenens, & Smahel, 2014) has shown the online resilience of kids and how they cope with online risks. Most children do not feel bothered when confronted with online risks. However, children who find it difficult to manage their emotions, conduct and social behaviour in the 'offline world' are more likely to feel bothered and upset in the 'online world'. Individual differences were once again apparent in this study. Children with psychological problems are less resilient online – online risks upset them more often and more intensely. Moreover, they tend to be passive instead of actively trying to solve the problem. Three online risks were investigated: exposure to sexual content, online bullying and sexting.

Research confirms that an approach that focuses on mediation and monitoring tends to be more appropriate to stimulate children's online resilience, so parents should be encouraged to stay nearby while their child goes online, talk regularly about the child's online activities, use the Internet together with their child, give advice on safer Internet use, and check what their children do online. Regardless of the type of online risk, emotional stability helps children to be more resilient to online threats. Across all ages, children who are self-confident and free from emotional and social problems are less likely to feel bothered by sexual content, online bullying or sexting. Moreover, among those with psychological problems, the intensity of harm related to online risks is stronger and the negative emotions remain for a longer period of time.

Staksrud and Livingstone (2009) argue that research on the risks associated with children's use of the Internet is often undertaken with the aim of informing policies of risk prevention. Yet paralleling the effort to map the nature and extent of online risk is a growing unease that the goal of risk prevention tends to support an over-protective, risk-averse culture that restricts the freedom of online exploration that society encourages for children in other spheres. It is central to adolescence that teenagers learn to anticipate and cope with risk – in short, to become resilient. Staksrud and Livingstone's pan-European study showed that in Northern European countries with high Internet access, parental perception of likelihood of online risk to their child was negatively associated with their perceived ability to cope. Surveys conducted among children in Norway, Ireland and the United Kingdom, areas seen as at relatively 'high risk', found that although the frequency of exposure to perceived online risks, especially content risk, is fairly high, most children adopt either positive strategies such as seeking help from a friend or, more commonly, neutral strategies such as ignoring the experience, as a way of coping. Nevertheless, they did find that a minority of young people did take risks by circulating risky content among their friends. Whatever their approach to the risky life experiences, most young people used coping strategies that excluded adult involvement. Significant differences in both risk and coping are found by gender and age across these countries, pointing to different styles of youthful risk management

In the final report form EU Kids Online project (Livingstone & Haddon, 2009) important individual differences were identified in risk exposure and behaviour. Livingstone and Haddon point out that although children in higher status families generally have more ready access to the Internet than those children in families of lower socio-economic status, it is the latter children and adolescents that are more exposed to risk online. This is yet another seemingly counterintuitive finding that makes planning effective remedial action more difficult.

Less puzzling is the emergence once more of gender differences in the type and frequency of a person's involvement in risky behaviour. Livingstone and Haddon (2009) report that boys were more likely to encounter, or indeed initiate, conduct risks (child as actor) while girls were more affected by content (child as recipient) and contact (child as participant) risks. Boys were more likely to seek out offensive or violent content, to meet somebody offline that they have met online and to give out personal information. Girls had a greater tendency to be upset by offensive, violent and pornographic material, to chat online with strangers, to receive unwanted sexual comments and to be asked for personal information though they are wary of providing it to strangers. Both sexes face the risk of being cyber bullied. While older teenagers encountered more online risks than younger children, the impact of facing such risks by pre-teens and young teens was a concern that as yet has been little researched.

So are Emotional Intelligence and Resilience the Key to Reducing Risk?

Emotional intelligence is a double-edged sword. Emotions play a major role in any individual's life and people interpret events as positive or negative mainly based on evoked emotional reactions. Essentially emotions are *self-regulating processes that permit rapid responses and adaptations to: situations of personal concern* (Kappas, 2011. p. 17). Emotions provide us with vital information for making sense of our inner experience and navigating the social environment (Abe, 2011). Typically emotions have properties that lead to self-termination – Kappas quotes the example of the emotion of fear engendered by a spider. If the spider is trodden and killed the specific emotion episode (fear of the spider) is terminated. However, this is not always the case as an individual may seek not to extinguish but to avoid the stimulus generating the emotion, for example, if the fear of flying prevents a business executive working appropriately (negative effect) but it can also be positive if it reduces confrontation, for example, by taking a new route home from school to avoid a waiting bully.

The ability to express and control our own emotions is important, but so is our ability to understand, interpret and respond to the emotions of others. Emotional intelligence refers to the ability to perceive, control and evaluate emotions to discriminate among them and to use this information to guide one's thinking and actions (Salovey & Mayer, 1990, p. 189). Their four-factor model sums up emotional intelligence as:

- Perceiving emotions: to accurately perceive any emotion.
- Reasoning with emotions: to use those perceptions to promote thinking and cognitive activity.

- Understanding emotions: to understand why a specific emotion is being expressed.
- Managing emotions: by responding appropriately to the emotions of others.

Management and regulation of emotion is the highest and most complex level of emotional intelligence, while perception, reasoning and understanding underpin the ability to regulate one's own and others' emotions. Emotional clarity (the ability to discriminate clearly between feelings) and emotional repair (the ability to regulate negative moods and prolong positive ones) are related to higher emotional adjustment (Berking, Orth, et al., 2008; Fernández-Berrocal & Extremera, 2008). However, a high level of attention to, and monitoring of, one's own feelings and emotions has been indicated as a precursor of ruminative thinking (Ramos, Fernández-Berrocal, & Extremera, 2007) and self-focused attention (Shulman & Hemenover, 2006), both variables have consistently been associated with negative affect and emotional distress (Nolen-Hoeksema, Wisco & Lyubomisrsky, 2008). Romanelli, Cain, and Sith (2006) describe this succinctly: *emotional intelligence might be defined as the set of skills people use to read, understand, and react effectively to emotional signals sent by others and oneself.*

So people who are capable of expressing and understanding emotions, assigning meaning to emotional experience and regulating their feelings will be better adjusted, psychologically and socially (Ciarrochi, Chan, et al., 2001). Yet while some researchers suggest that emotional intelligence can be learned and strengthened, others claim it is an inborn characteristic. This is the age-old nature/nurture debate that has consequences. If emotion is perceived as a unique, immutable mental state then emotion regulation is difficult. However, the more emotion is seen as an emergent phenomenon that is constructed from our personal goals then emotion regulation becomes possible. Whichever view you take of emotion there is now a body of evidence that shows that emotion regulation has important consequences for heath and adaptive functioning (Tamir, 2011). For those of us working with the young the latter instrumental view of emotion offers a plausible way to support them.

A further debate around the concept of emotional intelligence highlighted by Côté, DeCelles, et al. (2011, p. 1071) concerns the degree to which such intelligence is a benign characteristic. They ask the question: *does emotional intelligence promote behaviour that strictly benefits the greater good, or can it also advance interpersonal deviance?* Drawing from research on how the effective regulation of emotion promotes goal achievement, they showed that individuals with higher emotion-regulation knowledge exhibited greater pro-social behaviour in a social dilemma but were more Machiavellian when asked to respond to a workplace scenario. Thus, emotion-regulation knowledge has both a positive side and a negative side:

> Increasing emotional competence is not always beneficial for establishing and maintaining harmonious relationships. For example, even though a well-developed empathic sense might keep aggressors from attacking their victims, they might as well use it to enhance the effectiveness of their attacks.
>
> (Denham, 2007, p. 32)

Emotional intelligence is not necessarily a force for good: while it aids much valued empathetic behaviour, it also allows us to manipulate others. Yet engendering emotional intelligence in the young should not be viewed as an educational panacea so where do we go from here? Not having a high enough level of emotional intelligence places a child at risk. An extreme example of this is found in the difficulties children on the autistic spectrum disorder have in making friends and adapting to school (Dillon & Underwood, 2012). As a first step we should be looking out for those children with low emotional intelligence and poor regulation skills. Telltale signs can, but do not always, include:

- exhibiting a limited range of emotions
- coping poorly with stressful experiences
- having outbursts of negative emotions including tantrums
- showing aggressive or ego-centric behaviours beyond that which is normal for the age group
- being generally socially less competent
- being less productive in the classroom.

Children need to develop emotional intelligence but that does not mean they will behave well. Unless they are socially skilled they will certainly have difficulties in school and elsewhere. So if emotional intelligence is not a panacea should we focus on risk resilience? Resilience is an interactive concept that refers to a relative resistance to environmental risk experiences, or the overcoming of stress or adversity. As such, it differs from both social competence and positive mental health. Resilience differs from traditional concepts of risk and protection in its focus on individual variations in response to comparable experiences. The focus here is on individual differences and the causal processes that they reflect, rather than on resilience as a general quality.

Because resilience in relation to childhood adversities may impact adolescence and adulthood, a life-span trajectory approach is needed. Also, because of the crucial importance of gene-environment interactions in relation to resilience, a wide range of research strategies spanning psychosocial and biological methods is needed. Five main implications stem from the research to date:

1. resistance to hazards may derive from controlled exposure to risk (rather than its avoidance)
2. resistance may derive from traits or circumstances that are without major effects in the absence of the relevant environmental hazards
3. resistance may derive from physiological or psychological coping processes rather than external risk or protective factors
4. delayed recovery may derive from 'turning point' experiences in adult life
5. resilience may be constrained by biological programming or damaging effects of stress/adversity on neural structures.

How do We Cultivate a State of Emotional Intelligence and Risk Resilience?

There is evidence that parental monitoring of children's media can reduce the negative effects of media exposure on children. Gentile, Nathanson, et al. (2012) investigated parental monitoring of their children's media use. Data was gathered from 1,323 elementary/primary school children, their parents and teachers. The self-report data obtained from those children, parents and teachers helped to identify four distinct types of monitoring of TV viewing and video game playing:

- co-use of the technology particular when watching TV
- limit setting on amount of time that the child was allowed to view or play with each technology
- limit setting on type of content that could be watched or game that could be played
- active mediation.

Co-playing video games, however, is done more by parents who themselves play video games and believe that playing can have beneficial effects (Nikken & Jansz, 2006). There were differences in level and type of monitoring, even within the restricted age range; they found that parents are more likely to monitor their younger children's media use than their older children's media use.

When we combine our results with those of other studies, we see that parental monitoring decreases in frequency as children approach middle to late childhood (Gentile, et al., 2012). But parental monitoring alone may not be sufficient to tackle the issue of risk. It is likely that a much more structured approach to raising awareness of risk and resilience may be needed to educate our young. For instance, there are now a number of websites offering advice and support to parents and teachers interested in the development of emotional intelligence and risk resilience. For example, the Risk and Resilience Framework[1] originally developed within Wakefield Local Authority to provide a structured, multiagency approach to help reduce risk and improve good quality online communications was developed as a resource to support a range of professionals working with children and young people, including, early years workers, teachers and youth support workers, learning mentors, and social care and health practitioners. Part of this structured framework was to provide:

- a consistent, evidence-based and practical approach to promoting resilience and reducing risk of adverse outcomes;
- good quality interventions that promote resilience and reduce risk to all children and young people;
- a programme that is cohesive and developmental from 0 to 19 years; and
- an approach that puts the child or young person at the centre and focuses on their competences.

However, while this multiagency approach to improving resilience and reducing potential risk for all children and young people is seen as a positive step forward, this may be seen as an extreme form of risk resilience. In fact, there is some suggestion that most parents trust their children to use online resources and Internet sites safely. The report from the Ofcom (2012) survey suggests that the majority of parents with children between the ages of 5 and 15 years showed trust in their child to use the Internet safely (81%) and generally felt that the benefits of using the Internet clearly outweighed the potential risks (65%). It appears that while children may well be at risk from unsolicited communications (email, chat forums, sexual messages); the identification of risky material (pornography); or instances of cyber-bullying from others. The majority of young adults are well-equipped to deal with those situations in a well-informed, mature and efficient manner. Indeed, Bryce and Fraser's (2013) indepth study shows a general acceptance that there is risk and that it is just an unfortunate feature of online interactions. Their focus groups, consisting of young people aged 9 to 19 in the United Kingdom, showed that many of these youngsters were confident that they could defend themselves effectively against cyber-bullying, that is that they had the necessary awareness and agency to manage online risk responsibly. This

[1]https://www.riskandresilience.org.uk

is of course true for the majority of young people but as they point out there is a need to identify the characteristics of those young people who may be particularly vulnerable to victimization in order to design strategies that can stimulate coping skills and resilience to cyber-bullying for specific groups of young people. Our focus should, therefore, be to help promote and encourage these skills further and to improve risk resilience and emotional intelligence by working closely with individual learners and relying on multiagency support if and when appropriate.

Risks, Skills and Opportunities

This chapter has alluded to some of the potential risks in allowing children exposure to the Internet, relating to both physical and psychological difficulties with cyber-bullying, sleep deprivation and health risks. Rather than focus on these perceived risks, we have considered how we can instil confidence and resilience in the current generation to overcome the perceived difficulties that arise from their online activities. A number of practical steps can be taken to ensure safer use of digital technologies online, for example, providing easily available detailed guidelines on dealing with key issues with mobile technologies, mobile phones and the Internet and increaseing the awareness of cyber-bullying (Willard, 2006). There are also opportunities to raise a greater awareness among younger children about cyber-bullying, especially with the development of educational programmes with anti-bullying materials and educational workshops within schools (Samara & Smith, 2008). Although cyber-bullying shares many characteristics with traditional forms of bullying there are a number of unique and potentially damaging features, for example, the anonymity and lack of face-to-face social cues that can encourage persistence and escalation of harassment (Dehue, et al., 2008; Dehue, Bolman, et al., 2012). Yet bullying intervention programmes can help. Lereya, Samara, and Wolke's (2013) critical review of the literature suggests that for a bullying intervention programme to be effective it must look beyond the school gate and draw in the support of the family. Unwanted sexual solicitation needs to be addressed through raising awareness of potential risks among parents and educators. Strengthening home–school initiatives such as through workshops, training sessions as well as increasing the amount of advice offered to parents can all help to ameliorate these risk factors (Hasebrink, Görzig, et al., 2011). More importantly, allowing children to take control and autonomy in their use of the Internet and to take responsibility for their own Internet security seems a positive approach to reducing risk. The message should be one of empowerment rather than restriction (Banyard & Underwood, 2012).

Conclusions

There are some concerns that our adult fears may actually be damaging to the very people we seek to protect. Tynes (2007) sums this concern up in 'Internet safety gone wild? sacrificing the educational psychosocial benefits of online social environments'. She argues that online communities supported by SNSs are critical to adolescents sharing and receiving information about themselves and topics of interest. Further the Council for Exceptional Children (CEC)[2] maintains that those children with exceptional talents are avid users of the Internet. One reason for this is that it may be their only social outlet. The current dilemma regards how educators and parents allow children the freedom to explore new digital technology yet at the same time protect them from potential harm and unwarranted risks. As Crook (2008, p. 10) advocates: *safe internet use involves balancing perceived benefits against acceptable risks*. Most young adults, as well as children, appear to be aware of their own safety and clearly understand the associated risks when using online resources (Crook, 2008; Sharples, et al., 2009). This suggests that young adults are perhaps less naive, less susceptible and less vulnerable than the social media would perhaps lead us to believe. There is a growing need not to restrict the use of digital technologies, but to educate adults and young people about the potential risks and to allow them to make informed choices about their use of technology. Our own research has shown that schools that offer open but monitored Internet access tend to produce risk-aware and therefore potentially safer cohorts of young people who are more likely to have the skills to protect themselves beyond the school gate (Underwood, et al., 2008).

[2] http://www.cec.sped.org/

Chapter Eleven
The Future of Learning

Introduction

In this book *Learning and the e-generation* we have questioned the impact of digital technologies on learners and their learning process. In contrast to a number of excellent texts addressing this question, we have focused specifically on the ways in which technology is influencing basic skills such as language, communication and problem-solving and how such changes impact the way people learn. As we noted in the introduction, the perception that digital technologies are deskilling this and future generations of learners continues to be a concern both within educational circles and society in general. Throughout this text we have questioned whether this concern is valid or whether it is time to accept that change is inevitable and by doing so focus on how to exploit the many benefits that accrue from using these digital technologies.

There is little doubt that the rise in digital technologies is having an effect on how people go about their daily lives and it would seem self-evident that changes in how we learn are inevitable. Learners are now engaged with an increasingly complex, problem-orientated and intellectually challenging digital world and these experiences are promoting a new subset of skills. We have of course come down on the side of accepting that change is inevitable, however there is some truth in the assertion that the net generation is not honing many of the skills that previous generations have valued. While the basic skills of language, communication and decision-making remain central to our human endeavour, the tools we use to support those skills have continued to evolve. For previous generations the move from adolescence to adulthood,

Learning and the E-Generation, First Edition. Jean D. M. Underwood and Lee Farrington-Flint.
© 2015 Jean D. M. Underwood and Lee Farrington-Flint. Published 2015 by John Wiley & Sons, Ltd.

whether at 21 or latterly 18 years of age, was marked by the purchase of a high-quality watch. Today many individuals do not own a watch or if they do it is a piece of jewellery rather than a timepiece. The smart phone tells the time and offers so much more at the touch of an icon. What need is there for anything else? As this study has illustrated increased connectivity and more mobile technologies clearly offer so much more than previous technologies and this generation of learners is taking full advantage of the opportunities afforded by them. The key question concerns how our ability to embrace these digital technologies is shaping the cognitive, social and emotional skills of our current generation, which is the focus of this final chapter.

The Skills of the Net Generation

A key aim of this study has been to assess how technology has changed the cognitive, social and affective aspects of learning and a primary focus on the impact of technology on the individual learner. It remains clear that we now have a generation of learners that are fully immersed in digital technologies and these are often referred to as *digital natives, net generation, Google generation* or the *millenials* (Bennett, 2012). Each of these terms has been used synonymously to highlight the significance and importance of new technologies within the lives of many young people. For some, new technologies have been such a defining feature in the lives of our younger generation that they predict a fundamental change in the way in which young people communicate, socialize, create and learn. For others, technology is so rapidly changing that it remains difficult to keep abreast of new advances. It is likely that the rhetoric around 'digital natives' will encourage dramatic educational reforms because traditional education systems do not, and cannot, cater for the needs and interests of its young people. Yet it is clear that this digital divide is much more than a simple generational difference in the access to, and use of, technology. The digital divide also concerns the perceived benefits from using these technologies and whether similar gains in educational learning can be found across all users. From this perspective an understanding of the factors that have led to individual or group differences in how and why students embrace technological change becomes essential. Notwithstanding claims that the digital native myth is perpetuated by the wider moral and ideological debates over young people and their digital technology (Selwyn, 2009, 2011), and how this rhetoric may portray a pessimistic view about embedding technology into educational institutions (Helsper & Eynon, 2010), we can see that many young learners are changing as a result of their willingness to engage with such technology.

Native speakers of technology are quite clearly fluent in the digital language of computers, video games, and the Internet. Prensky (2005) acknowledges how the skills and abilities students acquire outside the classroom are far more refined that we could ever have thought. This has led to numerous sources debating the relevance of the competencies of digital natives and the extent to which these skill sets evolve through our digital lives (see Palfrey & Gasser, 2008). It remains apparent that our young people generally have a much better idea of what the future is bringing than we do. But in reality how are these natives engaging with new ways of learning? As we have seen within the previous chapters, learners are already busy adopting new systems for communicating (instant messaging), sharing (blogs), buying and selling (eBay), coordinating (wikis), searching (Google), reporting (camera), socializing (chat rooms), exchanging (peer-to-peer technology) and creating (Flash) (see, Bennett, 2012). These functionalities are readily accepted and exploited by the young and are having a profound effect on their patterns of behaviour, including their responses to formal education. They often embrace many of these features as possible tools for collaboration, communication and learning without any formal instruction to do so and these are activities that are part of their natural, everyday engagement with technology (Underwood, 2007; Underwood, et al., 2008, 2009).

The immersion in the digital world of technology is beginning very early. For example, in Gillen's (2002) study of the telephone discourse of three- and four-year-olds, the children were seen to enact spontaneous telephone play and through their imaginary conversation were seen to develop complex conventions of 'telephone talk'. Even young children are well equipped with the functionalities of the iPad and mobile phone (Falloon, 2013). Children furthermore often redefine themselves and others though such interactions with the technology and new technologies seem commonplace within the home. While there may be some ongoing debate on how digital technologies can fit into the lives of young children, young children's reliance on digital devices such as iPhones, iPads and game consoles are rapidly becoming a reality in early childhood settings and many children's homes (Smith, 2002; Verenikina & Kervin, 2011).

Perhaps the biggest change has been the shift within the types of online social interactions, often encouraged through social networking activities, and the way in which individuals broadcast themselves across the net. With the increased popularity of smart phones learners have a wealth of communication tools simply at the touch of a button. This has resulted in the widespread use of the hybrid language of digital texts seen in synchronous online communication, emails and text messages that reflect the creation of new orthographic features of informal and more abbreviated forms of written language (see Wood, et al., 2013, for a detailed discussion). For the first time in human history, a majority of the world's adult population is playing an active role in the culture of reading as well as of writing. Social media networks have become an effective vehicle for change, not least because what they offer is an arena of typed conversation (Chatfield, 2013). It is clear that learning and instruction need to adapt to these new literacies emerging with the move from traditional print-based media to digital, hybrid and multilingual forms (Razfar & Yang, 2010). This is proving painful for many given that *text speak* is not an accepted mode of communication in the majority of schools or other formal educational contexts and is often considered to be damaging the traditional conventions of literacy.

The introduction of new tools designed to enhance social communication allows learners to communicate with a range of individuals at any given time. Instant messaging, a popular tool for communication, allowed one-to-one dialogue in real-time, encouraged spontaneous discussions with friends and immediate responses (Paolillo, 1999). One-to-many types of interaction and the increased popularity of Twitter and Facebook have replaced this focus on one-to-one exchanges. This shift in moving towards a much more public form of communication appears to encourage young people to broadcast news to a wider community of friends, acquaintances and more worryingly strangers (Underwood, et al., 2011). Facebook and other SNSs provide a clear example of an individual's tendency to blend the personal with the public and an unrestricted form of social communication that provides greater freedom of expression, opportunities for collaboration, discussion and reflection (Davies & Merchant, 2009; Deed & Edwards, 2011). Despite concerns that Facebook, text messaging and other communication tools may be a distraction for our students, they show real potential to transform the learning experience for many individuals (McCarroll & Curran, 2013).

As these tools develop they modify the human skill set. So we find that handwriting has deteriorated in favour of email, text or instant messaging. The skill of essay writing is sorely missing in many of our undergraduate students as they arrive at university and they turn to the Internet as a source for providing immediate access to information and, sadly, from a teacher's point of view, for some, completed essays (Matthews, 2013). Such skills have been replaced by the bullet point and the development of story boarding and presentation skills and the keyboard not the pen, and images not words, are now king. But engagement with new technologies is shaping how we think, learn and react to challenges. These changes to the skill set are even more pronounced when we consider cognitive capabilities of the net generation and how they interact with video-games, virtual environments and multimodal learning environments. Multitasking through video-game playing can have real benefits and promote divided attention skills, and a refinement of behavioural, cognitive and affective skills that are needed to engage within a digitally rich social environment. For some, these may be seen simply as highly addictive or time-wasting activities yet for others they provide real opportunities to enhance students' cognition and learning. For example, while some multitaskers have been shown to perform poorly in certain cognitive tasks involving task-switching, selective attention and working memory, this may not always be detrimental. There is some suggestion that heavy media multitaskers performed better in a multisensory integration task and showed sustained improvements in engaging with parallel processing and attentional switching (Lui & Wong, 2012), skills that are inevitably important within many contexts in formal education. The benefits of technology for improving cognition can be found in the allure of video games. We know that video games can promote behavioural, cognitive and emotional engagement within learners (Appleton, 2008) as well as helping disenfranchised individuals back into education through the recognition of their role as expert gamers (Sandford & Williamson, 2006). Through the process of trial-and-error, video games may well promote effective learning and knowledge acquisition. As Shin and colleagues (2012) suggest, games can promote discovery learning and impact on the many essential processes that underpin it, which include finely attuned attentional skills, increased problem solving and more sophisticated forms of reasoning ability. Yet despite such evidence, there is so little emphasis on using gaming as a pedagogical tool within formal education.

Throughout the text we have gauged the opportunities for learner development through their growing access to new technology while noting some of the not inconsiderable risks of learning in digital worlds. Some of these risks include the detrimental effects of multitasking on educational outcomes, evidence of academic malpractice and cheating among students, the way in which video games are eroding young people's social lives and the deterioration of traditional literacy standards through a rise in texting and instant messaging. We have also briefly discussed how educators may need to allay parental concerns of online risks and how Internet harassment and bullying victimization is a growing concern for all involved. While there may be some criticism that we have not explicitly dealt with the urgent issue of cyber-bullying and associated malpractices, this was a conscious decision. It is a topic that requires its own indepth treatise and is beyond the scope of this text, which focuses primarily on learners and their learning journey.

Bridging the Home–School Divide

There is evidence that the divide between home and school technological practices still remains. Of course, there remains a minority of students who still do not have access to digital technologies within the home (Madell & Muncer, 2004; Underwood, Ault, et al., 2006 Underwood, Baguley, et al., 2007, 2009, 2010), and as a result, they lack the affordances that these new technologies can offer. But it is not simply access to technology that creates this divide, but also the uptake by the young and the convergence of functionality of the technologies.

There are often discrepancies between the types of technologies used within the home and those used within the classroom. Often technology at home is seen as a vehicle for promoting social practices, like gaming, and communicating with friends. For many individuals, the out-of-school digital world is richly populated and the school digital world often suffers by comparison. There are attempts to bridge this divide. While the increasing use of VLEs and other technological support as tools to dissolve the barriers between home and school learning environments is to be welcomed, there is a persistent core of pupils that is unable to take advantage of these initiatives (see Somekh & Underwood, 2007). Furthermore, as our own research has consistently shown, teachers are open to the implementation of new technologies but are constrained by the lack of funding or the lack of additional training that is currently required to fully integrate these tools into the curriculum (Underwood, Baguley, et al., 2008, 2009). It is not that teachers are reluctant to bridge this home–school divide it is simply that the institutional or government constraints are preventing the successful implementation of exciting new technologies into the classroom.

Returning to our main theme, our collective extolling of the affordances of these technologies at the expense of teaching and learning processes provides a partial explanation as to why technology has yet to be universally accepted in the classroom as they are in the world beyond the school gate. Day and Lloyd (2007) present a good example of this. They describe a class in which the teacher has identified the value of a wiki to support students' collaborative writing. From their observations they can see the identified technology affordance is clearly present and some students are producing collaborative text. However, a number of students are not involved, with some preferring to work on paper and have face-to-face discussions. So while these technologies may have educational potential, Maddux and Cummings (2004) argue that they are introduced as 'silver bullets' to solve educational ills rather than being embedded in educational theory and process, and in this role of educational panacea they have little chance of meeting the unrealistic initial expectations that are generated.

On the basis of our earlier investigations (Underwood, Baguley, et al., 2007, 2008;) we acknowledged that while learning occurs both in formal as well as informal settings, many students' technological world is likely to be richer outside school than inside the classroom. There is strong evidence for this suggestion. We know that the amount of time spent on ICT at home greatly exceeds that spent on ICT at school (Somekh, et al., 2002). We also know that many families are using technology much more to prepare their child for formal education. For example, Neumann and Neumann (2013) describe the versatile functions of tablet devices and their apps for alphabet matching, phonics games and personalized stories, which can be a valuable tool for promoting early literacy acquisition. In fact, nearly 72 per cent of apps are aimed at pre-school children, and more than 50 per cent of the top-selling apps target primary school children (Shuler, et al., 2012). Children's interactions with digital texts in out-of-school settings have revealed that they engage with the technology in a playful way with agency, and creativity (Burnett, 2010) as well as using iPads to promote personalized storytelling opportunities (Kucirkova, Messer, Sheehy, & Flewitt, 2013). This suggests a positive link between new technologies and home-based educational learning.

However, technology can also affect family dynamics especially if we consider the impact of young people's Internet use on the family as a whole. Having access to technology in the home may be less positive in some circumstances. There are conflicting findings as to whether young people's Internet use in the home has a deleterious impact on family time and communication. For example, it has been shown to reduce family time leading in turn to a weakening of family ties (Mesch, 2003; Nie, Hillygus, & Erbring, 2002). However, other studies show little or no reduction in family time (Kraut, et al., 2002). Lee and Chae's (2007) research further complicates the picture as it confirms the reduction in family time but found that this did not cause a reduction in the levels of communication within the family. They argue that Internet time may in fact replace passive rather than active family time and so is not deleterious. Further, while game-playing reduces family time and family communication, the use of the Internet as an information source or for homework posed little threat to family coherence. Clearly, as the evidence suggests, there may well be a strong need to consider the impact of technology not just within school but also within the home and how children's early social and educational practices are evolving with the introduction of these new technologies.

While there may be evidence of the successful use of technology within the home, still this does not address how teachers and parents can help overcome the home–school digital divide. It is not simply adding more technology into the classroom, but transforming the learning space to allow for greater flexibility in the choice of technology and how students learn that will encourage greater access between home and school.

Can Psychological Theory Inform Educational Practice?

A second theme of this book has been to ask to what extent psychological theory can illuminate the educational debate? Specifically we have drawn together the many theories of learning in order to understand when and why learning is or is not successful. We have shown that psychological theories can focus on a range of skills required by the learner, which relate to the behavioural, cognitive and affective dimensions of learning. We have also suggested that there is now a greater willingness to accept that psychological theory might have a place in developing pedagogic practice due to recent developments in the fields of cognition, education and neuroscience. As part of the student's journey, there is a wider recognition that we need to move away from our focus on content to a better awareness of the process in our attempts to maintain and promote learning or academic success.

One of the key difficulties is establishing what is meant by academic or pedagogic success. For some, success may relate to supporting disenchanted learners' return to the educational system, for others success can be defined by an improvement in a learner's attentional or behavioural skill. The notion of educational success varies across individuals and groups, and while not everybody sees success in national test scores such as SATs and GCSEs as the gold standard of learning, many teachers and educators often do. Based on their own work on Integrated Learning Systems, Wood, et al. (1999, p. 99) suggest that we need to further refine our claims about the impact of teaching and learning outcomes and our assessment of *what a 'learning gain' means*. To some extent, these gains should be focussed on learner attributes rather than solely on academic test scores.

There are those who are very sympathetic to the technology-supported play-way-to-learning. For example, Klopfer and Osterweil (2011) show:

> sympathy for those who favour unrestrained gaming over schooling. We see enormous creativity in gamers. Mastering a game involves entering into often chaotic environments, learning through trial and error, observation, analysis and systematic testing … the culture of problem solving that surrounds gaming reveals the very dispositions desired in the twenty-first century workforce.
>
> (Klopfer and Osterweil, 2011, p. 154)

However, the counter argument is also prevalent for example, Kirschner, et al. (2006) advocate that:

> after a half-century of advocacy associated with instruction using minimal guidance, it appears that there is no body of research supporting the technique. In so far as there is any evidence from controlled studies, it almost uniformly supports direct, strong instructional guidance rather than constructivist-based minimal guidance during the instruction of novice to intermediate learners.
>
> (Kirscher et al., 2006, p. 83)

The amount of flexibility and autonomy students should have within the confines of their own learning is an important distinction between these quotes. The debates about the content and process of learning and the value of digital technology as a tool to achieve those learning goals: *are often driven by personal belief and opinion, rather than being empirically reasoned and informed* (Selwyn, 2011, p. 88). However, in looking for commonalities in the many seemingly disparate learning theories we are endeavouring to make some small steps towards a more reasoned debate on the value of learning technologies. Utopian hopes and perception of technology: *often lead policy makers and practitioners to ignore general theoretical perspectives about teaching and learning* (Sutherland, et al., 2004, p. 413). Acknowledging the complexity of the relationships within the learning system is, perhaps, the first step in addressing the effective use of technology as it removes the polarization of perceptions for and against technology's role as a learning tool. This step leads to an appreciation that digital technologies are neither inherently good nor bad, and neither effective nor ineffective. Each learner and teacher can influence the learner's experience for themselves and for those around them. The difficulty lies in how to structure this learning experience. One way to embrace technology is to consider the use of instructional designs that focus not just on the use of technology, but on incorporating technology in a way that manages or supports the cognitive load and the flow of information for learners and the cognitive requirements of the task (Kester, Kirschner, & Merriënboer, 2005).

It is clear that physiological, cognitive and affective responses to learning also remain an important and enduring issue. Technology as a tool for learning requires a clear investment of cognitive skills on behalf of the learner. Learning requires attention and practices (perseverance) as well as a degree of reasoning and problem solving, but each of these skills also requires the emotional engagement of the learner (motivation). Such engagement comes from individuals seeing an activity as relevant to themselves and achievable by themselves. This raises the question of why these digital tools are not readily incorporated into educational provision in schools, given their appealing and enticing nature. There are many who question the importance of such technologies for education, especially in improving language, literacy and problem-solving skills and we highly recommend a greater focus on the positive affordances of these new technologies and a commitment to the reskilling of our current generation of learners to ensure their future success (see Selwyn, 2006).

Promoting Educational Change

The final issue concerns how we can support and promote educational reform through the implementation of these digital technologies? There is some recognition that the human skill set is changing; yet the link between the social and educational uses of technology is far from established. As noted in Chapter 1, vociferous arguments have been put forward to support the conclusion that ICT is a drain on our educational system (see Cuban, 2001; Oppenheimer, 2003) and a feeling that the technology is not bringing about the educational gains once expected. Although the usefulness of digital technologies in education is open to debate, few would challenge the major impact of digital technologies on our everyday lives. So why is the evidence so hard to find within educational settings? Watson (2001) for one has argued that such assumptions around the advances in technology within society often sit uncomfortably with teachers' own professional judgements and educational practices. The discontinuity between teachers and digital technology may be more deep-seated than simply a clash with professional practice. Those who choose to teach are characteristically book lovers and it is not age or gender, but membership of the teaching profession that is the defining characteristic of low involvement with new technological innovations (Sandford, et al., 2006).

But why is this change to education deemed important? Even if we consider the basic skills, such as reading and writing, then it becomes quite apparent that the skill set currently taught in schools fails to meet learners' everyday literacy practices. No longer do we see students turning to textbooks to find information or using a notepad and pen to record ideas. Instead, students turn to the iPad or notebook for note-taking and refer to a range of Internet sites for expert guidance and advice. According to some, the ability to use digital media requires skills that are inherently different from those required of conventional print and therefore require us to reskill (Gilster, 1997). This is certainly true when we consider the multimodal textual landscape of digital literacy (Kress, 2010), which involves the need to incorporate multiple sign systems into our everyday literacy activities (videos, images, multimedia) and skills in deciphering often complex, visual representations to extract meaningful information. The use of multiple information systems is a difficult skill for many, and whether we encourage the use of blogs to promote digital literacy activities and peer-collaboration within the classroom, or interpret visual representations, these are skills that are well beyond the conventional views of literacy. Without doubt, there is a clear recognition that this immersion in digital technology can shift the goals of education and require students to acquire a new contemporary skill set and it is only when students, teachers and institutions work together that any notable learning gains can be identified.

Learner, Teacher and School Level Characteristics

We have illustrated the effects of technology on the individual learner within this new digital age. As learning becomes more individualized, learner-centred, collaborative and ubiquitous across the lifespan, new technologies are becoming more personalized, user-centred, mobile, networked and durable. However, successful implementation of digital technology within the school environment does require a much more focused effort on behalf of the learner, the teacher and the institution. Underwood, Baguely, et al. (2008) summed this up in a learning equation, which suggests that effective learning is the direct result of valuable learning opportunities provided by the school and teacher as well as an individual's own investment in the learning process (see Figure 11.1). In essence, both opportunity and investment need to occur on all three levels to ensure successful implementation of digital technology to support and enhance the learning process.

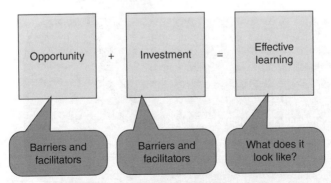

Figure 11.1. Learning equation developed by Underwood, Baguely et al. (2008) to capture personalized learning in schools.

If we are to consider that both opportunity and investment are the main components of success, then effective learning cannot happen without effective implementation not only by schools, but also by teachers and by the learners themselves (Somekh & Underwood, 2007; Underwood, Baguley, et al., 2007, 2008, 2010). In this sense, digital technologies can be considered as a toolkit, which can provide opportunities for learning both at the school and classroom level. At the school level, technology needs to be available, accessible and built into the curriculum to create a greater synergy between school and home educational culture and ethos. A top-down institutional policy regarding the whys and hows of embedding technology into the classroom is required.

Even at the classroom level there needs to be focus on integrating technologies to support the learning process (see Figure 11.2). Such integration is a complex process. 'Classroom orchestration' is the metaphor currently in vogue when we talk about an alignment of the design of technology learning experiences with pedagogic practice (Nussbaum, Dillenbourg, et al., 2013). Technology needs to be firmly embedded into the educational curriculum at the classroom level before any substantial gains can be identified. Successful embedding of learning technologies is predicated on: *appropriate, well-supported and focused human intervention, good learning design or pedagogical input and the sensitive handling of the process over time* (Salmon, 2005, p. 203). The potentials of technology, at the classroom level, can help to promote the differentiation of assessment to fit the students' needs and allow a more personalized learning experience by recognizing different

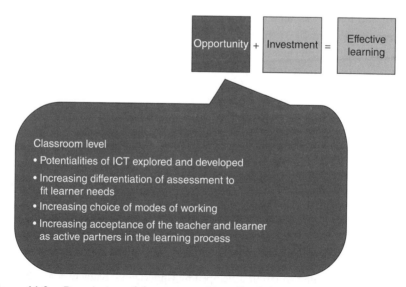

Figure 11.2. Description of the opportunities afforded at the classroom level

modes of learning. While technology may have the potential to shift the goals of learning and to make the learning process more authentic and engaging for students, this can only occur if the technology is focussed on enhancing the learning process itself. However, as we are aware from our own investigations (Underwood, Baguley, et al., 2009, 2010) some teachers lack the skills necessary to assess the value of different technologies and knowledge regarding the best ways to incorporate such technology into their teaching, while for others, they may need convincing of the potential benefits of using these digital tools (see also Gray, Ryan, & Coulon, 2004).

As we know, change does not always occur immediately. While there is a demand for immediacy, that change should have an impact here and now, this is unlikely to occur in any meaningful way when technology is first introduced into the educational process. Teachers may lack the experience or time to fully consider how and where these new technologies can be embedded into the classroom activities but additional support, guidance and freedom to experiment with new approaches could be beneficial. In a series of longitudinal studies we have identified what we call the technology dip (Underwood & Dillon, 2004, 2011). This is a dip in pedagogical risk taking by teachers following the introduction of new technologies. Until there is alignment of teachers' beliefs and practices and the newly acquired technology skills, teachers necessarily focus on acquiring the new technology skill-set. Recovery from that dip and the ensuing benefits take about 2 years but when this happens measurable learning gains alongside positive learner and teacher attitudes emerge (Underwood & Dillon, 2011). As technology becomes ubiquitous one might expect this dip to disappear but of course this will only occur if the technology stabilizes and its use become routine. Whether this change will result in low-level or advanced pedagogies is a question that can only be addressed once the technology is embedded within teaching and learning activities in the school curriculum.

However, providing opportunities on their own cannot guarantee success. Beyond these opportunities, there also needs to be a focus on investment. From an individual learner-level perspective, technology may encourage changes in learner behaviours in that the individual sees them as being relevant, stimulating and motivating. In essence, individual learners need to show some investment in their own learning on both a cognitive and affective level if digital technology is going to enhance their learning for the better (see Figure 11.3). However, the simple relationship between enjoyment and motivation, espoused as the key benefit of computers in classrooms, will not guarantee success. Often performance breaks down if the learner does not accept or embrace challenge or take some responsibility for their learning (Underwood, Baguley, et al., 2010).

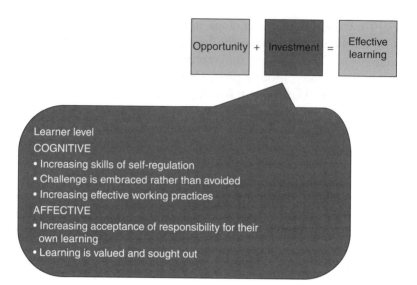

Figure 11.3. Descriptions of the cognitive and affective skills afforded at the individual learner level

However, it is perhaps pertinent to note that not all learners benefit from an e-learning experience. For example, Chandra and Lloyd (2008) found e-learning led to lower performance scores for high-performing girls but brought measurable learning benefits to low-achieving boys who showed marked improvement. The use of technologies tends to be less effective, or indeed ineffective, when the goals for their use are unclear. There needs to be an increased recognition of students regulating their learning.

With an increased focus on the learner, there may be a priority to ensure the promotion of personalized or self-regulated learning (SRL) and to prioritize the individual needs of the learner as a step toward to improving the educational experiences of children (Banyard, et al., 2006). Learners need to set their own goals and to think about the skills and strategies required to achieve them. The ability to monitor progress towards learning rather than outcome is indicative of du Boulay's (2000) shift from a focus on the content to the processes of learning. As we know, self-efficacy is positively related to self-regulatory strategies such as planning, monitoring, and regulating strategies and has been shown to lead to academic success (Pintrich, 2000). This self-regulation, coupled with an active approach to learning may be the key to observing actual gains in learning. From a constructivist approach, it is recognized that active learning is far more beneficial than being a passive recipient of information. However, concerns over deep and surface learning come to the fore. While deep learning is often seen as the gold standard for education, we know that a learner who can strategically move between surface and deep learning, depending on the nature of the information, will make better gains overall (Entwistle, 2000). There is also recognition of students' self-reflection on their own personal mode of learning and how pedagogy can embrace and incorporate learning activities that cater for visual, auditory and kinaesthetic learning styles (Sharp, et al., 2008). There is some pedagogic potential for allowing greater flexibility in the choice of medium in which learners can select, edit and produce material for classroom activities and assessment (Underwood, Baguley, et al., 2007, 2008, 2009). Given this freedom of choice, learners may take greater responsibility for their own role within learning and recognize the value of learning as a process rather than simply an outcome.

Many Possibilities but No Certainties

Technology is equipping our current generation of students with new skills for communication, collaboration and learning. Yet the gap between the use of technology both within and outside education remains apparent. While so many of the young are immersed within this technology, it begs the question why these technologies are not being integrated within mainstream educational settings? There is a worldwide imperative to exploit the opportunities afforded by new digital technologies for teaching and learning but this is not accompanied by the recognition that technology will transform the learning environment. Throughout this study, we have illustrated how technology does have the potential to shift the goals of learning and to make the learning process more authentic and engaging, but this can only occur if the technology is focussed on enhancing the learner and their own learning process. Providing opportunities within the home or school context may not be sufficient to promoting change. The technologies need to have a pedagogical focus and allow the learner to make an investment in their own learning. An attempt to embed technology necessarily involves some level of disturbance to the educational system and the extent that these perturbations are tolerated will affect the level of acceptance of the technology. If the acceptance is low then for some learners the educational system will become increasingly irrelevant and they will carve out a learning environment for themselves, dipping into the formal system only when they see the need. The move towards integrating digital technology into the classroom requires a greater emphasis on redesigning curriculam at the school and teacher level and a better understanding of the true affordances that this technology can provide. Despite some innovative examples of incorporating technology in the school setting, we still have some way to go and perhaps the starting point is to identify the new skills that are being acquired through such digital technologies.

References

Abe, J. A. (2011). Positive emotions, emotional intelligence and successful experiential learning. *Personality & Individual Differences, 51*: 817–22.

Adachi, P. J. C., & Willoughby, T. (2011). The effect of violent video games on aggression: Is it more than just the violence? *Aggression and Violent Behavior, 16*: 55–62.

Adachi, P. J. C., & Willoughby, T. (2012). Do video games promote positive youth development? *Journal of Adolescent Research, 28*: 155–65.

Agarwal, R., & Prasad, J. (1998). A conceptual and operational definition of personal innovativeness in the domain of information technology. *Information Systems Research, 9*: 204–15.

Aguilar-Roca, N. M., Williams, A. E., & O'Dowd, D. K. (2012). The impact of laptop-free zones on student performance and attitudes in large lectures. *Computers & Education, 59*: 1300–08.

Ainsworth, S. (1999). The functions of multiple representations. *Computers & Education, 33*: 131–52.

Ainsworth, S. (2006). DeFT: A conceptual framework for considering learning with multiple representations. *Learning and Instruction, 16*: 183–98.

Ainsworth, S. (2008). The educational value of multiple-representations when learning complex scientific concepts. In J. Gilbert, M. Reiner & M. B. Nakhleh (eds.), *Visualization: Theory and practice in science education* (pp. 191–208). New York: Springer.

Ainsworth, S., Bibby, P., & Wood, D. (2002). Examining the effects of different multiple representational systems in learning primary mathematics. *The Journal of the Learning Sciences, 11*: 25–61.

Ainsworth, S., & Loizou, A. (2003). The effects of self-explaining when learning with text or diagrams. *Cognitive Science, 27*: 669–81.

Ainsworth, S., Prain, V., & Tytler, R. (2011). Drawing to learn in science. *Science, 33*: 1096–7.

Ainsworth, S., & Van Labeke, N. (2004). Multiple forms of dynamic representation. *Learning and Instruction, 14*(3): 241–55.

Learning and the E-Generation, First Edition. Jean D. M. Underwood and Lee Farrington-Flint.
© 2015 Jean D. M. Underwood and Lee Farrington-Flint. Published 2015 by John Wiley & Sons, Ltd.

Akbulut, Y., Uysal, Ö., Odabasi, H. F., & Kuzu, A. (2008). Influence of gender, program of study and PC experience on unethical computer using behaviors of Turkish undergraduate students. *Computers & Education, 51*: 485–92.

Anderman, E. M., & Murdock, T. (2007). *Psychology of academic cheating.* San Diego: Elsevier.

Anderson, T. (2004). Towards a theory of online learning. In T. Anderson & F. Elloumni (eds.), *Theory and practice of online learning* (pp. 33–60). Alberta: Athabasca University Press.

Annetta, L. A., Minogue, J., Holmes, S. Y., & Cheng, M. (2009). Investigating the impact of video games on high school students' engagement and learning about genetics. *Computers & Education, 53*: 74–85.

Appleton, J. J. (2008). Student engagement with school: Critical conceptual and methodological issues of the construct. *Psychology, 45*: 369–86.

Appleton, J. J., Christenson, S. L., & Furlong, M. J. (2008). Student engagement with school: Critical conceptual and methodological issues of the construct. *Psychology in the Schools, 45*: 369–86.

Atchley, P., & Warden, A. (2012). The need of young adults to text now: Using delay discounting to assess informational choice. *Journal of Applied Research in Memory and Cognition, 1*: 229–34.

Attwood, R. (2007). Libraries dump 2m volumes. *The Times Higher Education Supplement, 1*:820: 1. Retrieved from http://www.timeshighereducation.co.uk/news/libraries-dump–2m-volumes/311092.article

Austin, M. J., & Brown, L. D. (1999). Internet plagiarism: Developing strategies to curb student academic dishonesty. *The Internet and Higher Education, 2*: 21–33.

Baddley, A. D., & Hitch, G. J. (1974). Working memory. In G. A. Bower (ed.), *The psychology of learning and motivation: Advances in research and theory* (pp. 47–89). New York: Academic Press.

Baker, M., & Lund, K. (1997). Promoting reflective interactions in a CSCL environment. *Journal of Computer Assisted Learning, 13*: 175–93.

Baker, R., Corbett, A., Koedinger, K., & Wagner, A. (2004). Off-task behavior in the cognitive tutor classroom: when students "game the system." *Proceedings of the ACM CHI 2004: Computer-Human Interaction (CHI'04)*, Vienna, Austria (pp. 383–90).

Balajthy, E. (2005). Text-to-speech software for helping struggling readers. *Reading Online, 8*: 1–9.

Banyard, P., & Underwood, J. D. M. (2012). E-learning: The dark side? *E-learning, 28*: 1–8.

Banyard, P., Underwood, J. D. M., Kerlin, L., & Stiller, J. (2011). Virtual learning environments: Personalising learning or managing learners? In M. Thomas (ed.), *Digital education: Opportunities for social collaboration. Digital education and learning* (pp. 123–42). New York: Palgrave Macmillan.

Banyard, P., Underwood, J. D. M., & Twiner, A. (2006). Do enhanced communication technologies inhibit or facilitate self-regulated learning? *European Journal of Education, 41*: 473–89.

Barks, A., Searight, H. R., & Ratwik, S. (2011). Effects of text messaging on academic performance. *Journal of Pedagogy and Psychology, 4*: 4–9.

Baron, N. (2004). Rethinking written culture. *Language Sciences, 26*: 57–96.

Baron, N. (2010). *Always on: Language in an online and mobile world*. New York: OUP.

Barrett, E. S., & Patton, J. H. (1983). Impulsivity: Cognitive, behavioural and psychophysiological correlates. In M. Zuckerman (ed.), *Biological bases of sensation seeking, impulsivity and anxiety* (pp. 77–112). Hillsdale, NJ: Erlbaum.

Barrett, J., & Underwood, J. D. M. (1997). Beyond numeracy. In J. D. M. Underwood & J. Brown (eds.), *Integrated learning systems in UK schools* (pp. 67–78). London: Heinemann.

Bartlett, J., & Miller, C. (2011). *Truth, lies and the Internet: A report into young people's digital fluency*. London: Demos.

Barton, D. (1994). *Literacy: An introduction to the ecology of written language*. Oxford, Blackwell.

Başoğlu, E. B., & Akdemir, Ö. (2010). A comparison of undergraduate students' English vocabulary learning: using mobile phones and flash cards. *The Turkish Online Journal of Educational Technology*, 9: 1–7.

Bennett, S. (2012). Digital natives. In Z. Yan (ed.), *Encyclopedia of cyber behaviour*, 1: 212–19. Hershey, PA: IGI Global.

Bennett, S., Bishop, A., Dalgano, B., Waycott, J., & Kennedy, G. (2012). Implementing Web 2.0 technologies in higher education: A collective study. *Computers & Education*, 59: 524–34.

Berking, M., Orth, U., Wupperman, P., Meier, L. L., & Caspar, F. (2008). Prospective effects of emotion-regulation skills on emotional adjustment. *Journal of Counseling Psychology*, 55: 485–94.

Beschorner, B., & Hutchison, A. (2013). iPads as a literacy teaching tool in early childhood. *Online Submission*, 1: 16–24.

Bessière, K., Fleming Seay, A., & Kiesler, S. (2007). The ideal elf: Identity Exploration in world of warcraft. *Cyberpsychology & Behavior*, 10: 533–34.

Bessière, K., Kiesler, S., Kraut, R., & Boneva, B. (2008). Effects of internet use and social resources on changes in depression. *Information, Communication & Society*, 11: 47–70.

Biancarosa, G., & Griffiths, G. G. (2012). Technology tools to support reading in the digital age. *The Future of Children*, 22: 139–60.

Biggs, J. B., & Watkins, D. A. (2001). The paradox of the Chinese learner and beyond. In J. B. Biggs & D. A. Watkins (eds.), *Teaching the Chinese learner: Psychological and pedagogical perspectives* (pp. 3–23). Hong Kong: CERC

Bilic-Zulle, L., Frkovic, V., Turk, T., Azman, J., & Petrovecki, M. (2005). Prevalence of plagiarism among medical students. *Croatian Medical Journal*, 46: 126–31.

Birkets, S. (2006). *The Gutenberg elegies: The fate of reading in an electronic age*. London: Faber and Faber.

Black, B., & Wood, A. (2003). Utilising information communication technology to assist the education of individuals with Down syndrome. *Down Syndrome Issues and Information*. Retrieved from http://www.down-syndrome.org/information/education/technology/?page=4

Blake, N. F. (1969). *Caxton and his world*. London: Andre Deutsch.

Boesch, M. C., Wendt, O., Subramanian, A., & Hsu, N. (2013). Comparative efficacy of the Picture Exchange Communication System (PECS) versus a speech-generating device: Effects on requesting skills. *Research in Autism Spectrum Disorders*, 7: 480–93.

Bolin, A. U. (2004). Self-control, perceived opportunity, and attitudes as predictors of academic dishonesty. *Journal of Psychology, 138*: 101–14.

Bonds-Raacke, J., & Raacke. J. (2010). Myspace and Facebook: Identifying dimensions of uses and gratifications for friend networking sites. *Individual Differences Research, 8*: 27–33.

Bondy, A. S., & Frost, L. A. (1994). The picture exchange communication system. *Focus on autism and other developmental disabilities, 9*: 1–19.

Borland, J. (2007). A smarter web. *Technology Review*. Retrieved from http://www.technologyreview.com/Infotech/18306/

Bos, van den W., van Dijk, E., Westenberg, M., Rombouts, S. A., & Crone, E. A. (2009). What motivates repayment? Neural correlates of reciprocity in the Trust Game. *Social Cognitive and Affective Neuroscience, 4*: 294–304.

Boulay du B. (2000). Can we learn from ITSs? In G. Gauthier, C., Frasson & K. VanLehn, K. (eds.), *Intelligent tutoring systems: Proceedings of 5th International Conference, ITS 2000, Montreal*, number 1839. Lecture Notes in Computer Science, 9–17.

Boyd, D. M., & Ellison, N. B. (2007). Social network sites: Definition, history, and scholarship. *Journal of Computer-Mediated Communication, 13*: 210–23.

Brady, B., & Dutta, K. (2012). 45,000 caught cheating at Britain's universities. *The Independent on Sunday*, 11 March. Retrieved from http://www.independent.co.uk/news/education/education-news/45000-caught-cheating-at-britains-universities-7555109.html

Brandon, D. P., & Hollingshead, A. B. (1999). Collaborative learning and computer-supported groups. *Communication Education, 48*: 109–26.

Bransford, J. D., Barron, B., Pea, R., Meltzoff, A., Kuhl, P., Bell, P., ... Sabelli, N. (2006). Foundations and opportunities for an interdisciplinary science of learning. In K. Sawyer (ed.), *The Cambridge handbook of the learning sciences* (pp. 19–34). New York: CUP.

Bransford, J. D., Brown, A. L., & Cocking, R. R. (2000). *How people learn: Brain, mind, experience, and school*. Washington: National Academy Press.

Brian, M. (2012). Apple: 1.5 million iPads are used in educational programs, with over 20,000 education apps. *TNW Blog*, 19 Jan. Retrieved from http://thenextweb.com/apple/2012/01/19/apple-1-5-million-ipads-in-use-in-educational-programs-offering-over-20000-education-apps/

Broadbent, D. (1957). A mechanical model for human attention and immediate memory. *Psychological Review, 64*: 205–15.

Brown, B. S., Weible, R. J., & Olmosk, K. E. (2010). Business school deans on student academic dishonesty: A survey. *College Student Journal, 44*: 299–308.

Brown, J. S., & Adler, R. P. (2008). Open education, the long tail, and learning 2.0. *Educause Review, 43*: 16–20.

Brown, J. S., Collins, A., & Duguid, P. (1989). Situated cognition and the culture of learning. *Educational Researcher, 18*: 32–42.

Brown, R. P., Budzek, K., & Tamborski, M. (2009). On the meaning and measure of narcissism. *Personality & Social Psychology Bulletin, 35*: 951–64.

Bryce, J., & Fraser, J. (2013). It's common sense that it's wrong: Young people's perceptions and experiences of cyberbullying. *Cyberpsychology, Behavior, and Social Networking, 16*: 783–7.

Bryce, J., & Haworth, J. T. (2002). Well-being and flow in a sample of male and female office workers. *Leisure Studies, 21*: 249–63.

Buckingham, D. (2006). Defining digital literacy: What do young people need to know about digital media? *The Nordic Journal of Digital Literacy, 1*: 263–76.

Buckingham, D. (2007). Digital media literacies: Rethinking media education in the age of the Internet. *Research in Comparative and International Education, 2*: 43–55.

Buckingham Shum, S., & Ferguson, R. (2010). Towards a social learning space for open educational resources. *OpenED2010: Seventh Annual Open Education Conference.* Retrieved from http://oro.open.ac.uk/23351/1/

Burgoon, J. K., Bonito, J. A., Ramirez, A., Dunbar, N. E., Kam, K., & Fischer, J. (2002). Testing the interactivity principle: Effects of mediation, propinquity, and verbal and nonverbal modalities in interpersonal interaction. *Journal of Communication, 52*: 657–77.

Burke, M., Kraut, R., & Marlow, C. (2011). Social capital on Facebook: Differentiating uses and users. *Proceedings of the ACM CHI 2011: Computer-Human Interaction 2011. Vancouver, BC, Canada.*

Burnett, C. (2010). Technology and literacy in early childhood educational settings: A review of research. *Journal of Early Childhood Literacy, 10*: 247–70.

Bus, A. G., Verhallen, M. J. A. J., & de Jong, M. T. (2009). How onscreen story-books contribute to early literacy. In A. G. Bus, & S. B. Neuman (eds.), *Multimedia and literacy development: Improving achievement for young learners* (pp. 153–67). New York: Routledge.

Bushnell, C., Kemp, N., & Martin, F. H. (2012). Text-messaging practices and links to general spelling skill: A study of Australian children. *Australian Journal of Educational & Development Psychology, 11*: 27–38.

Caine, R. N., & Caine, G. (1990). Understanding a brain-based approach to learning and teaching. *Educational Leadership, 48*: 66–70.

Camacho, L., & Spackman, A. (2011). Transitioning to e-books: Usage and attitudes among business faculty. *Journal of Business & Finance Librarianship, 16*: 33–45.

Carrier, L. M., Cheever, N. A., Rosen, L. D., Benitez, S., & Chang, J. (2009). Multitasking across generations: Multitasking choices and difficulty ratings in three generations of Americans. *Computers in Human Behavior, 25*: 483–9.

Cavendish, S., Underwood, J. D. M., Lawson, T., & Dowling, S. (1997). When and why do pupils learn from ILS? In J. Underwood and J. Brown (eds.), *Integrated learning systems in UK schools* (pp. 40–53). London: Heinemann.

Chakroff, J. L., & Nathanson, A. I. (2008). Parent and school interventions: Mediation and media literacy. In S. L. Calvert & B. J. Wilson (eds.), *The handbook of children, media, and development,* (pp. 552–76).Oxford: Blackwell.

Chandra, V., & Lloyd, M. (2008). The methodological nettle: ICT and student achievement. *British Journal of Educational Technology, 39*: 1087–98.

Chatfield, T. (2013). Viewpoint: Why do tech neologisms make people angry? *BBC Magazine,* 2 Apr. 2013. Retrieved from http://www.bbc.co.uk/news/magazine-21956748

Chen, S. H. A., & Bernard-Opitz, V. (1993). Comparison of personal and computer-assisted instruction for children with autism. *Mental Retardation, 31*: 368–76.

Chera, P., & Wood, C. (2003). Animated multimedia 'talking books' can promote phonological awareness in children beginning to read. *Learning and Instruction, 13*: 33–52.

Child Exploitation and Online Protection Centre (CEOP) (2012). *Threat assessment of child sexual exploitation and abuse 2012*. London: Child Exploitation and Online Protection Centre. Retrieved from http://ceop.police.uk/Documents/ceopdocs/CEOPThreatA_2012_190612_web.pdf

Chiong, C., Ree, J., and Takeuchi, L. (2012). *Print books vs. E-books*. Report for Joan Ganz Cooney Center. Retrieved from http://www.joanganzcooneycenter.org/publication/quickreport-print-books-vs-e-books/

Chou, H-T. G., & Edge, N. (2012). They are happier and having better lives than I am: The impact of using Facebook on perceptions of others' lives. *Cyberpsychology, Behavior and Social Networking, 15*: 1–5.

Ciampa, K. (2012). Reading in the digital age: Using electronic books as a teaching tool for beginning readers. *Canadian Journal of Learning and Technology, 28*(2): 1–26.

Ciarrochi, J., Chan, A., Caputi, P., & Roberts, R. (2001). Measuring emotional intelligence (EI). In J. V. Ciarrochi, J. P. Forgas, & J. D. Mayer (eds.), *Emotional intelligence in everyday life* (pp. 25–44). Philadelphia: Psychology Press.

Cingel, D. P., & Sundar, S. (2012). Texting, techspeak, and tweens: The relationship between text messaging and English grammar skills. *New Media & Society, 14*: 1304–20.

Clark, H. H., & Brennan, S. E. (1991). Grounding in communication. *Perspectives on Socially Shared Cognition, 13*: 127–49.

Codey, R. (2011). The high cost of addiction. *RAAFsafe magazine*. Retrieved from http://www.defence.gov.au/health/health-e-checkup/Health_Tips/RAAFSafe_411_Addiction.pdf

Coleman, J. S. (1988). Social capital in the creation of human capital. *The American Journal of Sociology, 94*: 95–120.

Comaskey, E. M., Savage, R. S., & Abrami, P. (2009). A randomised efficacy study of web-based synthetic and analytic programmes among disadvantaged urban Kindergarten children. *Journal of Research in Reading, 32*: 92–108.

Connell, C., Bayliss, L., & Farmer, W. (2012). Effects of e-book readers and tablet computers on reading comprehension. *International Journal of Instructional Media, 39*: 131–40.

Connell, J. P., & Wellborn, J. G. (1991). Competence, autonomy, and relatedness: A motivational analysis of self-system processes. In M. R. Gunnar & L. A. Sroufe (eds.). *Self Processes and Development*. (pp. 43–77). Hillsdale, NJ: Erlbaum.

Connolly, T. C., Boyle, E. A., Hainey, T., MacArthur, E., & Boyle, J. M. E. (2012). A systematic literature review of empirical evidence on computer games and serious games. *Computers & Education, 59*: 661–86.

Contarello, A., & Sarrica, M. (2007). ICTs, social thinking and subjective well-being. The Internet and its representation in everyday life. *Computers in Human Behavior, 23*: 1016–32.

Coren, A. (2011). Turning a blind eye: Faculty who ignore student cheating. *Journal of Academic Ethics, 9*: 291–305.

Côté, S., DeCelles, K. A., McCarthy, J. M., Van Kleef, G. A., & Hideg, I. (2011). The Jekyll and Hyde of emotional intelligence: Emotion-regulation knowledge facilitates both prosocial and interpersonally deviant behavior. *Psychological Science, 22*: 1073–80.

Crabtree, J., & Roberts, S. (2003). *Fat pipes, connected people-rethinking broadband Britain*. London: iSOCIETY.

Crook, C. (2008). *Web 2.0 technologies for learning: The current landscape – opportunities, challenges and tensions.* Coventry: BECTA.

Crystal, D. (2006). *Language and the Internet.* Cambridge: CUP.

Crystal, D. (2008). *Txtng: the gr8 db8.* Oxford: OUP.

Crystal, D. (2012). *Spell it out: The story of English spelling.* London: Profile.

Csikszentmihalyi, M. (1990). *Flow: The psychology of optimal experience.* New York: Harper & Row.

Csikszentmihalyi, M. (2002). *Flow: The classic work on how to achieve happiness.* London: Rider.

Csikszentmihalyi, M., & Csikszentmihalyi, I. (1975). *Beyond boredom and anxiety: The experience of play in work and games.* San Francisco: Jossey-Bass.

Cuban, L. (2001). *Oversold and underused: computers in the classroom.* Harvard: HUP.

Cuban, L., Kirkpatrick, H., & Peck, C. (2001). High access and low use of technologies in high school classrooms: Explaining an apparent paradox. *American Educational Research Journal, 38*: 813–34.

Davies, C., & Good, J. (2009). *Harnessing technology: the learner and their context: choosing to use technology: How learners construct their learning lives in their own contexts: key findings from the first year of research.* Coventry: BECTA.

Davies, H., & O'Sullivan, O. (2002). Literacy and ICT in the primary classroom: The role of the teacher. In A. Loveless & B. Dore (eds.), *ICT in the primary school* (pp. 106–7). Buckingham: Open University Press.

Davies, J. (2012). Facework on Facebook as a new literacy practice. *Computers & Education, 5*: 19–29.

Davies, J., & Merchant, G. (2009). *Web 2.0 for schools: Learning and social participation.* New York: Peter Lang.

Day, D., & Lloyd, M. M. (2007). Affordances of online technologies: More than the properties of the technology. *Australian Educational Computing, 22*: 17–21.

Deci, E. L., & Ryan, R. M. (2000). The "what" and "why" of goal pursuits: Human needs and the self-determination of behavior. *Psychological Inquiry, 11*: 227–68.

Deed, C., & Edwards, A. (2011). Unrestricted student blogging: implications for active learning in a virtual text-based environment. *Active Learning in Higher Education, 12*: 11–21.

Dehue, F., Bolman, C., & Völlink, T. (2008). Cyberbullying: Youngsters' experiences and parental perception. *Cyber Psychology & Behavior, 11*: 217–23.

Dehue, F., Bolman, C., Völlink, T., & Pouwelse, M. (2012). Cyberbullying and traditional bullying in relation with adolescents' perception of parenting. *Journal of CyberTherapy & Rehabilitation, 5*: 25–34.

Denham, S. A. (2007). Dealing with feelings: How children negotiate the worlds of emotions and social relationships. *Cognition, Brain & Behavior, 11*: 1–48.

Denti, L., Barbopuolos, I., Nilsson, I., Holmberg, L., Thulin, M., Wendeblad, M, & Davidsson, E. (2012). Sweden's largest Facebook study. Retrieved from https://gupea.ub.gu.se/bitstream/2077/28893/1/gupea_2077_28893_1.pdf

DePaoli, J., Brunell, A. B., Staats, S., & Hupp, J. (Jan. 2010). *Why narcissists don't deserve our admiration: A study of narcissism and integrity in a college sample.* Poster session presented at the annual meeting of the Society for Personality and Social Psychology, Las Vegas.

Deters, F. G., & Mehl, M. R. (2013). Does posting Facebook status updates increase or decrease loneliness: An online social networking experiment. *Social Psychological and Personality Science, 4*: 579–86.

Dey, R., Jelveh, Z., & Ross, K. W. (2012). Facebook users have become much more private: A large-scale study, *4th IEEE International Workshop on Security and Social Networking (SESOC)*. Lugano, Switzerland.

Diamond, M. C. (2001). Response of the brain to enrichment. *New Horizons for Learning*. Received from http://www.newhorizons.org/neuro/diamond_brain_response.html

Dickey, M. D. (2005). Engaging by design: How engagement strategies in popular computer and video games can inform instructional design. *Educational Technology Research and Development, 53*: 67–83.

Diekhoff, G. M., LaBeff, E. E., Shinohara, K., & Yasukava, H. (1999). College cheating in Japan and the United States. *Research in Higher Education, 40*: 343–53.

Diener, E., & Seligman, M. E. P. (2002). Very happy people. *Psychological Science, 13*: 80–83.

Dillon, G., & Underwood, J. (2012). Computer mediated imaginative storytelling in children with autism: Capturing the imagination of the autistic mind. *Human Computer Studies, 70*: 169–78.

Doige, N. (2007). *The brain that changes itself: Stories of personal triumph from the frontiers of brain science*. New York: Penguin.

Dooley, J. J., Pyżalski, J., & Cross, D. (2009). Cyberbullying versus face-to-face bullying. *Journal of Psychology, 217*: 182–8.

Drave, W. (2000). *Teaching online*. River Falls, WI: LERN Books.

Drew, B., & Waters, J. (1986). Video games: Utilization of a novel strategy to improve perceptual motor skills and cognitive functioning in the non-institutionalized elderly. *Cognitive Rehabilitation, 4*: 26–31.

Driscoll, D. (2002). The ubercool morphology of internet gamers: A linguistic analysis. *Undergraduate Research Journal for the Human Sciences*. Retrieved from http://www.kon.org/urc/driscoll.html

Drouin, M. A. (2011). College students' text messaging, use of textese and literacy skills. *Journal of Computer Assisted Learning, 27*: 67–75.

Drouin, M. A., & Davis, C. (2009). R u txting? Is the use of text speak hurting your literacy? *Journal of Literacy Research, 41*: 46–47.

Dunlap, J. C., & Lowenthal, P. R. (2009). Tweeting the night away: Using Twitter to enhance social presence. *Journal of Information Systems Education, 20*: 129–35.

Durkin, K., Conti-Ramsden, G., & Walker, A. J. (2010). Computer-mediated communication in adolescents with and without a history of specific language impairment (SLI). *Computers in Human Behaviour, 26*: 176–85.

Durkin, K., Conti-Ramsden, G., & Walker, A. J. (2011). Txt lang: texting, textism use and literacy abilities in adolescents with and without specific language impairment. *Journal of Computer-Assisted Learning, 27*: 49–57.

Dye, M. W., & Bavelier, D. (2010). Differential development of visual attention skills in school-age children. *Vision Research, 50*: 452–9.

Dye, M. W., Green, C. S., & Bavelier, D. (2009). The development of attention skills in action video game players. *Neuropsychologia, 47*: 1780–9.

Egenfeldt-Nielsen, S. (2006). Overview of research on the educational use of video games. *Digital Kompetanse, 3*: 184–213.

Egenfeldt-Nielsen, S., Smith, J. H., & Tosca, S. P. (2008). *Understanding video games: The essential introduction*. London: Routledge.

Eisenhart, M. (2005). Hammers and saws for the improvement of educational research. *Educational Theory, 55*: 245–61.

Elliott, C., Livengood, K., & McGlamery, M. (2012) iPads and struggling readers. *Society for Information Technology & Teacher Education International Conference*. Location, Mar. 2012. Place of publication, Publisher, pp. 4079–83. Austin, TX.

Ellison, N. B., Steinfield, C., & Lampe, C. (2007). The benefits of Facebook "friends": Social capital and college students' use of online social network sites. *Journal of Computer-Mediated Communication, 12*: 1143–68.

Entwistle, N. (2000). Promoting deep learning through teaching and assessment: conceptual frameworks and educational contexts. *TLRP Conference, Leicester*. Retrieved from http://www.tlrp.org/pub/acadpub/Entwistle2000.pdf

Ericsson, A. K., Charness, N., Feltovich, P., & Hoffman, R. R. (2006). *Cambridge handbook on expertise and expert performance*. Cambridge: CUP.

Ericsson, K. A., & Smith, J. (1991). *Toward a general theory of expertise*: prospects and limits. Cambridge: CUP.

Etter, S., Cramer, J. J., & Finn, S. (2006). Origins of academic dishonesty: Ethical orientations and personality factors associated with attitudes about cheating with information technology. *Journal of Research in Technology in Education, 39*: 133–55.

Facer, K., Furlong, J., Furlong, R., & Sutherland, R. (2003). *Screenplay: children and computing in the home*. London: RoutledgeFalmer.

Falloon, G. (2013). Young students using iPads: App design and content influences on their learning pathways. *Computers & Education, 68*: 505–21.

Feng, J., Lazar, J., Kumin, L., & Ozok, A. (2010). Computer usage by children with Down syndrome: Challenges and future research. *ACM Transactions on Accessible Computing, 2*: 13.

Ferguson C. J., & Olson C. (2013). Video game violence among 'vulnerable' populations: The impact of violent games on delinquency and bullying among children with clinically elevated depression or attention deficit symptoms. *Journal of Youth and Adolescence*. doi 10.1007/s10964-013-9986-5

Fernández-Berrocal, P., & Extremera, N. (2008). A review of trait meta-mood research. *International Journal of Psychology Research, 2*: 39–67.

Ferragina, E. (2012). *Social capital in Europe: A comparative regional analysis*. Cheltenham: Edward Elgar.

Festl, R., Sharkow, M., & Quandt, T. (2012). Problematic computer game use among adolescents, younger and older adults. *Addiction, 108*: 593–9.

Fidler, R. F. (1997). *Mediamorphosis: Understanding new media*. Thousand Oaks, CA: Sage.

Fisch, S. M. (2000). A capacity model of children's comprehension of educational content on television. *Media Psychology, 2*: 63–91.

Fisher, M., & Baird, D. E. (2005). Online learning design that fosters student support, self-regulation, and retention. *Campus-Wide Information Systems, 22*: 88–107.

Flint, A., Clegg, S., & Macdonald, R. (2006). Exploring staff perceptions of student plagiarism. *Journal of Further and Higher Education, 30*: 145–56.

Flores, M., Musgrove, K., Renner, S., Hinton, V., Strozier, S., Franklin, S., & Hil, D. (2012). A comparison of communication using the Apple iPad and a picture-based system. *Augmentative and Alternative Communication, 28*: 74–84.

Foehr, U. G. (2006). *Media multitasking among American youth: Prevalence, predictors and pairings*. Kaiser Family Foundation Report. Menlo Park, CA: Kaiser Family Foundation.

Foerde, K., Knowlton, B. J., & Poldrack, R. A. (2006). Modulation of competing memory systems by distraction. *Proceedings National Academy of Science, 103*: 11,778–83.

Fong, G. (2006). Adapting COTS games for military experimentation. *Simulation & Gaming, 37*: 452–65.

Fontana, L. (1997). Online learning communities. In P. H. Martorella (ed.), *Interactive technologies and the social studies: emerging issues and applications* (pp. 1–26). Albany: New York Press.

Fox, A. B., Rosen, J., & Crawford, M. (2009). Distractions, distractions: Does instant messaging affect college students' performance on a concurrent comprehension task? *Cyberpsychology & Behavior, 12*: 51–53.

Fredericks, J. A., Blumenfeld, P. C., & Paris, A. H. (2004). School engagement: Potential of the concept, state of the evidence. *Review of Educational Research, 74*: 59–109.

Freitas, de S., & Liarokapis, F. (2011). Serious games: A new paradigm for education? In Ma. Minhua, A. Oikonomou & L. C. Jain (eds.), *Serious games and edutainment applications* (pp. 9–23). London: Springer

Freitas, de S., & Oliver, M. (2006). How can exploratory learning with games and simulations within the curriculum be most effectively evaluated? *Computers & Education, 46*: 249–64.

Friere, P. (1994). *Pedagogy of hope* reliving "Pedagogy of the oppressed". New York: Continuum.

Fromkin, V., Rodaman, R., & Hyams, N. (2013). *An introduction to language* (10th edn.). Boston: Wadsworth.

Fuchs, D., Fuchs, L. S., Thompson, A., Sveson, E., Yen, Y., Al Otaiba, S., … Saenz, L. (2001). Peer-assisted learning strategies in reading. *Remedial and Special Education, 22*: 15–21.

Fuchs, T., & Woessmann, L. (2005). Computers and student learning: Bivariate and multivariate evidence on the availability and use of computers at home and at school. Ifo Working Paper No. 8, Ifo Institute for Economic Research at the University of Munich.

Gardner, H. (1993). *Multiple intelligences: The theory in practice*. New York: HarperCollins.

Garris, R., Ahlers, R., & Driskell, J. E. (2002). Games, motivation, and learning: A research and practice model. *Simulation and Gaming, 33*: 441–67.

Garrison, D. R., & Anderson, T. (2003). *E-learning in the 21st century*. London: RoutledgeFalmer.

Gee, J. (2003). *What video games have to teach us about learning and literacy*. New York: Palgrave Macmillan.

Gehlen-Baum, V., & Weinberger, A. (2012). Notebook or Facebook? How students actually use mobile devices in large lectures. *Lecture Notes in Computer Science, 7563*: 103–12.

Gehring, D., & Pavela, G. (1994). *Issues and perspectives on academic integrity*. Washington: National Association of Student Personnel Administrators.

Gentile, D. A., & Gentile, J. R. (2008). Violent video games as exemplary teachers: A conceptual analysis. *Journal of Youth and Adolescence, 37*: 127–41.

Gentile, D. A., Nathanson, A. I., Rasmussen, E. E., Reimer, R. A., & Walsh, D. A. (2012). Do you see what I see? Comparing parent and child reports of parental monitoring of children's media. *Family Relations, 61*: 470–87.

Gerdeman, R. D. (2000). Academic dishonesty and the community college. Los Angeles: ERIC Digest ED447840.

Gillen, J. (2002). Moves in the territory of literacy? The telephone discourse of three- and four-year-olds. *Journal of Early Childhood Literacy, 2*: 21–43.

Gilster, P. (1997). *Digital literacy.* New York: Wiley.

Goodwyn, A. (2013a). Machines to think with? E-books, Kindles and English Teachers, the much prophesied death of the book revisited. *Changing English, 20*: 148–59.

Goodwyn, A. (2013b). Reading is now "cool": A study of English teachers' perspectives on e-reading devices as a challenge and an opportunity. *Educational Review.* doi: 10.1080/00131911.2013.768960.

Goswami, U. (2006). Neuroscience and education: From research to practice? *Nature Reviews Neuroscience, 7*: 406–13.

Granovetter, M. S. (1973). The strength of weak ties. *American Journal of Sociology, 78*: 1360–80.

Gray, D. E., Ryan, M., & Coulon, A. (2004). The training of teachers and trainers: Practices, skills and competences in the use of eLearning. *European Journal of Open, Distance and E-learning, 2004/II.*

Green, C. S., & Bevalier, D. (2003). Action video games modify visual selective attention. *Nature, 423*: 534–7.

Green, C. S., & Bavelier, D. (2006). Enumeration versus multiple object tracking: The Case of action video game players. *Cognition, 101*: 217–45.

Green, C. S., & Bavelier, D. (2007). Action video game experience alters the spatial resolution of attention. *Psychological Science, 18*: 88–94.

Green, H., & Hannon, C. (2007). *Their space: education for a digital generation.* London: Demos.

Greenberg, A. L., Tomaino, M. A. E., & Charlop, M. H. (2012). Assessing generalization of the picture exchange communication system in children with autism. *Journal of Developmental and Physical Disabilities, 24*: 539–58.

Greenfield, P. M. (2009). Technology and informal education: What is taught, what is learned. *Science, 323*: 69–71.

Greenfield, P. M., deWinstanley, P., Kilpatrick, H., & Kaye, D. (1994). Action video games and informal education: Effects on strategies for dividing visual attention. *Journal of Applied Developmental Psychology, 15*: 105–23.

Greenfield, P. M., & Subrahmanyam, K. (2003). Online discourse in a teen chat room: New codes and modes of coherence in a visual medium. *Journal of Applied Developmental Psychology, 24*: 713–38.

Greenhow, C., & Gleason, B. (2012). Twitteracy: Tweeting as a new literacy practice. *The Educational Forum, 76*: 464–78.

Greeno, J. G. (1998). The situativity of Grossen, B., & Carnine, D. (1990). Translating research on initial reading instruction into classroom practice. *Interchange, 21*: 15–23.

Griffith, J. L., Voloschin, P., Gibb, G. D., & Bailey, J. R. (1983). Differences in eye-hand motor coordination of videogame users and non-users. *Perceptual and Motor Skills, 57*: 155–8.

Gross, R., & Aquisti, A. (2005). Information revelation and privacy in online social networks: (The Facebook case). Pre-proceedings version. *ACM Workshop on*

Privacy in the Electronic Society, pp. 71–80. Retrieved from http://www.heinz.cmu.edu/~acquisti/papers/privacy-facebook-gross-acquisti.pdf

Grosseck, G., & Holotescu, C. (2008). Can we use Twitter for educational activities? *4th International Scientific Conference, eLearning and software for education*. Bucharest, 17–18 Apr. 2008. Retrieved from http://www.cblt.soton.ac.uk/multimedia/PDFsMM09/Can%20we%20use%20twitter%20for%20educational%20activities.pdf

Grossen, B., & Carnine, D. (1990). 1989 Winner of CLD's award for outstanding research: diagramming a logic strategy: Effects on difficult problem types and transfer. *Learning Disability Quarterly, 168–182*.

Grüsser, S. M., Thalemann, R., & Griffiths, M. D. (2006). Excessive computer game playing: Evidence for addiction and aggression? *CyberPsychology & Behavior, 10*: 290–2.

Guan, S. S. A., & Subrahmanyam, K. (2009). Youth Internet use: Risks and opportunities. *Current Opinion in Psychiatry, 22*: 351–6.

Gulli, C., Kohler, N., & Patriquin, M. (2007). The great university cheating scandal. Retrieved from http://www.macleans.ca/general/the-great-university-cheating-scandal/

Haitiva, N. (1989). Students' conceptions and attitudes towards specific features of a CAI system. *Journal of Computer-Based Instruction, 19*: 56–63.

Hancock, V., & Betts, F. (2002). Back to the future preparing learners for academic success in 2004. *Learning and Leading with Technology, 29*: 10–13.

Hancox, B. (2005). Growing 'couch potatoes': Television, computers and childhood obesity- a response to Gard. *Children's Issues, 9*: 32–36.

Happ, C., Melzer, A., & Steffgen, G. (2013). Superman vs. BAD Man? The effects of empathy and game character in violent video games. *Cyberpsychology. Behavior and Social Networking, 16*: 774–8.

Hargrave, A. C., & Sénéchal, M. (2000). A book reading intervention with pre-school children who have limited vocabularies: The benefits of regular reading and dialogic reading. *Early Childhood Research Quarterly, 15*: 75–90.

Hargreaves, D., Beere, J., Swindells, M., Wise, D., Desforges, C., Goswami, U., ... Lownsbrough, H. (2005, April). About learning: Report of the learning-working group. Demos. Retrieved from http://www.demos.co.uk/files/About_learning.pdf?1240939425

Harper, H., Helmer, J., Lea, T., Chalkiti, K., Emmett, S., & Wolgemuth, J. (2012). ABRACADABRA for magic under which conditions? Case studies of a web-based literacy intervention in the Northern Territory. *The Australian Journal of Language and Literacy, 35*: 33–50.

Hart, M., & Friesner, T. (2004). *Plagiarism and poor academic practice – A threat to the extension of e-learning in higher education?* Retrieved from http://www.apfei.edu.au/resources/bibliography/plagiarism-and-poor-academic-practice-threat-extension-e-learning-higher-educ

Hasebrink, U., Görzig, A., Haddon, L., Kalmus, V., & Livingstone, S. (2011). Patterns of risk and safety online. In-depth analyses from the EU Kids Online survey of 9–16 year olds and their parents in 25 countries, 2009–11. Retrieved from http://www.lse.ac.uk/media@lse/research/EUKidsOnline/EU%20Kids%20II%20%282009-11%29/EUKidsOnlineIIReports/D5%20Patterns%20of%20risk.pdf

Hativa, N. (1989). Students' conceptions of and attitudes towards specific features of a CAI system. *Journal of Computer-Based Instruction, 16*: 81–89.

Hay, I., & Fielding-Barnsley, R. (2007). Facilitating children's emergent literacy using shared reading: A comparison of two models. *Australian Journal of Language and Literacy, 30*: 191–202.

Hayward, B., Alty, C., Pearson, S., & Martin, C. (2003). *Young people and ICT 2002: findings from a survey conducted in autumn 2002*. London: Department for Education and Skills.

Healy, A. (2000). Visual literacy: Reading and the contemporary text environment. In R. Campbell & D. Green (eds.), *Literacies and learners: Current perspectives* (pp. 155–72). Hazelbrook, NSW: Prentice Hall.

Hecker, L., Burns, L., Elkind, J., Elkind, K., & Katz, L. (2002). Benefits of assistive reading software for students with attention disorders. *Annals of Dyslexia, 52*: 244–72.

Helsper, E. J., & Eynon, R. (2010). Digital natives: where is the evidence? *British Educational Research Journal, 36*: 503–20.

Hendershott, A., Drina, P., & Cross, M. (2000). Towards enhancing a culture of academic integrity. *NASPA Journal, 37*: 587–97.

Henning, M. A., Ram, S., Malpas, P., Shulruf, B., Kelly, F., & Hawken, S. J. (2013). Academic dishonesty and ethical reasoning: Pharmacy and medical school students in New Zealand. *Medical Teacher, 35*: e1211–17.

Hew, K. F. (2011). Students' and teachers' use of Facebook. *Computers in Human Behavior, 27*: 662–76.

Hibbing, A. N., & Rankin-Erikson, J. (2003). A picture is worth a thousand words: Using visual imagery to improve comprehension for middle school struggling readers. *The Reading Teacher, 56*: 758–70.

Higgins, E. T. (1987). Self-discrepancy: A theory relating self and affect. *Psychological Review, 94*: 319–40.

Hinman, L. M. (2002). Academic integrity and the World Wide Web. *ACM SIGCAS Computers and Society, 32*: 33–42.

Holmes, W. (2011). Using game-based learning to support struggling readers at home. *Learning, Media and Technology, 36*: 5–19.

Honey, P., & Mumford, A. (2000). *The learning styles helper's guide*. Maidenhead: Peter Honey.

Huffaker, D. (2005). The educated blogger: Using weblogs to promote literacy in the classroom. *AACE Journal, 13*: 91–8.

Hughes, J. M. C., & McCabe, D. L. (2006). Understanding academic misconduct. *Canadian Journal of Higher Education, 36*: 49–63.

Hunter, A. G. (2012). Text comparison software for students: an educational development tool or quick 'text checker' – examining student use and perceptions of value. Retrieved from http://archive.plagiarismadvice.org/documents/conference2012/finalpapers/Hunter_fullpaper.pdf

Hutchison, A., Beschorner, B., & Schmidt-Crawford, D. (2012). Exploring the use of the iPad for literacy learning. *The Reading Teacher, 66*: 15–23.

Hutchison, A., & Reinking, D. (2011). Teachers' perceptions of integrating information and communication technologies into literacy instruction: A national survey in the US. *Reading Research Quarterly, 46*: 308–29.

Inal, Y., & Cagiltay, K. (2007). Flow experiences of children in an interactive social game environment. *British Journal of Educational Technology, 38*: 455–64.

James, W. (1890). *The principles of psychology*. London: Macmillan.

Jenkins, H. (2006). *Convergence culture*. New York: NYU Press.

Jenkinson, J. (2009). Measuring the effectiveness of educational technology: What are we attempting to measure? *Electronic Journal of e-Learning, 7*: 273–80.

Jensen, L. A., Arnett, J. J., & Feldman, S. S. (2002). It's wrong, but everybody does it: Academic dishonesty among high school and college students. *Contemporary Educational Psychology, 27*: 209–28.

Jernigan, C., & Mistree, B. F. T. (2009). Gaydar: Facebook friendships expose sexual orientation. *First Monday, 14*: 10. Retrieved from http://firstmonday.org/ojs/index.php/fm/article/view/2611/2302

Johnson, D., Jones, C., & Burns, J. (2013). Beyond the beat-em-up: Video games are good for young people. *The Conversation* (Australia). Retrieved from http://theconversation.com/beyond-the-beat-em-up-video-games-are-good-for-young-people-16231

Johnson, G. M. (2012). Comprehension of standard English text and digital textism during childhood. *The Internet Journal of Language, Culture & Society, 35*: 1–6.

Johnson, L., Levine, A., & Smith, R. (2009). *Horizon Report: 2009 K-12 Edition*. Austin, TX: New Media Consortium.

Johnson, S. (2005). *Everything bad is good for you: How popular culture is making us smarter*. London: Allen Lane.

Johnson, W. L. (2007). Serious use of a serious game for language learning. *Frontiers in Artificial Intelligence and Applications, 158*: 67.

Jonassen, D. (1992). Objectivism versus constructivism: Do we need a new philosophical paradigm? *Education Technology Research and Development, 39*: 5–14.

Jonassen, D. H., Howland, J., Moore, J., & Marra, R. M. (2003). *Learning to solve problems with technology: A constructivist perspective* (2nd edn.). Upper Saddle River, NJ: Merrill.

de Jong, M. T., & Bus, A. G. (2002). Quality of book-reading matters for emergent readers: An experiment with the same book in a regular or electronic format. *Journal of Educational Psychology, 94*: 145–55.

de Jong, M. T., & Verhallen, M. J. (2013). Video storybooks: A way to empower children at risk. In A. Samir & O. Korat (eds.), *Technology as a support for literacy achievements for children at risk* (pp. 33–45). Dordtrecht, Netherlands: Springer Science and Business Media.

Jones, C., Ramanau, R., Cross, S., & Healing, G. (2010). Net generation or digital natives: Is there a distinct new generation entering university? *Computers & Education, 54*: 722–32.

Jones, D. L. (2011). Academic dishonesty: Are more students cheating? *Business Communication Quarterly, 74*: 141.

Josephson Institute of Ethics (2012). The ethics of American youth: 2012. Retrieved from http://charactercounts.org/programs/reportcard/2012/index.html

Jump, P. (2013). A plague of plagiarism at the heart of politics. *Times Higher Education Supplement*, 16 May, pp. 1–3.

Junco, R., & Cotten, S. R. (2011). Perceived academic effects of instant messaging use. *Computers & Education, 56*: 370–8.

Kagohara, D. M., van der Meer, L., Ramdoss, S., O'Reilly, M. F., Lancioni, G. E., Davis, T. N., & Sigafoos, J. (2013). Using iPods and iPads in teaching programs for individuals with developmental disabilities: A systematic review. *Research in Developmental Disabilities, 34*: 147–56.

Kappas, A. (2011). Emotion and regulation are one! *Emotion Review, 3*: 17–25.

Karemaker, A. M., Pitchford, N. J., & O'Malley, C. (2010a). Does whole-word multimedia software support literacy acquisition? *Reading and Writing, 23*: 31–51.

Karemaker, A., Pitchford, N. J., & O'Malley, C. (2010b). Enhanced recognition of written words and enjoyment of reading in struggling beginner readers through whole-word multimedia software. *Computers & Education, 54*: 199–208.

Katz, J., & Aspden, P. (1997). A nation of strangers? *Communications of the ACM, 40*: 81–86.

Katzer, C., Fetchenhauer, D., & Belschak, F. (2009). Cyberbullying: Who are the victims? A comparison of victimization in internet chatrooms and victimization in school. *Journal of Media Psychology, 21*: 25–36.

Keller, J., Bless, H., Blomann, F., & Kleinböhl, D. (2011). Physiological aspects of flow experiences: Skills-demand-compatibility effects on heart rate variability and salivary cortisol. *Journal of Experimental Social Psychology, 47*: 849–52.

Kester, L., Kirschner, P. A., & van Merriënboer, J. J. (2005). The management of cognitive load during complex cognitive skill acquisition by means of computer-simulated problem solving. *British Journal of Educational Psychology, 75*: 71–85.

Kiili, K. (2005). Digital-game based learning: Toward an experiential gaming model. *Internet and Higher Education, 8*: 13–24.

Kiili, K. (2007). Foundation for problem-based gaming. *British Journal of Educational Technology, 38*: 394–404.

King-Sears, M. E., Swanson, C., & Mainzer, L. (2011). Technology and literacy for adolescents with disabilities. *Journal of Adolescent & Adult Literacy, 54*: 569–78.

Kirschner, F., Pass, F., & Kirschner, P. A. (2009). A cognitive load approach to collaborative learning: United brains for complex tasks. *Educational Psychology Review, 21*: 31–42.

Kirschner, P. A., & Karpinski, A. C. (2010). *Facebook®* and academic performance. *Computers in Human Behavior, 26*: 1237–45.

Kirschner, P. A., Sweller, J., & Clark, R. E. (2006). Why minimal guidance during instruction does not work: An analysis of the failure of constructivist, discovery, problem-based, experiential, and inquiry-based teaching. *Educational Psychologist, 46*: 75–86.

Kirschner, P. A., & van Merriënboer, J. J. (2013). Do learners really know best? Urban legends in education. *Educational Psychologist, 48*: 169–83.

Klimmt, C., Hartmann, T., & Frey, A. (2007). Effectance and control as determinants of video game enjoyment. *CyberPsychology & Behavior, 10*: 845–8.

Klopfer, E., & Osterweil, S. (2011). Are games all child's play? In S. de Freitas & P. Maharg (eds.), *Digital Games and Learning* (pp. 153–71). London: Continuum.

Knox, C., & Anderson-Inman, L. (2001). Migrant ESL high school students succeed using networked laptops. *Learning and Leading with Technology, 28*(5): 18–22.

Koirala, H. P., & Goodwin, P. M. (2000). Teaching algebra in the middle grades using mathmagic. *Mathematics Teaching in the Middle School, 5*: 562–6.

Kolb, A., & Kolb, D. A. (2012). Kolb's learning styles. In N. M. Seel (ed.) *Encyclopedia of the Sciences of Learning* (pp. 1698–703). New York: Springer.

Korat, O. (2010). Reading electronic books as a support for vocabulary, story comprehension and word reading in kindergarten and first grade. *Computers & Education, 55*(1): 24–31.

Korat, O., Segal-Drori, O., & Klien, P. (2009). Electronic and printed books with and without adult support as sustaining emergent literacy. *Journal of Educational Computing Research, 41*: 453–75.

Korat, O., & Shamir, A. (2007). Electronic books versus adult readers: Effects on children's emergent literacy as a function of social class. *Journal of Computer Assisted Learning, 23*: 248–59.

Korat, O., & Shamir, A. (2008). The educational electronic book as a tool for supporting children's emergent literacy in low versus middle SES groups. *Computers & Education, 50*: 110–24.

Korat, O., & Shamir, A. (2012). Direct and indirect teaching: Using e-books for supporting vocabulary, word reading, and story comprehension for young children. *Journal of Educational Computing Research, 46*: 135–52.

Korat, O., Shamir, A., & Arbiv, L. (2011). E-books as support for emergent writing with and without adult assistance. *Education and Information Technologies, 16*: 301–18.

Kozma, B., & Russell, J. (1997). Multimedia and understanding: Expert and novice responses to different representations of chemical phenomena. *Journal of Research in Science Teaching, 34*: 949–68.

Kraus, J. (2002). Rethinking plagiarism: What our students are telling us when they cheat. *Issues in Writing, 13*: 80–95.

Krause, M. B. (2013). "A series of unfortunate events" the repercussions of print-literacy as the only literacy for talented boys. *Gifted Child Today, 36*: 236–45.

Kraushaar, J. M., & Novak, D. C. (2010). Examining the effects of student multitasking with laptops during the lecture. *Journal of Information Systems Education, 21*: 241–51.

Kraut, R., Kiesler, S., Boneva, B., Cummings, J., Helgeson, V., & Crawford, A. (2002). Internet paradox revisited. *Journal of Social Issues, 58*: 49–74.

Kress, G. (1997). *Before writing: Rethinking the paths to literacy.* London: Routledge.

Kress, G. (2003). *Literacy in the new media age.* London: Routledge.

Kress, G. (2010). *Multimodality.* London: Routledge.

Kucirkova, N. (2013). Children interacting with books on iPads: Research chapters still to be written. *Frontiers in Psychology, 4*: 995.

Kucirkova, N., Messer, D., Sheehy, K., & Fernández Panadero, C. (2014). Children's engagement with educational iPad apps: Insights from a Spanish classroom. *Computers & Education, 71*: 175–84.

Kucirkova, N., Messer, D., Sheehy, K., & Flewitt, R. (2013). Sharing personalised stories on iPads: A close look at one parent–child interaction. *Literacy, 47*(3): 115–22.

Kucirkova, N., Messer, D., & Whitelock, D. (2010). Sharing personalised books: A practical solution to the challenges posed by home book reading interventions. *Literacy Information & Computer Education Journal, 1*: 263–72.

Kucirkova, N., Messer, D., & Whitelock, D. (2012). Parents reading with their toddlers: The role of personalisation in book engagement. *Journal of Early Childhood Literacy, 13*(4): 445–70.

Kukulska-Hulme, A., & Shield, L. (2008). An overview of mobile assisted language learning: From content delivery to supported collaboration and interaction. *ReCALL, 20*: 271–89.

Labbo, L. D., & Kuhn, M. R. (2000). Weaving chains of affect and cognition: A young child's understanding of CD-ROM talking books. *Journal of Literacy Research*, 32: 187–210.

Labbo, L. D., & Reinking, D. (1999). Negotiating the multiple realities of technology in literacy research and instruction. *Reading Research Quarterly*, 34: 478–93.

Lajoie, S. P., & Derry, S. J. (2013). *Computers as cognitive tools*. London: Routledge.

Langdon, P., & Thimbleby, H. (2010). Inclusion and interaction: Designing interaction for inclusive populations. *Interacting with Computers*, 22: 439–48.

Lanham, R. A. (1995). Digital literacy. *Scientific American*, 273: 198–9.

Lankshear, C., & Knobel, M. (2003). New technologies in early childhood literacy research: A review of research. *Journal of Early Childhood Literacy*, 3: 59–82.

Lankshear, C., & Knobel, M. (2006). *New literacies: Changing knowledge in the classroom*. New York: McGraw-Hill International.

Lankshear, C., Knobel, M., & Curran, C. (2013). Conceptualizing and researching "new literacies.". *The Encyclopedia of Applied Linguistics*. Chichester: Wiley.

Larkin, J. H., & Simon, H. A. (1987). Why a diagram is (sometimes) worth ten thousand words. *Cognitive Science*, 11: 65–99.

Larson, R. W. (2000). Toward a psychology of positive youth development. *American Psychologist*, 55(1): 170.

Larson, R. W., Hansen, D. M., & Moneta, G. (2006). Differing profiles of developmental experiences across types of organized youth activities. *Developmental Psychology*, 42: 849.

Lea, M. R., & Jones, S. (2011). Digital literacies in higher education: exploring textual and technological practice. *Studies in Higher Education*, 36: 377–93.

Lee, J., Lin, L., & Robertson, T. (2012). The impact of media multitasking on learning. *Learning, Media & Technology*, 37: 94–104.

Lee, O., & Shin, M. (2004). Addictive consumption of avatars in cyberspace. *Cyberpsychology, Behavior and Social Networking*, 7: 417–20.

Lee, S-J., & Chae, Y-G. (2007). Children's Internet use in a family context: Influence on family relationships and parental mediation. *CyberPsychology and Behavior*, 10: 640–4.

Leenaars, F. A., van Joolingen, W. R., & Bollen, L. (2013). Using self-made drawings to support modelling in science education. *British Journal of Educational Technology*, 44: 82–94.

Lenhart, A., Arafeh, S., Smith, A., & Macgill, A. R. (2008). *Writing, technology and teens*. Washington: Pew Internet and American Life Project.

Lenhart, A., Kahne, J., Middaugh, E., Macgill, A. R., Evans, C., & Vitak, J. (2008). Teens, video games and civics: *Teens' gaming experiences are diverse and include significant social interaction and civic engagement*. Washington: Pew Internet and American Life Project.

Lereya, S. T., Samara, M., & Wolke, D. (2013). Parenting behavior and the risk of becoming a victim and a bully/victim: A meta-analysis study. *Child Abuse & Neglect*, 37(12): 1091–108.

Lerna, A., Esposito, D., Conson, M., Russo, L., & Massagli, A. (2012). Social–communicative effects of the Picture Exchange Communication System (PECS) in autism spectrum disorders. *International Journal of Language & Communication Disorders*, 47: 609–17.

Lewin, C. (2000). Exploring the effects of talking book software in UK primary classrooms. *Journal of Research in Reading, 23*: 149–57.

Lewin, C., Mavers, D., & Somekh, B. (2003). Broadening access to the curriculum through using technology to link home and school: A critical analysis of reforms intended to improve students' educational attainment. *Curriculum Journal, 14*: 23–53.

Lewis, C., & Fabos, B. (2005). Instant messaging, literacies and social identities. *Reading Research Quarterly, 40*: 470–501.

Liberman, M. (2012). Texting and language skills. *Language Log*, 2 Aug. 2012. @ 5:12. Retrieved from http://languagelog.ldc.upenn.edu/nll/?p=4099

Ling, R., & Baron, N. S. (2007). Text messaging and IM linguistic comparison of American college data. *Journal of Language & Social Psychology, 26*: 291–8.

Lippincott, J. (2005). Net generation students and libraries. In D. Oblinger & J. Oblinger (eds.), *Educating the net generation* (Ch. 13). Retrieved from www.educause.edu/educatingthenetgen/

Littleton, K., Wood, C., & Chera, P. (2004). Reading together: Computers and collaboration. In K. Littleton, D. Miell, & D. Faulkner (eds.), *Learning to collaborate: Collaborating to learn* (pp. 31–47). New York: Nova.

Littleton, K., Wood, C., & Chera, P. (2006). Interactions with talking books: phonological awareness affects boys' use of talking books. *Journal of Computer Assisted Learning, 22*: 382–90.

Livingstone, S. (2008). Taking risky opportunities in youthful content creation: Teenagers' use of social networking sites for intimacy, privacy and self-expression. *New Media & Society, 10*: 393–411.

Livingstone, S., & Haddon, L. (2009). *EU Kids Online: Final Report.* LSE, London: EU Kids Online. (EC Safer Internet Plus Programme Deliverable D6.5). Retrieved from http://www.lse.ac.uk/media@lse/research/EUKidsOnline/Home.aspx

Livingstone, S., & Helsper, E. (2008). Parental mediation of children's Internet use. *Journal of Broadcasting & Electronic Media, 52*: 581–99.

Loewenstein, G. F., Weber, E. U., Hsee, C. K., & Welch, N. (2001). Risk as feelings. *Psychological Bulletin, 127*: 267–86.

Lu, M. (2008). Effectiveness of vocabulary learning via mobile phone. *Journal of Computer Assisted Learning, 24*: 515–25.

Lui, K. F. H., & Wong, A. C. N. (2012). Does media multitasking always hurt? A positive correlation between multitasking and multisensory integration. *Psychonomic Bulletin & Review, 19*: 647–53.

Lunzer, E. A., & Gardner, K. (1979). *The effective use of reading.* London, Heinemann.

Lynch, L., Fawcett, A. J., & Nicolson, R. I. (2000). Computer-assisted reading intervention in a secondary school: An evaluation study. *British Journal of Educational Technology, 31*: 333–48.

Madden, M., & Lenhart, A. (2013). What teens said about social media, privacy, and online identity. *Pew Research Center*, 21 May 2013. Retrieved from http://www.pewinternet.org/Commentary/2013/May/Focus-group-highlights.aspx

Maddux, C. D., & Cummings, R. (2004). Fad, fashion and the weak role of theory and research in information technology in education. *Journal of Technology and Teacher Education, 12*: 511–33.

Madell, D., & Muncer, S. (2004). Gender differences in the use of the Internet by English secondary school children. *Social Psychology of Education, 7*: 229–51.

Maehr, M. L., & Meyer, H. A. (1997). Understanding motivation and schooling: Where we've been, where we are, and where we need to go. *Educational Psychology Review, 9*: 371–408.

Malone, T. W., & Lepper, M. (1987). Intrinsic motivation and instructional effectiveness in computer-based education. In R. E. Snow & M. J. Farr (eds.), *Aptitude learning and instruction* (pp. 223–53). Hillsdale, NJ: Erlbaum.

Manago, A. M., Taylor, T., & Greenfield, P. M. (2012). Me and my 400 friends: The anatomy of college students' Facebook networks, their communication patterns, and well-being. *Developmental Psychology, 48*: 369–80.

Margaryan, A., Littlejohn, A., & Vojt, G. (2011). Are digital natives a myth or reality? University students' use of digital technologies. *Computers and Education, 56*: 429–40.

Margolin, S. J., Driscoll, C., Toland, M. J., & Kegler, J. L. (2013). E-readers, computer screens, or paper: does reading comprehension change across media platforms? *Applied Cognitive Psychology, 27*: 512–19.

Marsh, J. (2004). The techno-literacy practices of young children. *Journal of Early Childhood Research, 2*: 51–66.

Marvin, C. (1988). *When old technologies were new. Thinking about electronic communications in the late nineteenth century.* New York: OUP.

Mason, L., Tornatora, M. C., & Pluchino, P. (2013). Do fourth graders integrate text and picture in processing and learning from an illustrated science text? Evidence from eye-movement patterns. *Computers & Education, 60*: 95–109.

Matthews, D. (2013). Essay mills: University course work to order. *Times Higher Educational Supplement*, 10 Oct. 2013. Retrieved from http://www.timeshigher-education.co.uk/features/essay-mills-university-course-work-to-order/2007934. fullarticle

Mayer, R. E. (1983). *Thinking, problem solving, cognition.* New York: Freeman.

Mayer, R. E. (2003). The promise of multimedia learning: using the same instructional design methods across different media. *Learning and Instruction, 13*: 125–39.

Mayer, R. E. (2005). *The Cambridge handbook of multimedia learning.* Cambridge: CUP.

Mayer, R. E., & Anderson, R. B. (1991). Animations need narrations: An experimental test of a dual-coding hypothesis. *Journal of Educational Psychology, 83*: 484–90.

Mayer, R. E., & Moreno, R. (1998). A split-attention effect in multimedia learning: Evidence for dual processing systems in working memory. *Journal of Educational Psychology, 90*: 312–20.

Mayer, R. E., & Moreno, R. (2002). Animation as an aid to multimedia learning. *Educational Psychology Review, 14*: 87–99.

Mayer, R. E., & Moreno, R. (2003). Nine ways to reduce cognitive load in multimedia learning. *Educational Psychologist, 38*: 43–52.

McCabe, D. L. (2005). The Center for Academic Integrity Assessment Project Surveys. June 2005. Retrieved from http://www.academicintegrity.org/cai_research.asp

McCabe, D. L., & Trevino, L. K. (1997). Individual and contextual influences on academic dishonesty: A multi-campus investigation. *Research in Higher Education, 38*: 379–96.

McCabe, D. L., Treviño, L. K., & Butterfield, K. D. (2001). Cheating in academic institutions: A decade of research. *Ethics and Behavior, 11*: 219–32.

McCarroll, N., & Curran, K. (2013). Social networking in education. *International Journal of Innovation in the Digital Economy, 4*: 1–15.

McClanahan, B., & Stojke, A. (2013). Mobile devices for struggling readers in the classroom. *Literacy Research, Practice and Evaluation, 3*: 143–64.

McClanahan, B., Williams, K., Kennedy, E., & Tate, S. (2012). A breakthrough for Josh: How use of an iPad facilitated reading improvement. *TechTrends, 56*: 20–28.

McFarlane, A., Sparrowhawk, A., & Heald, Y. (2002). *Report on the educational use of games.* Cambridge: TEEM.

McFarlane, C. (2013). iPads and their potential to revolutionize learning. In *World Conference on Educational Multimedia, Hypermedia and Telecommunications,* 24–28 June 2013, Victoria, Canada. 2013 (1): 1690–95.

McKenna, K., & Bargh, J. (1998). Coming out in the age of the Internet: Identity "demarginalization" through virtual group participation. *Journal of Personality & Social Psychology, 75*: 681–94.

McKenna, K., & Bargh, J. (2000). Plan 9 from cyberspace: The implications of the Internet for personality and social psychology. *Personality and Social Psychology Review, 4*: 57–75.

McKenna, M. C., Labbo, L. D., Reinking, D., & Zucker, T. A. (2003). Effective use of technology in literacy instruction. *Best Practices in Literacy Instruction, 2*: 307–31.

McKenna, M. C., Reinking, D., Labbo, L. D., & Kieffer, R. (1999). The electronic transformation of literacy and its implications for the struggling reader. *Reading & Writing Quarterly, 15*: 111–26.

McLoughlin, C., & Lee, M. J. (2007). Social software and participatory learning: Pedagogical choices with technology affordances in the Web 2.0 era. In *ICT: Providing choices for learners and learning. Proceedings ascilite Singapore* Dec. 2007, pp. 664–75.

Mehl, M. R., Vazire, S., Holleran, S. E., & Clark, C. S. (2010). Eavesdropping on happiness: Well-being is related to having less small talk and more substantive conversations. *Psychological Science, 21*: 539–41.

Menon. M. K., & Sharland, A. (2011). Narcissism, exploitative attitudes, and academic dishonesty: An exploratory investigation of reality versus myth. *Journal of Education for Business, 86*: 50–55.

Merchant, G. (2001). Teenagers in cyberspace: An investigation of language use and language change in internet chatrooms. *Journal of Research in Reading, 24*: 293–306.

Merchant, G. (2005). Digikids: Cool dudes and the new writing. *E-learning and Digital Media, 2*: 50–60.

Merchant, G. (2007). Writing the future in the digital age. *Literacy, 41*: 118–28.

Merrill, M. D. (1992). Constructivism and instructional design. In T. Duffy & D. Jonassen (eds.), *Constructivism and the technology of instruction: A conversation* (pp. 99–114). Hillsdale, NJ: Erlbaum.

Mesch, G. S. (2003). The family and the Internet: The Israeli case. *Social Science Quarterly, 84*: 1038–50.

Mesch, G. S. (2009). Social context and communication channel choice among adolescents. *Computers in Human Behaviour, 25*: 244–51.

Meyer, B. J. F., Wijekumar, K. K., & Lin, Y. (2011). Individualizing a web-based structure strategy intervention for fifth graders comprehension of nonfiction. *Journal of Educational Psychology, 103*: 140–68.

Meyer, B. J. F., Wijekumar, K., Middlemiss, W., Higley, K. Lei, P-W., Meier, C., & Spielvogel, J. (2010). Web-based tutoring of the structure strategy with or without elaborated feedback or choice for fifth- and seventh-grade readers. *Reading Research Quarterly, 45*: 62–92.

Meyer, D. E., Kieras, D. E., Lauber, E., Schumacher, E., Glass, J., Zurbriggen, E., ... Apfelblat, D. (1995). Adaptive executive control: Flexible multiple-task performance without pervasive immutable response-selection bottlenecks. *Acta Psychologica, 90*: 163–90.

Montag, C., Kirsch, P., Sauer, C., Markett, S., & Reuter, M. (2012). The role of the CHRNA4 gene in Internet addiction – A case-control study. *Journal of Addiction Medicine, 6*(3): 191–5. doi: 10.1097/ADM.0b013e31825ba7e7.

Moody, E. J. (2001). Internet use and its relationship to loneliness. *CyberPsychology & Behavior, 4*: 393–401.

Moon, J. (1999) How to ... stop students from cheating. *The Times Higher Education Supplement*, 3 Sept. 1999. Retrieved from http://www.timeshighereducation.co.uk/news/how-tostop-students-from-cheating/147580.article

Moore, M., & Calvert, S. (2000). Brief report: Vocabulary acquisition for children with autism: Teacher or computer instruction. *Journal of Autism and Developmental Disorders, 30*: 359–62.

Morgan, H. (2013). Multimodal children's E-books help young learners in reading. *Early Childhood Education Journal, 41*: 477–83.

Muldner, K., Burleson, W., van de Sande, B., & VanLehn, K. (2010). An analysis of gaming behaviors in an intelligent tutoring system. In V. Aleven, J. Kay & J. Mostow (eds.), *Intelligent Tutoring Systems: 10th International Conference, ITS 2010* (pp. 184–93). Heidelberg: Springer.

Mullen, R., & Wedwick, L. (2008). Avoiding the digital abyss: Getting started in the classroom with YouTube, digital stories, and blogs. *The Clearing House: A Journal of Educational Strategies, Issues and Ideas, 82*: 66–69.

Murdock, T. B., Beauchamp, A. S., & Hinton, A. M. (2008). Predictors of cheating and cheating attributions: Does classroom context influence cheating and blame for cheating? *European Journal of Psychology of Education, 23*: 477–92.

Nagi, K., Suesawaluk, P., & U-Lan, P. V. (2008). Evaluating interactivity of eLearning resources in a learning management system (LMS) – A case study of MOODLE, An open source platform. *Fifth International Conference on eLearning for Knowledge-Based Society. Bangkok, Thailand.*

Neuman, S. B. (2009). The case for multi-media presentation in learning: A theory of synergy. In A. G. Bus & S. B. Neuman (eds.), *Multimedia and literacy development: Improving achievement for young learners* (pp. 44–56). New York: Taylor & Francis.

Neumann, M. N., & Neumann, D. L. (2013). Touch screen tablets and emergent literacy. *Early Childhood Education Journal*. Retrieved from http://link.springer.com/article/10.1007%2Fs10643-013-0608-3

Newell, A., & Simon, H. A. (1972). *Human problem solving*. Upper Saddle River, NJ: Prentice-Hall.

Nie, N. H., Hillygus, D. J., & Erbring, L. (2002). Internet use in in interpersonal relations, and sociability: a time diary study. In B. Wellman & C. Haythornthwaite (eds.), *The Internet in everyday life* (pp. 215–43). Oxford: Blackwell.

Nikken, P., & Jansz, J. (2006). Parental mediation of children's videogame playing: A comparison of the reports by parents and children. *Learning, Media and Technology, 31*: 181–202.

Nolen-Hoeksema, S., Wisco, B. E., & Lyubomisrsky, S. (2008). Rethinking rumination. *Perspectives on Psychological Science, 5*: 400–24.

Northrop, L., & Killeen, E. (2013). A framework for using iPads to build early literacy skills. *The Reading Teacher, 66*: 531–7.

Novak, J. (1990). Concept mapping: A useful tool for science education. *Journal of Research in Science Teaching, 27*: 937–49.

Nussbaum, M., Dillenbourg, P., Dimitriadis, Y., & Roschelle, J. (2013). Classroom orchestration. *Computers & Education, 69*: 485–523.

Nuutinen, T., Ray, C., & Roos, E. (2013). Do computer use, TV viewing, and the presence of the media in the bedroom predict school-aged children's sleep habits in a longitudinal study. *BMC Public Health, 13*, 684 Retrieved from http://www.biomedcentral.com/1471-2458/13/684

Ofcom (2010). *UK children's media literacy*. Retrieved from http://stakeholders.ofcom.org.uk/binaries/research/media-literacy/ukchildrensml1.pdf

Ofcom (2012). *Digital lifestyles: Young adults aged 16–24*. Retrieved from http://stakeholders.ofcom.org.uk/binaries/research/media-literacy/young_digital_lifestyles.pdf

Ofqual (2011). Mobile phone for Christmas? – "Don't take it into the exam hall" warns regulator. Retrieved from http://www2.ofqual.gov.uk/news-and-announcements/130/533

Ofsted (2009a). The importance of ICT: Information and communication technology in primary and secondary schools, 2005/2008. Retrieved from http://www.ofsted.gov.uk/resources/importance-of-ict-information-and-communication-technology-primary-and-secondary-schools-20052008

Ofsted (2009b). Virtual learning environments: An evaluation of their development in a sample of educational settings. Retrieved from http://www.ofsted.gov.uk/resources/virtual-learning-environments-evaluation-of-their-development-sample-of-educational-settings

Olsen, A. N., Kleivset, B., & Langseth, H. (2013). E-book readers in higher education: Student reading preferences and other data from surveys at the University of Agder. *SAGE Open, 3*, 2. Retrieved from http://sgo.sagepub.com/content/3/2/2158244013486493.short

Olson, K. R., & Shaw, A. (2011). "No fair, copycat!": What children's response to plagiarism tells us about their understanding of ideas. *Developmental Science, 14*: 431–9.

Oppenheimer, O. (2003). *The flickering mind: The false promise of technology in the classroom and how learning can be saved*. Retrieved from http://www.citeulike.org/group/716/article/220562

Orji, R., Mandryk, R., Vassileva, J., & Gerling, K. (2013). Control your game-self: Effects of controller type on enjoyment, motivation, and personality in game. *CHI '13: Proceedings of the 31st International Conference on Human Factors in Computing Systems, Paris*. Retrieved from http://www.academia.edu/2697291/Tailoring_Persuasive_Health_Games_to_Gamer_Type

Orlandi, M. A., & Greco, D. (2004). A randomized double-blind clinical trial of EEG neurofeedback treatment for attention-deficit. *Presented at the Annual Meeting of the International Society for Neuronal Regulation, Fort Lauderdale, FL.*

Orosz, G., Farkas, D., & Roland-Lévy, C. (2013). Are competition and extrinsic motivation reliable predictors of academic cheating? *Frontiers in Psychology, 4*: 87. doi: 10.3389/fpsyg.2013.00087.

Oshima, N., Nishida, A., Shimodera, S., Tochigi, M., Ando, S., Yamasaki, S., ... Sasali, T. (2012). The suicidal feelings, self-injury, and mobile phone use after lights out in adolescents. *Journal of Pediatric Psychology, 37*: 1023–30.

Owens, C., & White, F. A. (2013). A 5-year systematic strategy to reduce plagiarism among first-year psychology university students. *Australian Journal of Psychology, 65*: 14–21.

Paivio, A. (1986). *Mental representations: A dual coding approach.* Oxford: OUP.

Palasinski, M. (2012). Implications of urban adolescent discourses of (un) happy slapping. *Safer Communities, 11*: 159–64.

Palasinski, M. (2013). Turning assault into a "harmless prank" – teenage perspectives on happy slapping. *Journal of Interpersonal Violence, 28*: 1909–23.

Palfrey, J. G., & Gasser, U. (2008). *Born digital: understanding the first generation of digital natives.* New York: Basic Books.

Palmer, S. (2006). *Toxic childhood: How the modern world is damaging our children and what we can do about it.* London: Orion.

Panoutsopoulos, H., & Sampson, D. G. (2012). A study on exploiting commercial digital games into school context. *Educational Technology & Society, 15*: 15–27.

Paolillo, J. (1999). The virtual speech community: Social network and language variation on IRC. *Journal of Computer-Mediated Communication, 4*(4). Retrieved from http://onlinelibrary.wiley.com/doi/10.1111/j.1083-6101.1999.tb00109.x/full

Papert, S. (1980). *Mindstorms: Children, computers, and powerful ideas.* New York: Basic Books.

Paraskeva, F., Mysirlaki, S., & Papagianni, A. (2010). Multiplayer online games as educational tools: Facing new challenges in learning. *Computers & Education, 54*: 498–505.

Parish-Morris, J., Mahajan, N., Hirsh-Pasek, K., Golinkoff, R. M., & Collins, M. F. (2013). Once upon a time: Parent–child dialogue and storybook reading in the electronic era. *Mind Brain Education, 7*: 200–11. doi: 10.1111/mbe.12028.

Parsons, S., & Mitchell, P. (2002). The potential of virtual reality in social skills training for people with autistic spectrum disorders. *Journal of Intellectual Disability Research 46*: 430–43.

Pashler, H., McDaniel, M., Rohrer, D., & Bjork, R. (2008). Learning styles concepts and evidence. *Psychological Science in the Public Interest, 9*: 105–19.

Passey, D., Rogers, C., Machell, J., & McHugh G. (2003). *The motivational effect of ICT on pupils.* Research Report RR523. London: Department for Education and Skills.

Pennebaker, J. W., & Chung, C. K. (2011). Expressive writing and its links to mental and physical health. In H. S. Friedman (ed.), *Oxford handbook of health psychology* (pp. 417–37). New York: OUP.

Pfister, H. R., & Mühlpfordt, M. (2002). Supporting discourse in a synchronous learning environment: The learning protocol approach. In G. Stahl (ed.), Computer support for collaborative learning: foundations for a CSCL community. Proceedings of CSCL2002. Hillsdale: Erlbaum.

Phipps, L., Cormier, D., & Stiles, M. (2008). Reflecting on the virtual learning systems–extinction or evolution? Retrieved from http://www.seda.ac.uk/resources/files/publications_11_eddev9_2.pdf

Pierce, T. (2009). Social anxiety and technology: Face-to-face communication versus technological communication among teens. *Computers in Human Behavior, 25*: 1367–72.

Pintrich, P. R. (1999). The role of motivation in promoting and sustaining self-regulated learning. *International Journal of Educational Research, 31*: 459–70.

Pintrich, P. R. (2000). Multiple goals, multiple pathways: The role of goal orientation in learning and achievement. *Journal of Educational Psychology, 92*: 544–55.

Plester, B., & Wood, C. (2009). Exploring relationships between traditional and new media literacies: British preteen texters at school. *Journal of Computer-Mediated Communication, 14*: 1108–29.

Plester, B., Wood, C., & Bell, V. (2008). Txt msg n school literacy: does texting and knowledge of text abbreviations adversely affect children's literacy attainment? *Literacy, 42*: 137–44.

Plester, B., Wood, C., & Joshi, P. (2009). Exploring the relationship between children's knowledge of text abbreviations and school literacy outcomes. *British Journal of Developmental Psychology, 27*: 145–61.

Plowman, L., Stevenson, O., Stephen, C., & McPake, J. (2012). Preschool children's learning with technology at home. *Computers & Education, 59*: 30–37.

Prensky, M. (2001). Digital natives, digital immigrants part 1. *On the Horizon, 9*: 1–6.

Prensky, M. (2005). Listen to the natives. *Educational Leadership, 63*: 8–13.

Prensky, M. (2006). *"Don't bother me, Mom, I'm learning!": how computer and video games are preparing your kids for 21st century success and how you can help!* St. Paul, MN: Paragon House.

Priest, J., Coe, R., Evershed, B., & Bush, N. (2004). *An exploration of the use of ICT at the Millennium Primary School, Greenwich*. Retrieved from http://dera.ioe.ac.uk/1602/1/becta_2004_greenwichschool_report.pdf

Przybylski, A. K., Murayama, K., DeHaan, C. R., & Gladwell, V. (2013). Motivational, emotional, and behavioural correlates of fear of missing out. *Computers in Human Behavior, 29*: 1841–8.

Punamäki, R., Wallenius, M., Nygård, C., Saarni, L., & Rimpelä, A. (2007). Use of information and communication technology (ICT) and perceived health in adolescence: The role of sleeping habits and waking-time tiredness. *Journal of Adolescence, 30*: 569–85.

Purdy, J. P. (2005). Calling off the hounds: Technology and the visibility of plagiarism. *Pedagogy, 5*: 275–96.

Rainie, L., Smith, A., & Duggan, M. (2013). Coming and going on Facebook. *Pew Research Center's Internet and American Life Project*. Retrieved from http://www.winthropmorgan.com/wp-content/uploads/2013/03/Education-Advocacy%20Toolkit/PIP_Coming_and_going_on_facebook.pdf

Ramdoss, S., Lang, R., Mulloy, A., Franco, J., O'Reilly, M., Didden, R., & Lancioni, G. (2011). Use of computer-based interventions to teach communication skills to children with autism spectrum disorders: A systematic review. *Journal of Behavioral Education, 20*: 55–76.

Ramos, N., Fernández-Berrocal, P., & Extremera, N. (2007). Perceived emotional intelligence facilitates cognitive-emotional processes of adaptation to an acute stressor. *Cognition & Emotion, 21*: 758–72.

Razfar, A., & Yang, E. (2010). Digital, hybrid, & multilingual literacies in early childhood. *Language Arts, 88*: 114–24.

Reichle, J. (2011). Evaluating assistive technology in the education of persons with severe disabilities. *Journal of Behavioral Education, 20*(1): 77–85.

Reid, G. (2011). *Dyslexia. A complete guide for parents and those who help them* (2nd edn.). Oxford: Wiley-Blackwell.

Reid, G., Strnadová, I., & Cumming, T. (2013). Expanding horizons for students with dyslexia in the 21st century: universal design and mobile technology. *Journal of Research in Special Educational Needs, 13*: 175–81.

Reinders, H., Thomas, M., & Warschauer, M. (eds.). (2012). *Contemporary computer-assisted language learning*. London: Bloomsbury.

Reinking, D. (2005). Multimedia learning of reading. In R. Mayer (ed.) *The Cambridge Handbook of Multimedia Learning* (pp. 355–76). Cambridge: CUP.

Reinking, D., Labbo, L., & McKenna, M. (2000). From assimilation to accommodation: a developmental framework for integrating digital technologies into literacy research and instruction. *Journal of Research in Reading, 23*(2): 110–22.

Reitsma, P. (1988). Reading practice for beginners: Effects of guided reading, reading-while-listening, and independent reading with computer-based speech feedback. *Reading Research Quarterly, 23*: 219–35.

Resnick, P. (2001). Beyond bowling together: Socio-technical capital. In J. Carroll (ed.). *HCI in the new millennium* (pp. 647–72). New York: Addison-Wesley.

Revelle, R., Reardon, E., Green, M. M., Betancourt, J., & Kotler, J. (2007). The use of mobile phones to support children's literacy learning. In Y. deKort et al. (eds). *Lecture Notes in Computer Science, 4744*: 253–8.

Ricci, C. M., & Beal, C. R. (2002). The effect of interactive media on children's story memory. *Journal of Educational Psychology, 94*(1): 138–44.

Richards, R., McGee, R., Williams, S. M., Welch, D., & Hancox, R. J. (2010). Adolescent screen time and attachment to parents and peers. *Archives of Pediatrics and Adolescent Medicine, 164*: 258–62.

Rideout, V. J., Ulla, M. A., Foehr, G., & Roberts, D. F. (2010). *Generation M2: Media in the lives of 8- to 18-year-olds*. Menlo Park, CA: Kaiser Family Foundation.

Roberts, D. F., Foehr, U. G., & Rideout, V. (2005). *Generation M: Media in the lives of 8–18 year-olds*. Washington: Kaiser Family Foundation.

Robertson, L. A., McAnally, H. M., & Hancox, R. J. (2013). Childhood and adolescent television viewing and antisocial behavior in early adulthood. *Pediatrics, 131*(3): 439–46.

Roblyer, M. D., McDaniel, M., Webb, M., Herman, J., & Witty, V. (2010). Findings on Facebook in higher education: A comparison of college faculty and student uses and perceptions of social networking sites. *The Internet and Higher Education, 13*: 134–40.

Rockinson-Szapkiw, A. J., Courduff, J., Carter, K., & Bennett, D. (2013). Electronic versus traditional print textbooks: A comparison study on the influence of university students' learning. *Computers & Education, 63*: 259–66.

Romanelli, F., Cain, J., & Sith, K. M. (2006). Emotional intelligence as a predictor of academic and/or professional success. *American Journal of Pharmaceutical Education, 70*(3): 69.

Rosen, L. D. (2007). *Me, MySpace, and I: parenting the net generation.* New York: Palgrave Macmillan.

Rosen, L. D., Carrier, L. M., & Cheever, N. A. (2013). Facebook and texting made me do it: Media-induced task-switching while studying. *Computers in Human Behavior, 29*: 948–58.

Rosen, L. D., Chang, J., Erwin, L., Carrier, L. M., & Cheever, N. A. (2010). The relationship between "textisms" and formal and informal writing among young adults. *Communication Research, 37*: 420–40.

Rosenstock, I. M. (1974). The health belief model and preventive health behavior. *Health Education & Behavior, 2*: 354–86.

Rubinstein, J. S., Meyer, D. E., & Evans, J. E. (2001). Executive control of cognitive processes in task switching. *Journal of Experimental Psychology: Human Perception and Performance, 27*: 763–97.

Russoniello, C. V., Fish, M., & O'Brien, K. (2013). The efficacy of casual videogame play in reducing clinical depression: A randomized controlled study. *Games for Health, 2*: 341–6.

Ryan, T., & Xenos, S. (2009). Who uses Facebook? An investigation into the relationship between the big five, shyness, narcissism, loneliness, and Facebook usage. *Computers in Human Behaviour, 27*: 1658–64.

Salary.com (2012). Why & how your employees are wasting time at work. Retrieved from http://business.salary.com/why-how-your-employees-are-wasting-time-at-work/

Salmon, G. (2005). Flying not flapping: A strategic framework for e-learning and pedagogical innovation in higher education institutions. *ALT-J: Research in Learning Technology, 13*: 201–18.

Salomon, G., & Perkins, D. N. (1989). Rocky roads to transfer: Rethinking mechanism of a neglected phenomenon. *Educational Psychologist, 24*: 113–42.

Salomon, G., Perkins, D. N., & Globerson, T. (1991). Partners in cognition: Extending human intelligence with intelligent technologies. *Educational Researcher, 20*: 2–9.

Salovey, P., & Mayer, J. (1990). Emotional intelligence. *Imagination, Cognition and Personality, 9*: 185–211.

Samara, M., & Smith, P. K. (2008). How schools tackle bullying, and the use of whole school policies: Changes over the last decade. *Educational Psychology, 28*: 663–76.

Sanbonmatsu, D. M., Strayer, D. L., Medeiros-Ward, N., & Watson, J. M. (2013). Who multi-tasks and why? Multi-tasking ability, perceived multi-tasking ability, impulsivity, and sensation seeking. *PloS One, 8*: e54402.

Sandford, R., Uiksak, M., Facer, K., & Rudd, T. (2006). *Teaching with games: Using commercial off-the-shelf computer games in formal education.* Bristol: Nesta Futurelab.

Sandford, R., & Williamson, B. (2006). *Games and learning: A handbook from Futurelab.* Bristol: Futurelab.

Savage, R. S., Abrami, P., Hipps, G., & Deault, L. (2009). A randomized controlled trial study of the ABRACADABRA reading intervention program in grade 1. *Journal of Educational Psychology, 101*: 590.

Savage, R., Abrami, P., Piquette, N., Wood, E., Deleveaux, G., Sanghera-Sidhu, S., & Burgos, G. (2013). A (Pan-Canadian) cluster randomized control effectiveness trial of the ABRACADABRA web-based literacy program. *Journal of Educational Psychology, 105*: 310–28.

Schiano, D. J., Chen, C. P., Isaacs, E., Ginsberg, J., Gretarsdottir, U., & Huddleston, M. (2002). Teen use of messaging media. *Proceedings of the ACM CHI 2002: Computer-Human Interaction (CHI'02)*. Minneapolis, MN, pp. 594–5.

Schmidt, M. E., & Vandewater, E. A. (2008). Media and attention, cognition and school achievement. *The Future of Children, 18*: 63–85.

Schnabel, J. (2009). Media research: The black box. *Nature, 459*: 765–8.

Schneps, M., Thomson, J., Chen, C., Sonnert, G., & Pomplun, M. (2013). E-readers are more effective than paper for some with dyslexia. *PloS one, 8*(9): e75,634.

Schneps, M., Thomson, J., Sonnert, G., Pomplun, M., Chen, C., & Heffner-Wong, A. (2013). E-readers configured for short lines facilitate reading in those who struggle. *Journal of Vision, 13*: 789–9.

Schreibman, L., & Stahmer, A. C. (2013). A randomized trial comparison of the effects of verbal and pictorial naturalistic communication strategies on spoken language for young children with autism. *Journal of Autism and Developmental Disorders, 44*(5): 1244–51.

Schroeder, S., Richter, T., McElvany, N., Hachfeld, A., Baumert, J., Schnotz, W., ... Ulrich, M. (2011). Teachers' beliefs, instructional behaviors, and students' engagement in learning from texts with instructional pictures. *Learning and Instruction, 21*: 403–15.

Schüler, J. (2012). The dark side of the moon. In Stefan Engeser (ed.), *Advances in flow research* (pp. 123–37). New York: Springer.

Sclater, N. (2010). eLearning in the Cloud. *International Journal of Virtual and Personal Learning Environments, 1*: 10–19.

Segal-Drori, O., Korat, O., Shamir, A., & Klein, P. S. (2010). Reading electronic and printed books with and without adult instruction: Effects on emergent reading. *Reading and Writing, 23*: 913–30.

Segers, E., Nooijen, M., & de Moor, J. (2006). Computer vocabulary training in kindergarten children with special needs. *International Journal of Rehabilitation Research, 29*: 343–5.

Segers, E., & Verhoeven, L. (2002). Multimedia support of early literacy learning. *Computers & Education, 39*: 207–21.

Segers, E., & Verhoeven, L. (2004). Computer-supported phonological awareness intervention for kindergarten children with specific language impairment. *Language, Speech, and Hearing Services in Schools, 35*: 229.

Seifert, T. A., Pascarella, E. T., Goodman, K. M., Salisbury, M. H., & Blaich, C. F. (2010). Liberal arts colleges and good practices in undergraduate education: Additional evidence. *Journal of College Student Development, 51*: 1–22.

Selwyn, N. (2006). Exploring the "digital disconnect" between net-savvy students and their schools. *Learning, Media and Technology, 31*: 5–17.

Selwyn, N. (2008). Not necessarily a bad thing: A study of online plagiarism amongst undergraduate students. *Assessment & Evaluation in Higher Education, 33*: 465–79.

Selwyn, N. (2009a). Challenging educational expectations of the social web: A web 2.0 far? *Nordic Journal of Digital Literacy, 4*: 72–82.

Selwyn, N. (2009b). Faceworking: Exploring students' education-related use of Facebook. *Learning, Media & Technology, 34*: 157–74.

Selwyn, N. (2011). *Education and technology: Key issues and debates.* London: Continuum.

Şendag, S., Duran, M., & Fraser, R. (2012). Surveying the extent of involvement in online academic dishonesty (e-dishonesty) related practices among university students and the rationale students provide: One university's experience. *Computers in Human Behavior, 28*: 849–60.

Shaffer, D. W. (2006). Epistemic frames for epistemic games. *Computers & Education, 46*: 223–34.

Shamir, A., Korat, O., & Fellah, R. (2013). Promoting emergent literacy of children at risk for learning disabilities: Do E-books make a difference? In Adina Shamir & Ofra Korat (eds.), *Technology as a Support for Literacy Achievements for Children at Risk* (pp. 173–85). Dordrecht: Springer.

Shamir, A., & Shlafer, I. (2011). E-books effectiveness in promoting phonological awareness and concept about print: A comparison between children at risk for learning disabilities and typically developing kindergarteners. *Computers & Education, 57*: 1989–97.

Sharp, J. G., Bowker, R., & Byrne, J. (2008). VAK or VAK-uous? Towards the trivialisation of learning and the death of scholarship. *Research Papers in Education, 23*: 293–314.

Sharples, M. (2010). Web2.0 technologies for learning at key stages 3 and 4. Learning Sciences Research Institute. Retrieved from http://dera.ioe.ac.uk/1474/1/becta_2008_web2_currentlandscape_litrev.pdf

Sharples, M., Graber, R., Harrison, C., & Logan, K. (2009). E-safety and Web 2.0 for children aged 11–16. *Journal of Computer Assisted Learning, 25*(1): 70–84.

Sharples, M., Taylor, J., & Vavoula, G. (2005). Towards a theory of mobile learning. *Proceedings of mLearn 2005*(1): 1–9.

Shaw, R., Grayson, A., & Lewis, V. (2005). Inhibition, ADHD, and computer games: The inhibitory performance of children with ADHD on computerized tasks and games. *Journal of Attention Disorders, 8*: 160–8.

Shea, V. (1994). *Netiquette.* San Francisco: Albion Books.

Shin, N., Sutherland, L. M., Norris, C. A., & Soloway, E. (2012). Effects of game technology on elementary student learning in mathematics. *British Journal of Educational Technology, 43*: 540–60.

Shuler, C., Levine, Z., & Ree, J. (2012). *iLearn II: An analysis of the education category of Apple's app store.* New York: Joan Ganz Cooney Center at Sesame Workshop. Retrieved from http://joanganzcooneycenter.org/upload_kits/ilearnii.pdf

Shulman, T., & Hemenover, S. (2006). Is dispositional emotional intelligence synonymous with personality? *Self and Identity, 5*: 147–71.

Shute, V., & Ventura, M. (2013). *Stealth assessment measuring and supporting learning in video games. The John D. and Catherine T. MacArthur Foundation Reports on Digital Media and Learning.* Cambridge, MA: MIT Press.

Sia, C. L., Tan, B. C., & Wei, K. K. (2002). Group polarization and computer-mediated communication: Effects of communication cues, social presence, and anonymity. *Information Systems Research, 13*: 70–90.

Sifry, D. (2006). State of the blogosphere, February 2006 Part 1: On blogosphere growth. *Sifry's Alerts*, 6 Feb. Retrieved from http://www.sifry.com/alerts/archives/000419.html

Silverman, R., & Hines, S. (2012). Building literacy skills through multimedia. In A. M. Pinkham, T. Kaefer & S. B. Neuman (eds.), *Knowledge development in early childhood* (pp. 242–58). New York: Guilford.

Sim, R. (1997). Interactivity: A forgotten art? *Computers in Human Behavior, 13*: 157–80.

Simon, C. A., Carr, J. R., McCullough, S. M., Morgan, S. J., Oleson, T., & Ressel, M. (2003). The other side of academic dishonesty: The relationship between faculty scepticism, gender and strategies for managing student academic dishonesty. *Assessment & Evaluation in Higher Education, 28*: 194–207.

Simpson, A., Walsh, M., & Rowsell, J. (2013). The digital reading path: Researching modes and multidirectionality with iPads. *Literacy, 47*: 123–30.

Slusarek, M., Velling, S., Bunk, D., & Eggers, C. (2001). Motivational effects on inhibitory control in children with ADHD. *Journal of American Academy of Child and Adolescent Psychiatry, 40*: 355–63.

Small, G., & Vorgan. G. (2009). *iBrain: Surviving the technological alteration of the modern mind.* New York: HarperCollins.

Smith, A. (2012). The rise of the "connected viewer". Pew Research Center, 17 July 2012. Retrieved from http://pewinternet.org/Reports/2012/Connected-viewers.aspx

Smith, C. R. (2002). Click on me! An example of how a toddler used technology in play. *Journal of Early Childhood Literacy, 2*: 5–20.

Smith, S. D., & Caruso, J. B. (2010). The ECAR study of undergraduate students and information technology, 2010 (Research Study, Vol. 6). Boulder, CO: EDUCAUSE Center for Applied Research. Retrieved from http://www.educause.edu/ers1006

Smith, S. M., & Woody, P. C. (2000). Interactive effect of multimedia instruction and learning styles. *Teaching of Psychology, 27*: 220–3.

Somekh, B., Lewin, C., & Mavers, D. (2002). *Using ICT to enhance home school links: An evaluation of current practice in England.* Nottingham: Department for Education and Science.

Somekh, B., & Underwood, J. (2007). *Evaluation of the ICT Test Bed project: final report.* Coventry: BECTA.

Southwell, B. G., & Doyle, K. O. (2004). The good, the bad, or the ugly? A multi-level perspective on electronic game effects. *American Behavioral Scientist, 48*: 391–401.

Squire, K. (2003). Video games in education. *International Journal of Intelligent Simulations and Gaming, 2*: 49–62.

Squire, K. (2005). Changing the game: What happens when video games enter the classroom. *Innovate: Journal of Online Education, 1.* Retrieved from http://website.education.wisc.edu/kdsquire/tenure-files/manuscripts/26-innovate.pdf

Staksrud, E., & Livingstone, S. (2009). Children and online risk: powerless victims or resourceful participants? *Information, Communication and Society, 12*: 364–87.

Standen, P. J., & Brown, D. J. (2005). The use of virtual reality in the rehabilitation of people with intellectual disabilities, *Cyberpsychology & Behaviour, 8*: 272–82.

Statistic Brain (2012). Social networking statistics. Retrieved from http://www.statisticbrain.com/social-networking-statistics/

Staude-Müller, F., Hansen, B., & Voss, M. (2012). How stressful is online victimization? Effects of victim's personality and properties of the incident. *European Journal of Developmental Psychology, 9*: 260–74.

Stenning, K., & Oberlander, J. (1995). A cognitive theory of graphical and linguistic reasoning: Logic and implementation. *Cognitive Science, 19*: 97–140.

Stevens, J. M., Young, M. F., & Calabrese, T. (2007). Does moral judgment go offline when students are online? A comparative analysis of undergraduates' beliefs and behaviors related to conventional and digital cheating. *Ethics and Behavior, 17*: 233–54.

Straw, D. (2002). The plagiarism of generation "why not?" *Community College Week, 14*: 4–7.

Sugarman, D. B., & Willoughby, T. (2013). Technology and violence: conceptual issues raised by the rapidly changing social environment. *Psychology of Violence, 3*: 1–8.

Superby, J. F., Vandamme, J. P., & Meskens, N. (2006). Determination of factors influencing the achievement of the first-year university students using data mining methods. *Workshop on Educational Data Mining* (pp. 37–44).

Sutherland, R., Armstrong, V., Barnes, S., Brawn, R., Breeze, N., Gall, M., ... John, P. (2004). Transforming teaching and learning: Embedding ICT into everyday classroom practices. *Journal of Computer Assisted Learning, 20*: 413–25.

Sutherland-Smith, W. (2003). Hiding in the shadows: Risks and dilemmas of plagiarism in student academic writing, in conference papers, abstracts and symposia. *Australian Association for Research in Education, Coldstream, Vic.*, 1–18.

Suthers, D. D., & Hundhausen, C. D. (2003). An experimental study of the effects of representational guidance on collaborative learning processes. *The Journal of the Learning Sciences, 12*: 183–218.

Suwa, M., & Tversky, B. (2001). Constructive perception in design. In J. S. Gero & M. L. Maher (eds.), *Computational and cognitive models of creative design V.* (pp. 227–39). Sydney: Key Centre of Design Computing and Cognition, University of Sydney.

Sweetser, P., & Wyeth, P. (2005). GameFlow: A model for evaluating player enjoyment in games. *Computers in Entertainment (CIE), 3*(3): 3.

Sweller, J. (1988). Cognitive load during problem solving: Effects on learning. *Cognitive Science, 12*: 257–85.

Tagliamonte, S. A., & Denis, D. (2008). Linguistic ruin? LOL: Instant messaging and teen language. *American Speech, 83*: 3–34.

Tamir, M. (2011). The maturing field of emotion regulation. *Emotion Review, 3*: 3–7.

Telner, J. A., Wiesenthal, D. L., Bialystok, E., & York, M. (2008). Benefits of bilingualism and video game proficiency when driving and speaking on a cellular telephone. *Presented at International Conference on Traffic and Transport Psychology. Washington.*

Thomas, K., Grier, C., & Nicol, D. M. (2010). Unfriendly: Multi-party privacy risks in social networks. *Lecture Notes in Computer Science, 6205*: 236–52.

Thurlow, C. (2003). *Generation txt? The sociolinguistics of young people's text-messaging.* Retrieved from http://extra.shu.ac.uk/daol/articles/v1/n1/a3/thurlow2002003.html

Thurlow, C. (2006). From statistical panic to moral panic: The metadiscursive construction and popular exaggeration of new media language in the print media. *Journal of Computer-Mediated Communication, 11*: 667–701.

Tindell, D. R., & Bohlander, R. W. (2012). The use and abuse of cell phones and text messaging in the classroom: A survey of college students. *College Teaching, 60*: 1–9.

Tong, S. T., Van Der Heide, B., Langwell, L., & Walther, J. B. (2008). Too much of a good thing? The relationship between number of friends and interpersonal impressions on Facebook. *Journal of Computer-Mediated Communication, 13*: 531–49.

Topping, K., & Whiteley, M. (1993). Sex differences in the effectiveness of peer tutoring. *School Psychology International, 14*: 57–67.

Torgesen, J. K., Wagner, R. K., Rashotte, C. A., Herron, J., & Lindamood, P. (2010). Computer-assisted instruction to prevent early reading difficulties in students at risk for dyslexia: Outcomes from two instructional approaches. *Annals of Dyslexia, 60*: 40–56.

Trepte, S., & Reinecke, L. (2013). The reciprocal effects of social network site use and the disposition for self-disclosure: A longitudinal study. *Computers in Human Behavior, 29*: 1102–12.

Tversky, B. (2001). Spatial schemas in depictions. In M. Gattis (ed.), *Spatial schemas and abstract thought* (pp. 79–111). Cambridge, MA: MIT Press.

Tynes, B. M. (2007). Internet safety gone wild? Sacrificing the educational and psychosocial benefits of online social environments. *Journal of Adolescent Research, 22*: 575–84.

Umarji, R. (2005). Text-a-friend: the high-tech approach to cheating. Silver Chips online. Retrieved from http://silverchips.mbhs.edu/

Underwood, G., & Everatt, J. (1996). Automatic and controlled information processing: The role of attention in the processing of novelty. In O. Neumann & A. F. Sanders (eds.), *Handbook of Perception and Action. Attention* (Vol. 3, pp. 185–227). London: Academic Press

Underwood, G., & Underwood, J. D. M. (1998). Children's interactions and learning outcomes with interactive talking books. *Computers & Education, 30*: 95–102.

Underwood, J. D. M. (2000). A comparison of two types of computer support for reading development. *Journal of Research in Reading, 23*: 136–48.

Underwood, J. D. M. (2003). Student attitudes towards socially acceptable and unacceptable group working practices. *British Journal of Psychology, 94*: 319–37.

Underwood, J. D. M. (2006). *Digital technologies and dishonesty in examinations and tests*. London: QCA.

Underwood, J. D. M. (2007). Rethinking the digital divide. *European Journal of Education, 42*: 213–22.

Underwood, J. D. M. (2009). *The impact of digital technology: A review of the evidence of the impact of digital technologies on formal education*. Coventry: BECTA.

Underwood, J. D. M., Ault, A., Banyard, P., Bird, K. Dillon, G., Hayes, M., ... Twining, P. (2005). *The impact of broadband in school*. Coventry: BECTA

Underwood, J. D. M., Ault, A., Baguley, T., Banyard, P., Coyne, E., Farrington-Flint, L., & Selwood, I. (2006). *Impact 2007: Phase one*. Coventry: BECTA.

Underwood, J. D. M., Baguley, T., Banyard, P., Coyne, E., Farrington-Flint, L., & Selwood, I. (2007). *Impact 2007: Personalising learning with technology*. Coventry: BECTA.

Underwood, J. D. M., Baguley, T., Banyard, P., Dillon, G., Farrington-Flint, L., Hayes, M., ... Selwood, I. (2008). *Personalising learning*. Coventry: BECTA.

Underwood, J. D. M., Ault, A., Baguley, T., Dillon, G., Farrington-Flint, L., Hayes, M., & Selwood, I. (2010). *Understanding the impact of technology: Learner and school level factors*. Coventry: BECTA.

Underwood, J. D. M., Baguely, T., Banyard, P., Dillon, G., Farrington-Flint, L., Hayes, & Wright, M. (2009). *Personalising learning*. Coventry: BECTA

Underwood, J. D. M., & Banyard, P. (2008). Managers', teachers' and learners' perceptions of personalised learning: Evidence from Impact 2007. *Technology, Pedagogy and Education, 17*: 233–46.

Underwood, J. D. M., & Dillon, G. (2004). Maturity modelling: A framework for capturing the effects of technology. *Technology, Pedagogy and Education, 13*: 213–24.

Underwood, J. D. M., & Dillon, G. (2011). Chasing dreams and recognising realities: teachers' responses to ICT. *Technology, Pedagogy and Education, 20*: 343–56.

Underwood, J. D. M., Dillon, G., & Twining, P. (2007). *Test bed baseline questionnaire: Summary of findings year 4 2006*. Coventry: BECTA.

Underwood, J. D. M., Kerlin, L., & Farrington-Flint (2011). The lies we tell and what they say about use: Using behavioural characteristics to explain Facebook activity. *Computers in Human Behavior, 27*: 1621–6.

Underwood, J. D. M., & Okubayashi, T. (2011). Comparing the characteristics of text-speak used by English and Japanese students. *International Journal of Cyber Behavior, Psychology and Learning, 1*: 45–57.

Underwood, J. D. M., & Stiller, J. (2013). Does knowing lead to doing in the case of learning platforms? *Teachers and Teaching*. doi: 10.1080/13540602.2013.848569.

Underwood, J. D. M., & Szabo, A. (2004). Academic offences and e-learning: Individual propensities in cheating. *British Journal of Educational Technology, 34*: 467–78.

Underwood, J. D. M., & Underwood, G. (1990). *Computers and learning: Helping children acquire thinking skills*. Oxford: Blackwell.

Valkenburg, P. M., & Peter, J. (2009). The effects of instant messaging on the quality of adolescents' existing friendships: A longitudinal study. *Journal of Communication, 59*: 79–97.

Vancouver, J. B. (2000). Self-regulation in organizational settings: A tale of two paradigms. In M. Boekaerts, P. R. Pintrich, & M. Zeidner (eds.), *Handbook of self-regulation*. (pp. 303–41). San Diego: Academic Press.

Vandoninck, S., d'Haenens, L., & Smahel, D. (2014). *Preventive measures: How youngsters avoid online risks*. London: EU Kids Online.

Vannini, N., Enz, S., Sapouna, M., Wolke, D., Watson, S., Woods, S., & Schneider, W. (2011). "FearNot!": A computer-based anti-bullying-programme designed to foster peer intervention. *European Journal of Psychology of Education, 26*: 21–44.

Varnhagen, C., McFall, G. P., Pugh, N., Routledge, L., Sumida-McDonald, H., & Kwong, T. E. (2010), lol: new language and spelling in instant messaging. *Reading & Writing, 23*: 719–33.

Veater, H. M., Plester, B., & Wood, C. (2010). Use of text message abbreviations and literacy skills in children with dyslexia. *Dyslexia, 17*: 65–71.

Veen, W., & Vrakking, B. (2006). *Homo zappiens: Growing up in a digital age*. London, UK: Network Continuum Education.

Verenikina, I., & Kervin, L. (2011). iPads, digital play and preschoolers. *He Kupu, 2*: 4–19. Retrieved from http://www.hekupu.ac.nz/Journal%20files/Issue5%20October%202011/iPads%20Digital%20Play%20and%20Preschoolers.pdf

Verhallen, J., Bus, A. G., & de Jong, M. T. (2006). The promise of mulitmedia stories for kindergarten children at risk. *Journal of Educational Psychology, 98*: 410–19.

Vorderer, P., Klimmt, C., & Ritterfeld, U. (2004). Enjoyment: At the heart of media entertainment. *Communication Theory, 14*: 388–408.

Vosloo, S. (2009). The effects of texting on literacy: Modern scourge or opportunity? An issue paper from the Shuttleworth Foundation, Apr. 2009. Retrieved from http://www.siu-voss.net/Voslo__effects_of_texting_on_literacy.pdf

Vriend, J. L., Davidson, F. D., Corkum, P. V., Rusak, B., Chambers, C. T., & McLaughlin, E. N. (2013). Manipulating sleep duration alters emotional functioning and cognitive performance in children. *Journal of Pediatric Psychology, 38*: 1058–69.

Vygotsky, L. (1978). *Mind in society: The development of higher psychological processes*. M. Cole, V. John-Steiner, S. Scribner & E. Souberman (eds.). Harvard: HUP.

Walker, J. (2010). Measuring plagiarism: Researching what students do, not what they say they do. *Studies in Higher Education, 35*: 41–59.

Walther, J. B. (1996). Computer-mediated communication impersonal, interpersonal, and hyperpersonal interaction. *Communication Research, 23*: 3–43.

Walther, J. B. (2007). Selective self-presentation in computer-mediated communication: Hyperpersonal dimensions of technology, language, and cognition. *Computers in Human Behavior, 23*: 2538–57.

Watson, D. M. (2001). Pedagogy before technology: Re-thinking the relationship between ICT and teaching. *Education and Information Technologies, 6*: 251–66.

Watson, J. (2012). Soft teaching with silver bullets: Digital natives, learning styles, and the truth about best practices. *Proceedings of the 4th Annual Conference on Higher Education Pedagogy, Virginia Tech US* (pp. 175–6).

Weibel, D., Wissmath, B., Habegger, S., Steiner, Y., & Groner, R. (2008). Playing online games against computer- vs. human-controlled opponents: Effects on presence, flow, and enjoyment. *Computers in Human Behavior, 24*: 2274–91.

Weis, R., & Cerankosky, B. C. (2010). Effects of video-game ownership on young boys' academic and behavioral functioning: A randomized, controlled study. *Psychological Science, 21*: 463–70.

Weiser, E. B. (2001). The functions of internet use and their social and psychological consequences. *CyberPsychology & Behavior, 4*: 723–43.

Weller, M. (2010). The centralisation dilemma in educational IT. *International Journal of Virtual and Personal Learning Environments, 1*: 1–9.

Whitaker, J. L., & Bushman, B. J. (2009). Online dangers: Keeping children and adolescents safe. *Washington and Lee Law Review, 66*: 1053–63.

White, F., Owens, C., & Nguyen, M. (2012). Using a constructive feedback approach to effectively reduce student plagiarism among first-year psychology students. *Proceedings of The Australian Conference on Science and Mathematics Education*. Retrieved from http://ojs-prod.library.usyd.edu.au/index.php/IISME/article/view/6254

Whitley, B. E. (1998). Factors associated with cheating among college students: A review. *Research in Higher Education, 39*: 235–74.

Wijekumar, K. K., Meyer, B. J. F., & Lei, P. (2013). High-fidelity implementation of web-based intelligent tutoring system improves fourth and fifth graders content area reading comprehension. *Computers & Education, 68*: 366–79.

Willard, N. E. (2006). *Cyberbullying and cyberthreats: Responding to the challenge of online social cruelty, threats, and distress*. Center for Safe and Responsible Internet Use. Retrieved from http://www.accem.org/pdf/cbcteducator.pdf

Willett, R., Robinson, M., & Marsh, J. (2009). *Play, creativity and digital cultures*. London: Routledge.

Williams, K. D. (2009). Ostracism: A temporal need-threat model. *Advances in experimental social psychology, 41*: 279–314.

Williams, K. D., & Zadro, L. (2005). The social outcast: Ostracism, social exclusion, rejection, and bullying. In K. D. Williams, J. P. Forgas & W. von Hippel (eds.), *The social outcast: Ostracism, social exclusion, rejection and bullying* (pp. 19–34). New York: Psychology Press.

Williams, K. M., Nathanson, C., & Paulhus, D. L. (2010). Identifying and profiling scholastic cheaters: Their personality, cognitive ability, and motivation. *Journal of Experimental Psychology: Applied, 16*: 293.

Wise, B. W., & Olson, R. K. (1994). Computer speech and the remediation of reading and spelling problems. *Journal of Special Education Technology, 12*: 207–20.

Wise D., Olson, R., Annsett, M., Andrews, L., Terjak, M., Schneider, V., … Kriho, L. (1989). Implementing a long term computerized remedial reading program with synthetic speech feedback: hardware, software and real world issues. *Behavior Research Methods, Instruments and Computers, 21*: 173–180.

Wise, L. Z., Skues, J., & Williams, B. (2011). *Facebook in higher education promotes social but not academic engagement*. In G. Williams, P. Statham, N. Brown, & B. Cleland (eds.), *Changing Demands, Changing Directions. Proceedings ascilite Hobart* (pp.1332–42). Retrieved from http://www.ascilite.org.au/conferences/hobart11/downloads/LWise.pdf

Wolak, J., Finkelhor, D., Mitchell, K. J., & Ybarra, M. L. (2008). Online "predators" and their victims: Myths, realities, and implications for prevention and treatment. *American Psychologist, 63*: 111–28.

Wolak, J., Mitchell, K. J., & Finkelhor, D. (2007). Does online harassment constitute bullying? An exploration of online harassment by known peers and online-only contacts. *Journal of Adolescent Health, 41*: S51–8.

Wood, C. (2005). Beginning readers' use of "talking books" software can affect their reading strategies. *Journal of Research in Reading, 28*: 170–82.

Wood, C., Jackson, E., Hart, L., Plester, B., & Wilde, L. (2011). The effect of text messaging on 9- and 10-year-old children's reading, spelling and phonological processing skills. *Journal of Computer Assisted Learning, 27*: 28–36.

Wood, C., Kemp, N., & Plester, B. (2013). *Text messaging and literacy – the evidence*. London: Routledge.

Wood, C., Littleton, K., & Chera, P. (2005). Beginning readers' use of talking books: styles of working. *Literacy, 39*: 135–41.

Wood, C., Meacham, S., Bowyer, S., Jackson, E., Tarczynski-Bowles, M. L., & Plester, B. (2011). A longitudinal study of children's text messaging and literacy development. *British Journal of Psychology, 102*: 431–42.

Wood, C., Pillinger, C., & Jackson, E. (2010). Understanding the nature and impact of young readers' literacy interactions with talking books and during adult reading support. *Computers & Education, 54*: 190–8.

Wood, D., Underwood, J., & Avis, P. (1999). Integrated learning systems in the classroom. *Computers & Education, 33*: 91–108.

Yaw, J. S., Skinner, C. H., Parkhurst, J., Taylor, C. M., Booher, J., & Chambers, K. (2011). Extending research on a computer-based sight-word reading intervention to a student with autism. *Journal of Behavioral Education, 20*: 44–54.

Ybarra, M. L., Boyd, D., Korchmaros, J. D., & Oppenheim, J. K. (2012). Defining and measuring cyberbullying within the larger context of bullying victimization. *Journal of Adolescent Health, 51*: 53–8.

Yee, N., Bailenson, J. N., Urbanek, M., Chang, F., & Merget, D. (2007). The unbearable likeness of being digital: The persistence of nonverbal social norms in online virtual environments. *CyberPsychology & Behavior, 10*: 115–21.

Yoffie, D. B. (1997). *Competing in the age of digital convergence.* Boston, MA: Business School Press.

Zhang, H., Song, W., & Burston, J. (2011). Reexamining the effectiveness of vocabulary learning via mobile phones. *The Turkish Online Journal of Educational Technology, 10*: 203–14.

Zhang, J. (1997). The nature of external representations in problem solving. *Cognitive Science, 21*: 179–217.

Zhong, B., Hardin, M., & Sun, T. (2011). Less effortful thinking leads to more social networking? The associations between the use of social network sites and personality traits. *Computers in Human Behavior, 27*: 1265–71.

Zimmerman, B. J. (1989). A social-cognitive view of self-regulated academic learning. *Journal of Educational Psychology, 81*: 329.

Zull, J. E. (2002). *The art of changing the brain: Enriching the Practice of teaching by exploring the biology of learning.* Sterling, VA: Stylus Publishing.

Author Index

Subject Index

Learning and the E-Generation, First Edition. Jean D. M. Underwood and Lee Farrington-Flint.
© 2015 Jean D. M. Underwood and Lee Farrington-Flint. Published 2015 by John Wiley & Sons, Ltd.